Audrey Acton
Sept 98

EVAN JONES was born in Portland, Jamaica in 1927. He grew up on a banana farm, and was educated at Munro College and later at Haverford College in Pennsylvania and Wadham College, Oxford, where he was awarded [...] literature at the George [...] Connecticut. He moved [...] freelance writer ever since. His p[...] Man' and the 'Lament of the [...] ized widely. His television w[...] ries 'The Fight Against Slav[...] *King and Country* (1964), *Funeral in Berlin* (1966), *Escape to Victory* (1981) and *Champions* (1984). Other writing includes a biography of Las Casas, *Protector of the Indians* (Nelson, N.Y., 1958), *Junior Language Arts of the Caribbean* (Longman, 1977–1983), *Tales of the Caribbean* (Ginn & Co., 1984), and *Skylarking*, a novel for children (Longman, 1993), also published in France as *Aventures sur la planète Knos* (Musée Dapper, 1997). *Stone Haven* was originally published in 1993.

Evan Jones lives in London. He is married with two daughters, both writers.

EVAN JONES

STONE HAVEN

(Abridged)

Heinemann

Heinemann Educational Publishers
Halley Court, Jordan Hill, Oxford OX2 8EJ
A division of Reed Educational & Professional Publishing Ltd

Heinemann: A Division of Reed Publishing (USA) Inc.
361 Hanover Street, Portsmouth, NH 03801–3912, USA

MELBOURNE   AUCKLAND   FLORENCE
PRAGUE   MADRID   ATHENS   SINGAPORE
TOKYO   SAO PAULO   CHICAGO   PORTSMOUTH (NH)
MEXICO CITY   IBADAN   GABORONE
JOHANNESBURG   KAMPALA   NAIROBI

© Evan Jones 1993

First published by Institute of Jamaica Publications Ltd in 1993
Abridged version first published by Heinemann Educational Publishers in 1998

The right of Evan Jones to be identified as the author
of this work has been asserted by him in accordance with the
Copyright, Designs and Patents Act 1988.

British Library Cataloguing in Publication Data
A catalogue record for this book is available from the British Library.

Library of Congress Cataloging-in-Publication Data
Jones, Evan. 1927–
　　Stone haven / Evan Jones.
　　　p.   cm. — (CWS)
　　ISBN 0-435-98949-9
　　I. Title. II. Series: CWS (Series)
PR9265.9.J66S76   1998
813 — dc21　　　　　　　97-47723
　　　　　　　　　　　　CIP

AFRICAN WRITERS SERIES and CARIBBEAN WRITERS SERIES and
their accompanying logos are trademarks in the United States of America
of Heinemann: A Division of Reed Publishing (USA) Inc.

Cover design by Touchpaper
Cover illustration by Debbie Lush
Author photograph by Margret Randall

Phototypeset by SetSystems Ltd, Saffron Walden, Essex
Printed and bound in Great Britain by
Cox & Wyman Ltd, Reading, Berkshire

ISBN 0 435 98949 9

98 99 00 01 02   10 9 8 7 6 5 4 3 2 1

*To
Teacher
and to
Sunshine*

Chapter One

There was a light showing in the Girls' School, and when the buggy at last fell silent at the foot of the steps a door was opened and a lamp and a black face appeared in the opening.

'Is that you, Miss Alsina?'

'Yes, Myrtle. And I've brought Miss Neville with me.'

'The Lord be praised.'

Myrtle opened the door wider and, as the night was still and windless, ventured outdoors with the lamp to light the stairs and welcome the travellers.

'The girls is all sleeping,' said Myrtle.

The driver unpacked the two light travelling cases which had come on the buggy, carried them into the building, and set them down. The trunks had been left behind on the wharf to be fetched later.

'Thank you, Johnson,' said Alsina.

Grace, though she was too weary for mere manners, thought this was not quite enough, and added, 'You drove us very well.'

'Yes, mistress. Good night, mistress,' and he turned away.

Grace could hear him muttering to the mule as he led it away into the darkness.

'You want anything to eat or drink, Miss Alsina? You must be tired.'

'Do you, Grace?' Alsina asked.

'I'd like some water.'

Myrtle, lamp in hand, led the way down a narrow corridor punctuated by doors with iron knobs. They reached a bigger room, square, evidently the school dining room, for there were two long wooden tables with benches on either side. Myrtle put the lamp down, took the lid off a yabba, and fishing in it with a ladle produced a drink of cool, fresh water. Alsina also took a glass, and then Grace declined a second, on principle.

'Then goodnight,' said Alsina. 'It must be past midnight.'

'Oh, midnight gone long time, Miss Alsina. I cease to expect you before day.'

The lamp was on the move again, back down the corridor, Grace following, carrying her case. Myrtle pushed open the door of a cubicle, with a shuttered window, bare floor, and an iron bedstead. A white enamel ewer and basin stood on a washstand, with a square of yellow soap in a dish.

'Water is in the pitcher, mam, and the chamber pot under the bed. The sheets is clean.'

'Thank you.'

'Yes, Miss Neville.'

'Grace. You must call me Grace.'

'Yes, mistress. Welcome to Jamaica, mam,' said Myrtle, who knew her place.

Grace undressed in the warm, yellow lamplight but, modest even in private, she slipped the long nightdress over her head to remove her underthings in its shelter. Then she unpinned her hair, let it fall, and shook it loose. 'I'll not brush it tonight,' she thought, 'just this once. I'm so tired.' But even as she thought this, she was reaching for the brush, for the habit of virtue is the armour of saints, and sitting on the bed, she began the long, sensuous, rhythmic motion of brushing out her hair.

Alsina came in, just to make sure she was all right, and stood by the door, watching her.

'Be sure to cover up,' Alsina said. 'It'll be cooler before dawn when night breeze comes down from the hills.'

Grace stopped brushing, and let her hand rest palm upwards in her lap, the brush loose in her fingers.

'I can't wait,' she said, 'to see what it's like in the morning.'

'Then go to sleep,' said Alsina, and took the brush gently from her hand and put it by the ewer and basin.

Already, the lamp had attracted a little snowstorm of moths, and one settled on Alsina's wrist as she cupped her hand over the top of the shade to blow out the light. She went out in the darkness, and the door closed again.

The cubicle was intensely hot. The mattress was hard, stuffed with horsehair, and the sheets felt slightly damp from the sea air. Despite Alsina's advice, Grace decided to do her sweating on top of the sheets.

After a while, she rose and pushed the shutters further open, but this made no difference. She lay down again, resigned to death by melting.

There had been hot and sticky summer nights in Iowa. The difference here was the rich, moist smell of the vegetation, and the presence of the sea. Lying there, she could hear it whispering around the cliffs below the Girls' School, cliffs she had only vaguely discerned as the buggy had passed near them. She was too tired to sleep, and images of her journey succeeded each other behind her closed eyelids like pictures from a magic lantern. She saw Alsina and herself on the boat, her first sight of Jamaica, the wharf with all those half-naked black people, Port Antonio, the buggy road overhung with trees, the emerald sea, wooden shacks perched on foundation stones, women with their skirts tucked up washing clothes, small naked children, and men with machetes sharp enough for the murder of missionaries! Why had she come to this savage, frightful place?

She could have stayed home and found a husband as her father wanted, but she'd been cooking and washing and ironing and doing chores for a whole family ever since her mother died, and she didn't fancy keeping house all over again for someone else, not just yet. So when the call came from the Society of Friends, Quakers, for teachers to work in the mission field, she had accepted the call, and the challenge.

There was a convulsive shiver of brilliant white light filling the room and, in an instant, a tremendous explosion of sound, which echoed as loud as itself, and then rumbled and grumbled slowly away into silence. Grace lay, eyes open, sweating in the still heat, waiting. The lightning flashed again, and the thunder followed, and after a while again, though either it was not so close or one could get accustomed even to the noise God's cannon must have made when Satan angered him to war. Then there was another sound, between the fading thunder and the whispering of the sea, like a low, deep note on an organ, rising in volume, coming closer, then a fierce tapping on the wooden shingles above her head. The shutter banged in the first gust of wind, then everything was obscured by a new thunder as the rain filled the night with the noise of falling water.

Chapter Two

After the rain, the morning was sunny, with a fresh breeze coming in from the sea, tall palms bowing in the wind, and john crows circling overhead. The coast, which faced the north-east trades, was a series of coves and limestone cliffs, honeycombed by the waves. Small valleys, green and overgrown, alternated with breezy hill tops, each of which commanded a view of fifteen miles of coastline, rocky fingers reaching for the sea, and spray, rising and falling like the wings of giant butterflies.

The Girls' School at Happy Grove was on one of these hill tops, in an old great house. The lower floor was no more than a cellar above ground. In the days of slavery, it had served as fort and storehouse, now it was the home of rats and frogs and abandoned bits of rusted metal. Above was the dormitory for sixteen girls, with rows of iron bedsteads made in Birmingham. Grace had her little room, Alsina a slightly larger one. They shared an office and a verandah above the flight of steps which led down to the short, coarse grass of what might be a lawn, a playing field, or pasture for a goat, and was all three.

The girls were separated from the boys by a deep gully through which they walked every morning in a single file, escorted by Grace and Alsina, full-skirted white shepherdesses keeping a flock of little black sheep. The girls were scrubbed clean and neat as pins, their blouses sparkling white against their black skins and navy pinafores, and their feet encased in little white socks and button shoes. The rocky track led down from the Girls' School into a shaded, secret place of fern and towering bamboo, where they forded a stream by stepping stones. On the other side, they passed the government elementary school, a shed furnished with benches, open-sided, filled with thin-legged children chanting their lessons in a high-pitched chorus, conducted by a teacher with a guava switch.

Grace, Alsina, and the girls passed on, out of the sun, into the shade of an almond tree, into the sun once more, and up the path to the Boys' School, which consisted then of two buildings, side by side, oddly contrasted. The first was neoclassical, narrow and tall with white columns; the second was the old plantation house, the foundations shrouded in hibiscus, the louvres full of wasps and lizards.

The classrooms were in the basement of the Friends' church, which stood between the other buildings and the sea, exposed to sun and wind on the crest of a grassy knoll. It was of concrete, softened by ivy, with gothic windows and a bell-tower with a clock, and was the biggest church for fifty miles. Sited where it was, it looked like a strayed cathedral, or some enormous turtle that had climbed the cliff, its back to the sea, its neck to the side, squinting at the island with one round clockface of an eye.

Behind the school, tucked away in the coconuts, was the Mission Home, residence of the Friends' pastor, a pleasant, pagoda-like building with a red roof and cream painted walls, set in a garden of hibiscus and poinciana, and fenced to keep out the village goats.

Mr Montclair Hoffman, headmaster, had been its first pupil, a barefoot boy who had attached himself to the Founder, first as a yard boy, then as a student. The Board of Missions had sent him on a scholarship to Howard University in America, where he had graduated *summa cum laude*, and in gratitude he had returned to his old school.

Grace sat in on Mr Hoffman's classes, and marvelled at him, a piece of chalk in his carefully manicured fingers, his neck imprisoned in a white wing collar, the handkerchief in his breast pocket ready to dab the sweat from his high domed forehead. She listened to him discuss, in the purest accents, such irrelevancies as the accession of William and Mary, or the geological features of the Yorkshire Dales, while outside a donkey brayed, tethered under the almond tree.

Mr Hoffman, on his part, made it his particular care to look after his foreign staff. They were hard to get, almost impossible to replace and, given that the Lord had chosen them to carry his banner in a foreign field, they were surprisingly fragile. Some succumbed to melancholia, to loneliness, or to fear of the darkness and the drums. Some contracted malaria or typhoid, some disappeared to Kingston or went into business. Some went home. So he was quick to notice a change in Grace after a few months. Too delicate to discuss it with her, he mentioned it to Alsina, who spoke to Grace as they walked home after the Wednesday night prayer meeting.

'Mr Hoffman says Jamaican food must suit you.'
'You mean I'm getting fat.'
'He didn't say that.'
'Well, it's none of his business.'
'Only if it affects your work.'
'Well, it don't.'

And that was that. Grace would not discuss it further, though privately she worried. She had been furtively employed in letting out seams to accommodate swelling bosom, hips and waist. The path to the Girls' School seemed steeper, and breathing the humid air more difficult. She had even noticed, gravely contemplating her face in the mirror, that its whole outline had softened, and the high cheekbones, firm jaw and square forehead were all disappearing into an indeterminate full moon.

'Cheese,' she said to the mirror. 'Cheddar cheese.'

She'd never been fat before, never had time to put on weight, but here in Jamaica, doing the Lord's work, she was not allowed to do her own. Tucker, the yard boy, cleaned her shoes, Inez did her washing and ironing, and Myrtle cooked the meals. The girls waited on table, so Grace did not even lift a spoon except to her own mouth, and she was hungry all the time. It could have been the sea air, or the mountain air, or both, and the food seemed to be composed entirely of fat and starch. Myrtle's soups were thick, rich, and islanded with dumplings swimming in grease. Half a chicken or a plate of pork was always accompanied by six or seven vegetables, all starch: rice and peas, white yam, yellow yam, Irish potato, sweet potato, cocos, plantains, cho-choes, and other unknown things designed specifically to make her fat. On an island full of fruit there seemed to be no fruit but the banana, as starchy as a vegetable, in a green countryside no greens but callaloo boiled to a mess. There was always pudding, rice pudding or bread pudding, sponge cakes, fruit cakes, and coconut cakes, and bottled jams and sugar everywhere.

Grace decided Mr Hoffman was right. She was eating too much because she was homesick. She would consider her ways, and change them with God's help. She would eat less, and she would take exercise. As work was not allowed, she would have to play games, something she'd never done, nor thought of doing. With Mr Hoffman's permission, Grace became games mistress and taught rounders and netball, of which she knew nothing. For her own health, she played tennis.

The tennis court had been dug out of the slope in front of the Boys' School by pick and shovel. By dint of constant cutting with a machete, and rolling after rain, a combination of crab grass and weed had been pressed into a playable surface. When the teachers were to play, the boys competed for the honour of marking the lines with bucket and brush, putting up the tangled net, and serving as ball boys. A large barringtonia, with a bench around its trunk, served as a grandstand and umpire's chair, provided shade for the court, littered it with large, flat leaves, bombarded it with heart-shaped fruit and, on some mornings, decorated it with silken stamens, pink and white.

Grace played with Mr Hoffman against Ruthanna, a big-breasted girl from Kansas City, who taught science, and Mr Khadurian, an Armenian refugee who taught French and carpentry. The headmaster was neat and slow, while Mr Khadurian scooted around like a terrier. Ruthanna was the only one who had been taught the game, and her shots were ponderously correct. Grace was hopeless, flushed and overweight, hampered by skirts to her ankles and sleeves to her wrists. Her long hair was constantly escaping its pins and having to be recaptured. Nevertheless, she ran and served and stroked and volleyed in silent determination, as if her life depended on each shot. Ruthanna and Mr Khadurian prevailed.

'I'm sorry, partner, I've let you down,' said Mr Hoffman, not meaning it. Grace saw no reason to apologize, but thanked him for the game, while the Armenian and the girl from Kansas City beamed proudly at each other, and the ball boys perched on the bank, their arms resting on their raised knees, hoping for a resumption of this strange comedy at which they were not allowed to laugh.

The players were discussing the pros and cons of another set when a buggy, drawn by a mule and carrying two young men, turned into the school yard, rattled up the gravel path past the church and came to a stop by the tennis court.

'Hello, Montclair,' called out one of the young men, hopping down from the buggy. 'Are we too late for a game?'

'Not at all, my dear chap,' replied Mr Hoffman. 'You've come in good time.'

The newcomers were dressed in white, and had brought their

rackets, so there was no doubt the headmaster had invited them. These must be the Newtons, thought Grace, the ones with the banana plantation. Mr Hoffman introduced the brothers, Stanley and Harold, who greeted Grace with exaggerated politeness, Stanley in melodic Jamaican tones, but Harold in something like an English accent. They were both brown, slightly built, in their late twenties. They looked, in their white tennis clothes, like a pair of Indian princes, Grace thought, mail-order Indian princes. Harold, the younger brother, seemed more fun; he was already laughing and making some joke with Mr Hoffman. The mule and the buggy were led away into the shade, and the discussion of another set began, complicated now by the choice of partners. Everybody offered to be left out, but Mr Hoffman, as headmaster, claimed first right to self-sacrifice, which meant that Mr Khadurian must needs drop out in the interest of a mixed foursome. Harold generously offered to play with Grace, and Stanley was honoured to partner Ruthanna.

It was a bloodless victory, for though Harold played the occasional sensational shot, and clowned a lot, making Grace laugh in spite of herself, and Grace bustled and strained and sweated profusely inside her voluminous garments, they were no match for Ruthanna's slow correct returns, and the quick, dapper Stanley, whose wristy forehand made the ball slide on the crab grass like a cake of soap. Then Grace and Ruthanna sat on the bench under the barringtonia to watch the Newton brothers take on Mr Hoffman and Mr Khadurian, 'Teachers vs farmers', as Harold called it.

Grace hardly watched, intent on pulling bits of her wet blouse away from her skin, and gently shaking the cloth to dry it and herself. She shivered.

'You'll catch a chill,' said Ruthanna, anxious and knowledgeable, and she dispatched one of the boys to fetch towels. So, as the shadow of the barringtonia stretched across the court and toward the church, the two girls sat, huddled in towels, while the men darted back and forth in the hot evening, calling out the score, laughing, encouraging or congratulating, apologizing, and the ball-boys watched, their attitude respectful and the dark eyes in their black faces expressionless.

Afterwards, Harold proposed a picnic on the beach.
'What about Sunday morning?'

'Sunday is the Lord's day,' pronounced Mr Hoffman slowly, and Stanley, embarrassed for his brother, looked away.

'Wednesday is half-day,' suggested Grace, not wanting them to feel rejected.

'Then Wednesday it is,' said Stanley.

'Jolly good,' said Harold. 'We're very short of social life in this neck of the woods.'

Promptly at two o'clock on Wednesday, the Newton buggy turned into the gate of the Girls' School. The driver announced he had 'come fo' de 'oman teachahs dem'. The woman teachers, Ruthanna and Grace, for Alsina had pleaded a headache, with their bathing costumes rolled into towels and packed into a basket, climbed aboard and were borne slowly seaward. The school buggy, with Mr Hoffman and Mr Khadurian, and the mission buggy, with the Reverend and Mrs Robert Steere and two small, white children, joined them at the church gate.

In convoy, at a walk, the buggies proceeded along the cliff-top road which led past Sammy Ying's grocery store and a wooden cottage that housed the Newton's overseer. They crossed a piece of flat ground on which the Newtons allowed the village to play cricket, then descended to the floor of a valley choked with vegetation – a first level, shaded, composed of the large flat leaves of the banana, and out of this rose the pillars of coconut trunks supporting a second level, each palm a feather duster of bright leaves rippling green and yellow in the sun.

The buggies forded a stream, and proceeded down a muddy track between the bananas to the beach.

Harold, full of welcomes, came to assist the unloading. A labourer, under Stanley's supervision, was just completing a bathing hut, made of a bamboo frame and thatched with coconut fronds. The brothers were already in bathing costumes, Stanley in navy blue, Harold, rather more daring, in horizontal stripes. Grace noticed that the skin of their shoulders and calves was a creamy colour, much paler than the rich brown of their faces.

Harold escorted the girls to the changing room, as to a palace, while Stanley exchanged a word with the labourer, who, arming himself with a grass knife attached to a bamboo pole, moved off into the field.

While she was changing in the hot, dim, sweet-smelling cubicle, Grace heard the rustle and thud of coconuts being picked. When she came out, dressed for the first time in the bathing costume she had bought only because the Mission Board advised it, the labourer was coming back bringing in coconuts by the twos and threes, a couple under his arm and another stuck on the point of his machete.

The bathers gathered to watch him prepare them, as he deftly balanced the huge green nut in one hand and, spinning it around, trimmed the husk off one end with the machete and then, with a final flick of the wrist, took the crown off the exposed shell without spilling a drop of the pearly liquid within. Harold offered them round. Grace didn't like the taste at first, but it was refreshing, and she put it down carefully so as not to waste the rest. The labourer retrieved her coconut with a thrust of the machete, poured the water away, and split the thing in two with one stroke like a sword opening a man's head, exposing the coconut meat, still only half-formed, thin, soft and white. He cut a tiny slice of husk to make a spoon, and held up the halves to her.

'Mistress?'

He was barefooted, and the spread and hardness of his feet indicated that he always was; he wore a pair of patched, stained trousers and a bright blue shirt he had put on for the party. He was older than his wiry muscles would suggest. He had a short moustache and a missing tooth. His eyes were friendly.

'Mistress?'

'Thank you.'

Grace took the coconut and spoon, scooping the soft jelly out.

'It's not bad, is it?' said Harold, next to her. 'Meat and drink in the same dish. You can never go hungry in this little old country of ours.'

Grace agreed that it was delicious. She wasn't sure she liked Harold. He was friendly and attentive, but there was something about the voice and manner that grated on her. He didn't talk like a Jamaican, and although she'd never met an Englishman, she didn't think he talked like an Englishman either.

She and Ruthanna went for a walk along the beach. From a distance, they looked like a pair of emperor penguins, the skirts of their bathing costumes swaying as they walked, their tender white feet, protected by bathing slippers, treading over the pebbles and the sea-shells and through a breaking wave sliding up the sand. The beach was the closed end of a horseshoe bay, a gentle arc of pale yellow fringed with almond trees. Cliffs rose on both sides of the bay, so that the water was enclosed, shadowed, dark green. Beyond the reef, out at sea, it sparkled blue and white. Under the almond trees, the girls found a group of dugout canoes, resting on rollers, upturned against the rain. At the end of the beach, a stream flowed into the bay, with a green pool at its mouth.

Two washerwomen were standing in the water, their skirts tucked up and tied around their buttocks. One was rubbing brown soap into a pile of clothes, and the other beating out a garment on a flat white stone. They greeted the teachers with cheerful cries and called down upon them the blessings of the Lord.

The whole party went into the sea except for Mr Hoffman, who made a joke about it being unhealthy, but looked as if he thought it was undignified. Grace, Ruthanna, and Mrs Steere donned their bathing caps as they waded across the breakwater. Robert Steere, a muscular young man, struck off toward the reef with a fine, firm breaststroke. Wilma Steere asked Harold anxiously about sharks. He assured her they would not attack a preacher, at which she was not amused, and Stanley said sharks did not come inside the reef. At last Steere turned back and the girls could stop worrying about him.

Among the almond trees, the labourer had lighted a fire between three carefully arranged stones, filled a large black kettle from the stream, and sat waiting for it to boil. Two women, with trays on their heads, large trays covered with white linen, were coming down the cliff path at the end of the beach. Despite the steepness of the path, their arms swung loose at their sides, and the trays remained perfectly balanced. In the same way, they forded the stream, lifting their skirts as the water came up to their knees, ignoring the burden on their heads. The missionaries, all except Grace, had been in Jamaica long enough to take such miracles for granted, but she could hardly contain her amazement as the tea-bearers swayed lazily along the beach.

One of them handed a tablecloth to the labourer, who spread it on the grassy sand. With light, easy movements the trays came down and the linens were removed. There was a teapot, jugs and china cups, saucers and silver spoons; there were plates of salmon and cucumber sandwiches, tomato sandwiches, biscuits, Saltine crackers, guava jelly, processed cheese, sponge cake and fruit cake, and lemonade made with brown sugar and fresh limes. Harold invited the bathers to help themselves, and the party fell upon the feast like john crows on a dead donkey.

Later, when the women had departed and the labourer had thrown the coconut husks into a trench and kicked sand on the fire, and when the drivers, summoned from sleep under the almond trees, were harnessing the horses and the mule, the party walked through the banana field. Grace walked with Stanley.

'It doesn't look like a field to me. It looks like a jungle.'

'It needs weeding.'

'I didn't mean that, Mr Newton. It's just different. I was raised on a farm. In Iowa.'

'What did you grow?'

'Corn, and pigs, and cattle.'

'Beef, or dairy?'

'Dairy. Our fields were so very . . . neat.'

'You have winter, and the bush grows quickly here.'

'When will you reap this crop?'

'We reap all year long.'

He showed her a clump of bananas, five or six plants coming from the same root.

'This will be ready next week, and we reap it by cutting down the tree, this one in three months' time, and then this one after that . . .'

She watched him as he talked, slow, unhurried, explaining, drawing confidence from what he knew and what interested him. She thought of her father in a field of corn. How different they were, her father, tall, pink-faced, white-haired, with that sly humour of his, and this man, small, dark, intense, with no sense of humour that she could yet discern, talking about bananas. They were alike in some way, both growing from their native soil. Was that what it meant in the Bible, that God made Adam out of clay?

Well, she thought skittishly, she couldn't be made out of this man's rib. She was taller than he for a start.

Chapter Three

After six months, Grace's fat melted as fast as it had accumulated. Instead of the angular girl who had landed in Port Antonio, or the roly-poly Grace of the early months, a happy medium emerged, a full-figured, dark-haired beauty. Needle and thread were once more required to accommodate the change.

So employed, one Thursday afternoon, she was surprised to hear male voices in the yard below, and, looking out, to see Stanley and a black man with a ladder in deep conversation on the subject of Alsina's window.

'De sash-cord burs', sar.'

'You have cord?'

'No, sar.'

'How you come here without? I told you.'

'I jus' sen' a bwoy fo' some, sar.'

Stanley looked up to see Grace looking down at him.

'Good afternoon, Miss Neville.'

'Good afternoon, Mr Newton.'

'I hope you are well.'

'Thank you, and you?'

'Very well, thank you.'

Suddenly, and for some unaccountable reason, flustered, Grace withdrew.

'Isn't that nice of Mr Newton,' Grace said to Alsina at supper, 'to have our window mended?'

Alsina was not impressed. 'I asked him to send the carpenter some months ago, and I don't know why he had to come himself, do you?'

On Saturday, Grace went with Myrtle, the cook, to market in Manchioneal. On the way, they met the Newton buggy driving home to Williamsfield, carrying Stanley and an old black woman, who was presumably his cook, and market baskets full of vegetables. As the buggies passed, each with a wheel in the gutter, brushing the ferns growing on either bank, Grace smiled, and Stanley raised his hat.

Such encounters were both natural and accidental but Grace was taken aback when Stanley turned up in the Friends' church. She'd been told the Newtons were Anglican, and went to church in Manchioneal.

He had chosen a pew by the side door, exactly opposite to where she sat to play the organ. She had to look at him, or avoid looking at him by gazing at the keys, out of the window, or up at a bird fluttering from beam to beam, trapped in the rafters. During the time of silent prayer she closed her eyes, but all the while she felt that Stanley was watching her.

It made her impatient and annoyed, but Grace, who tried to be honest with herself, couldn't be sure whether she was annoyed at his impertinence, or annoyed because she was, in spite of herself, pleased. Afterwards, in the churchyard, when the boys and girls were rushing away to lunch, and the Reverend Steere, in his white suit and polka-dot tie, was shaking hands with the older Friends, black and white, she thought it would only be polite to speak to Stanley.

'Have you forsaken the Anglican church?'

'Far from it, but I come sometimes for a change, and to hear the Reverend Steere.'

'I hope you enjoyed it.'

'It was a fine sermon; "By their fruits ye shall know them".'

She had forgotten the text, and indeed had hated the sermon. Robert Steere was of the 'stream-of-life-flowing-over-the-pebbles-of-adversity' school of preaching, and though she had been brought up on it Grace couldn't help thinking from time to time that both God and the English language deserved something better. Stanley was still talking:

'. . . after all, we're neighbours, and I like to think of ourselves as friends of the Friends.'

That was the last she had to do with Stanley for a while, until his bearer, Tumpy, turned up at the Girls' School with a note. Tumpy was a young dwarf, devoted to Stanley, whose cast-off shirt he wore together with a pair of khaki shorts and tennis shoes in which a hole had been cut out of the uppers to allow a space for his little toe. His left leg was bent outwards at the knee, by rickets or by injury, but he was surprisingly agile. He said he'd wait for an answer, and retired to the shade of the poinciana tree.

Dear Miss Neville,
   If you can forgive the impertinence, I would like to call on you. I can't pretend to have serious matters to discuss, and yet you will probably find me boringly serious anyway. Never mind, I would consider it an honour.
                              Yours faithfully,
                              Stanley Newton

Tumpy waited. He sat through breakfast, and the departure of the girls. He sat while Inez hung the morning's washing on the line between the lime trees. He sat for another hour while the climbing sun scorched the brown grass around the deep pool of shade in which he waited. He waited until Miss Neville came out of the school and down the steps with a letter in her hand.

Dear Mr Newton,
   You may come to tea on Sunday at four o'clock if that would be convenient for you.
                              Yours sincerely,
                              Grace Neville

At five minutes to four on Sunday, Grace knew that Stanley would be late. The buggy had not yet left the Newton yard, and if it had, it had certainly not passed the church, and even if it had done that, it had not appeared on the cliff-top road below the Girls' School.

Grace had laid tea in the cool, airy study which opened on the stone verandah and had windows to the sea. She had put on the primrose frock that had hung unworn in the cupboard since her arrival. It had a square neckline and short sleeves. It fitted loosely at the waist with a smart belt on the hips and a scalloped hem which showed some four inches of calf above the ankle. Alsina hadn't sniffed when she saw it, but she had said, 'That's very pretty, Grace,' so that it sounded like a sniff.

Stanley was coming up the stone steps, neat and slim, wearing a three-piece brown suit and an expression of the utmost gravity. He shone from top to toe, his black hair parted and brushed as flat to his head as the curls would allow, and his brown shoes reflecting the sun. He had walked. He wasn't sweating because he had stopped in the gully below the school and taken off his jacket, to cool off. After a while, he had taken the watch from his waistcoat pocket and, realizing it was time, hurried on to make his entrance.

'You walked, Mr Newton.'

'That's right, yes.'

'I'm sorry.'

'No, no. I'm accustomed to it. It's the best way of seeing a field.' That, he thought, was a stupid remark. He wasn't seeing a field; he was coming to tea. 'Harold's using the buggy.' That wasn't much better.

'Sit down, Mr Newton.'

'... he's gone into Port Antonio. There was some sort of party there, a dinner dance. Some people called Marriott, a large family of girls. Poor old Marriott has to keep giving parties in the hope of marrying them off.'

'I hope you didn't miss the party for our sake.'

'Oh no, Miss Neville. The Marriotts, like the poor, are always with us.'

'Don't you think of us as permanent?'

'I hope so,' said Stanley sincerely. 'I don't know what we in Jamaica would do without you.'

He was really a nice young man, thought Alsina, and he had been very helpful about the window.

'You're looking very pretty, Miss Neville ... and I'd say the same for you, Alsina, except that you're spoken for.'

'Am I? This is news to me. By whom?'

'Doctor McIntosh. He has declared firm intention to marry you.'

'That old drunk. You know very well he's not allowed within ten miles of the school in case he corrupts the children.'

'Shall I tell him that when I see him?'

'You can tell him what you like, Mr Newton. I know you are only teasing.'

'You can take your coat off if you wish. It's quite warm.'

'No thanks. I'm very comfortable.'

And so he was, after the opening attack of nerves, comfortable. He entertained them with stories of the local society, the plantocracy, the people who mattered on the stretch of coast between Port Antonio and Morant Bay. They all sounded alike to Grace. They all seemed to consume copious quantities of rum, were all riddled with malaria, and heaven knows what else; they never seemed to do a stroke of work, indulging instead in gormandizing and the making of bastards; and were redeemed only by a gargantuan sense of the absurd.

'I'm surprised you waste your time on a couple of Quaker missionaries,' she said.

'My father was an Anglican missionary. He founded the Church at Manchioneal.'

'Oh, and where did he come from?'

'From Wales.'

'Have you been to Wales?'

'No. Not yet. One day.'

They talked about the migrations of families; how Alsina's family had moved from Scotland to Virginia, Kentucky, and Kansas; and Grace's family from England and from Germany, pausing in New York only long enough to find out where the land was, the rich dark land of Iowa; and Stanley's from Wales, from India and from Africa; and what a miracle it was that God should have led all three of them by such various paths to tea in that room, that particular afternoon, within sight and whisper of his eternal sea.

'That's all very well,' Alsina said, when Stanley had thanked them and departed. 'It's all very well to be friends with the Newtons, but it mustn't go any further.'

If she had said it looking out of the window, or down at the floor, and thereby indicated her shame, Grace would have felt better, but Alsina said it looking directly at her, in the voice of kind authority, her pale blue eyes focussing through the thick round spectacles. Suddenly Grace felt ashamed of the primrose dress.

'I don't know what you mean,' she replied, defiantly.

Alsina paused. 'A word to the wise is sufficient,' she said, and picked up *Thoughts from the Garden*. Grace busied herself collecting the tea things. Thank God it was Myrtle's day off, so she didn't have to call her to remove the tray. She could take it away herself and escape from Alsina into the empty kitchen.

What did Alsina mean? It was only too clear what Alsina meant. But would Alsina have said it if they had been teaching in a small town in Iowa and a young farmer had come to call? That was a good way of posing the question! She wouldn't! Well, she would if the man were known as a drinker, or a gambler, or if his family were a bad lot, if there were some kind of taint . . .

Grace decided that this last line of thought was unprofitable, and spent the rest of the afternoon with the third form arithmetic exercise books. But it did recur some days later when she had Saturday lunch, minced beef and rice, with the Reverend Steere and his wife.

'I hear you're walking out with Stanley Newton.'

'He came to tea with Alsina and myself. Do you object?'

'Of course not. I'm sure there's no harm in that, though there might be.'

'Why?'

'Some people have evil minds. If they thought you were encouraging him – you must be careful, Grace. Decent folk might say you were cheap.'

'Decent folk?'

'They might think you were available.'

'Is that what you think? That I am cheap, and available?'

'Of course not. I know you are as sensible as you are pretty,' he said, and touched her hand which was resting on the table.

'Other people,' she repeated, withdrawing her hand, 'what would other people think – that if I am friendly with a coloured man, I am cheap and available?'

'We're not talking about colour. We are all equal in the eyes of the Lord.'

'Yet I am cheap and available.'

'Of course not, but we must think of what folk will say.'

'Decent folk.'

'Grace, we few, we few Friends, we have to set an example. Anything we do or say is talked about, and magnified. We have to be careful.'

Grace, the knife in her hand, wondered what it would look like sticking out of his neck.

'I will be careful,' she said, 'and I will be Christian.'

Mr Hoffman and Grace were the two invited to Williamsfield when the Marriott girls came for the weekend.

The Marriott girls were nineteen or twenty, pretty girls with black hair, bobbed but defiantly curly. One was in pale blue, the other in green and white with organdy frills. Their smooth brown complexions were rouged and powdered. Their habitual expression was boredom, but anyone catching the eye of either of them was rewarded with the sweetest of smiles. They were both small-breasted, with slim waists, slightly larger at the hip, but attractively so, with good straight legs and neat ankles. They said nothing, sitting side by side, listening to the men and the music. Grace, looking at them, felt large and white and plain, and wished she hadn't come.

The men, as usual, were discussing the banana business, and De Roux, who was the harbour pilot, announced that the United Fruit Company were putting another ship on the Port Antonio run.

'Is that so?' said Stanley.

'Yes. If I had a piece of mountainside like yours, I'd get the axe in there, chop down all that bush and plant bananas, make a fortune.'

Harold shook his head. 'Easier said than done. It's a brute. Steep, you hear, steep! The land would wash away, man. No, man, what we have here in this parish is natural beauty. Natural beauty. God gave it to us to share with others, and to make money therefrom. I keep telling Stanley we should build a guest house. Travel is the new thing.'

Stanley said nothing. Harold turned to Grace for support. 'Don't you think so, Miss Neville?'

'It sounds good, but I don't know the ins and outs,' she replied.

'The United Fruit Company have the monopoly,' said Stanley cautiously. 'They already have a hotel. They bring the tourists in their own ships, and put them up in their own hotel.'

Harold was shaking his head vigorously, 'You only need a little imagination to break that monopoly.'

'Maybe so,' said Stanley, doubting it.

'Of course,' said Mr Hoffman, attempting a summary, 'any kind of progress is stifled by the shortage of skilled people. We are doing our best in our small corner, but until the elementary schools can teach people how to read . . .'

He broke off, rose respectfully, and vacated the rocking chair as a woman entered from the dining room, a small black woman, light-boned and wiry, in a full-skirted grey dress. It was the woman Grace had seen in the buggy on the way to Manchioneal market and had presumed was Stanley's cook. She seemed to be about fifty, her black hair streaked with grey. Her face, full and round in youth, was receding toward the bone, emphasizing the cheekbones, and making darker hollows around her eyes. The eyes themselves were pale, almost honey-coloured, marvellously bright in her black face. Grace realized she was looking at Stanley's mother.

'If you want anything done well,' Mama Newton was saying, 'you have to do it yourself. That stupid girl burn the rice and peas. Dinner soon ready.' She sat down in the rocking chair. 'Kitchen is very hot, you know, I'll catch cold in the shoulder from that open window. Montclair, just pass me that shawl.'

'Mama,' said Stanley, 'this is Grace Neville.'

Grace rose, and faced Mrs Newton across the room, ready to step forward and shake hands, as everyone seemed to do in Jamaica, but the older woman wasn't interested.

'Sit down, sit down, that's all right.' She settled the shawl around her shoulders. 'Harold, you going into the hotel business? Stick to what you know. Plant bananas.'

Harold laughed and changed the subject. The men talked about cricket, boring Grace into a daydream, a memory of Iowa afternoons, from which she was wakened by Stanley inviting her in to dinner.

Mama Newton served a roast suckling pig, with stuffing, rice and peas, and corn fritters, and an endless array of vegetables. She herself ate nothing, but sat at the head of the table encouraging the others.

After the baked bananas and the coconut cream, the Marriott girls and Grace sat on the verandah with cups of coffee. The sun had gone behind the house so the shade was moving slowly down the steps and across the yard. The wind had dropped, the land was still, and there was only the drowsy movement of the sea. The men had taken themselves off, but only as far as the pimento tree by the gate where they were absorbed in some deep and important discussion. Grace could only hear the usual low Jamaican mutter, punctuated by the occasional emphatic, high-pitched phrase or shriek of laughter. She thought she saw Harold offer a hip flask to De Roux, and was relieved to note that Mr Hoffman and Stanley seemed quite aloof from such goings on.

She turned her attention to the Marriott girls. The older one, Helen, was slightly taller, had a mole on her chin, and was definitely the more sensible. Cynthia, the one with the frills, clearly thought that she was the prettier, though Grace felt this was a matter of opinion.

Cynthia said she was a stenographer, and had taken the Pitman course, and that her shorthand speed was phenomenal. She wasn't actually working at the moment because there wasn't anything interesting to do in Port Antonio. Her father wanted her to sit in the wire cage in his shop and take money, and write bills, but she had sworn to leave home rather than do that. She might go to Boston, she said, she had an aunt there, but she wasn't sure she could stand the cold. Cynthia asked Grace which one of the men she thought most attractive. Grace said she thought they were both attractive, and changed the subject, but Cynthia would not be deterred.

'I'm going to marry one of them, but I haven't decided which one yet.'

'You'll marry the one that asks,' said Helen.

'Well, nobody is going to ask you,' retorted Cynthia.

Just then they heard the distinct chink-chink of cutlery on a plate coming from the dining room. Helen leaned forward in her chair to have a peek. It was, she whispered, Mama Newton, having her dinner. There, at the end of the table now cleared and polished but for one place, was Mama Newton, facing away from them, going at the roast pig and rice and peas in solitary splendour.

'Why?' asked Grace. 'Why does she do that? Why didn't she eat with us?'

Helen shrugged, not knowing.

'It's her teeth,' said Cynthia, 'she takes them out to eat, and she's shy.'

'You're making it up,' said Helen.

'God's truth,' said Cynthia, 'you don't see how pretty they are? Harold brought them from England for her, and she's very proud of them. She just don't want to wear them out.'

'Oh, Lawd,' said Helen, 'you're a terrible liar.'

Chapter Four

Harold, in a light brown suit, high collar, and tie with a gold tie-pin, his hair greased and flattened, was drifting down King Street. He was in no hurry. It was ten o'clock in the morning and already hot. He kept to the shady side of the street, under the colonnades of the Indian bazaars, the Portuguese jewellery stores, and the Syrian dry goods emporiums. He gave a penny to the legless beggar on the steps of Barclays Bank, but ignored the fruit-sellers and the sweet-sellers under the shade trees in front of the government buildings. Other pedestrians ignored him, a well-dressed, up from the country brown man about his lawful business. Harold paused to admire a long, low, touring car, loaded with Yankees off the cruise boat, as it negotiated the turn out of Harbour Street, blowing its horn and blasting the buggies and donkey carts and bicycles out of the way. It passed a tramcar coming the other way, its benches jammed full, and people standing on the steps and hanging off the sides like ants feeding on a fruit cake.

Harold's way led him into Love Lane, a gutter lined with buildings, and through the batwing doors of the Old Soldier's Bar and Restaurant. Three mulattoes with civilian manners and civilian bellies were already drinking rum though the barmaid was still sweeping up the cigar butts of the night before. Harold said, 'Mawnin', Rose,' and 'Morning, chaps,' and went straight on past the bar into the back yard. There, a stunted mango tree shaded a chicken coop and a latrine. A staircase led up to a verandah shaded by louvred shutters painted green. There was a round table, chairs, a washstand in the corner, and a small sideboard with drawers filled with poker chips and crisp new slippery playing cards, all neatly boxed and wrapped in cellophane.

Thomson was at the poker table having his breakfast, bare to the waist, his black shoulders fat and smooth. He was going grey and occasional white hairs showed also on his chest.

'Mawnin', Mass Harold.'

'Morning.'

'How is the bush?'

'The bush doesn't change.'

'Not much change in this blasted place either. You looking for a game.'

'No. Not today. Just passing.'

Thomson called for Rose without even turning his head, and she replied from the dark interior without showing herself. He told her to bring a new bottle of rum, some limes, and a pitcher of water.

'Cold water, you hear. Not tomorrow, today. You hear me?'

Rose did not reply.

Harold sat down.

'You can have coffee, if you prefer,' said Thomson.

'I've had coffee.'

Rose appeared with the drinks, and cleared away the remains of Thomson's breakfast. Thomson poured a rum, a large one, for Harold, and a small one for himself.

'Pity you're not playing today.'

'I can't afford it.'

'Shame, because Mass Albert is coming round, and that man is the worst poker player since the prodigal son.'

Yap Sing was coming up the stairs in a white linen suit. He owned a grocery store in Orange Street and was blessed with a father who spoke no English and a hard-working wife, so he was free to spend his days with friends who shared his interests. Two rums later, Ferdy arrived. He was a white man from an old Jamaican family. He had been in the war with Harold, that is, they had enlisted together, gone to England together, but Ferdy had gone to France and left his right arm there. He was freckled, thin, and hesitant of manner, but if he had enough to drink he was good company. His father had left him some money, and he had a young black girl at home who was unaccountably fond of him.

Harold was the life of the party. On his fourth rum he was telling the story about the goat at Pleasant Hill that gave birth to a kid with five fingers, and how the owner of the goat hanged himself.

They were all laughing when Mass Albert, fat, brown, and sweating under his straw boater, came up the stairs. Thomson ordered another bottle of rum and Harold reluctantly agreed to a couple of hands before lunch.

Thomson played carefully, limiting his betting and folding often, but he was a good host. He didn't tell stories during a hand, the rum bottle was always there, and beef patties or fish fritters or chicken sandwiches appeared at regular intervals. Yap Sing was in luck and winning steadily. Ferdy, cards in his one hand and cigar in his mouth, was breaking even. Harold and Mass Albert were down.

Harold had lost the week before, and the week before that, and he was worried about facing Stanley. Stanley would say nothing, he would press his lips together and look away, and then later, an hour, a day, or a week later, there would be some remark to their mother, something about him throwing away money Stanley was working so hard to earn.

He looked at his down card. It was the ace of hearts. They were playing five card stud, Thomson was dealing. The next was the queen of spades, and Harold went with the betting. The next was a ten, also a spade, and the next a deuce. Deuces were wild. Yap Sing, who had been building the pot, swore, and folded. So did Thomson. Ferdy stayed in for the last card and then he folded. Mass Albert and Harold sat looking at each other.

Mass Albert had two pair showing. Harold had the ten, queen, king of spades, and a wild card.

'Two pair,' said Thomson, 'four to a straight flush. Your bet, Mass Albert.'

'Double the pot,' said Mass Albert.

Harold smiled. He was beaten on the table, but with the ace of hearts he had a straight. Not good enough if Albert had the full house, but maybe he didn't, and maybe he could bluff the running flush.

'Double it again,' said Harold.

Thomson counted the pot. 'Three hundred and sixty. What you fellows using for money?'

'Cash,' said Mass Albert.

Harold asked for a piece of paper and wrote, 'I.O.U.' He left the next line blank, and below wrote, 'On the security of Williamsfield Estate'. He signed it, and passed it to Ferdy, who witnessed it.

'Yours is the last raise,' Thomson said to Albert.

'That can be changed by mutual agreement,' said Harold. 'Isn't that so, Mass Albert?'

Albert nodded.

'Two hundred.'

'Your two, and four,' said Harold, and put the bad I.O.U. on top of the pot.

Albert looked as if he were going to cry. 'Pshaw rass, man,' he said. 'You're a rass, man. I don't want you blasted land, Harold!'

He folded his cards, backed away from the table, knocking over his chair, and headed down the stairs. Harold sat still, staring at the pot. He picked up the I.O.U. and tore it in half.

'Just count it for me, Thomson. I'm going to spring a leak.'

Harold went down the staircase. He was dizzy. It was the rum, the heat, the swirling sky above the roofs of Kingston. He felt his knees going weak, and his balance going, and he grabbed at the banister to steady himself. Weaving slightly, and fumbling with the buttons of his flies, he circumnavigated the chicken coop and gained the shade of the mango tree. He doubled up, and vomited, a nasty, yellowish mess on the bare earth. With a rasping noise like a child with whooping cough he vomited again, the rest of the rum and Thomson's beef patties. He straightened, sweating, and dabbed at his mouth with a handkerchief. He felt better; he had splashed his two-tone shoes, but the money was still there.

In the gentleman's room of the Myrtle Bank Hotel, old Moses re-polished the shoes, and Harold washed away the sweat of honest toil. He lunched in the open air, shaded by a royal palm. There was white linen, and silver-plated cutlery. The diners at the other tables were all white people, colonial servants, top businessmen, or tourists down from the States. His vomiting fit, pure nerves, had left him hungry, so he had snapper, and roast beef, and ice cream, and a bottle of French champagne.

His luck was in, he thought. Would it be pushing it to go home by way of Port Antonio and ask Cynthia to marry him?

The school benefited enormously from Stanley's interest in Grace. Every week a cart arrived with bunches of green bananas, rejected for export and free of charge to the school kitchens. The school library, which was all of three book cases, received an encyclopaedia, and Mr Hoffman's request that the Newton beach be available for supervised swimming was granted immediately. Grace began to fear that the Newtons' own house, and even the labourers' huts which the property provided, would all fall into disrepair. Joubert, the carpenter, seemed perpetually employed at the school. There was nothing she could do to stem the flow of generosity, and in truth she did not want to. She became accustomed to his regular visits on errands real or imagined, to the unfailing cheerfulness of his manner, and his earnest care for the well-being of the school and of the church. These visits being purely innocent and well-intentioned, she could not understand why they produced such an epidemic of giggling among the girls. Never in front of her, she noticed, and she couldn't make up her mind which was worse, for the giggling to stop when she entered a room, or start after she'd left it. Grace was not a frivolous person and giggling irritated her.

Nevertheless, she found herself expecting his visits, even looking out for them, and more often than not, she was by her classroom window when his buggy turned into the gate. Or, knowing that he was somewhere in the school, she caught herself listening for the sound of his voice. Yet she was still unprepared for it when he turned up at the Wednesday night prayer meeting.

She knew that Stanley was charming in his own way, generous and concerned, and that many people had a good opinion of him, but only then did she realize that he was also cunning. There was no other word for it. He must have thought about it, and planned it. The children did not attend prayer meeting; it was a service for the community. This meant it was attended by the minister, the teachers, and those tradespeople – Joubert, the carpenter; Mrs Taylor, the seamstress; Carmichael, the butcher; and Mrs King, the shopkeeper – whose trade largely depended on the school.

The prayer meeting, she felt, was almost private, a few friends gathered by lamplight on the cedar benches in one corner of the church to sing hymns, read the Bible, and pray. Watching Stanley absorbed in his Bible, she knew that he knew Alsina had sprained her ankle the previous week, and so she was without an escort home along the path by the elementary school and down through the dark gully overgrown by ferns. She noticed that he had positioned himself so that when they all rose to shake hands he would be closer to her than Mr Khadurian or the Reverend Steere, and lifting her eyes from a contemplation of the psalms she saw through the church window that the moon was rising. Had he arranged that too?

They walked together down the hill away from the church in silence. The moon was bright enough for them to distinguish the bulk of the Girls' School on the hill in front, bright enough to give a shine to the coconut leaves, pick out the white spray on the cliffs, and paint a shade of purple in the sea; it was bright enough for them to see each other's faces, moon-dimmed and moon-enhanced.

'There's something I have to say to you . . .' Grace began.
'What is it?'
'Nothing. Never mind.'

Stanley waited in silence, broken by a rustle. Something large and heavy was moving on the other side of the fence, and then, in the half light, Grace saw the gleam of an eye and heard the animal's breathing.

Stanley was reassuring. 'Donkey. Strayed into the bottom of the mission garden. I'll chase it out on my way back.'

They were standing still, side by side, as if the dark presence of the donkey had robbed them of the ability to move. Grace could feel the beating of her heart, and she tried to control her breathing. She started to go, but he put out an arm to detain her, and turned her toward him, gentle but insistent. She stood stock still, and Stanley kissed her. There was a quick rush of kisses, given and taken in a passionate despair, and broken off before their sweetness could be tasted. Grace broke away with a small murmur, and he, already lucky, already blessed, did not try to stop her.

Stanley led the way through the gully, and she followed, stepping carefully. He walked beside her to the steps, and then they turned to look at each other once more. He took her hand for a moment, and she felt the firm pressure of his fingers. She went up the stairs, and opened the door as quietly as its creaking hinge would allow, and tiptoed into the sleeping building. When she got to her room, she knew that he was still there, standing below her window, but she did not look out. She waited until she knew that he had given up, that he was moving away toward the gully, and then she looked out, and watched him out of sight.

'It's no use praying, Grace,' she said to herself. 'You've got to settle this one for yourself.'

That was easier said than done. What could have possessed her?

Perhaps the thing that had startled them, rustling the bushes at the bottom of the mission garden, had been the devil himself. Nonsense. It was, as Stanley had said, a donkey, and she'd made an ass of herself. Oh dear. What was to be done? Well, nothing. Just pretend it hadn't happened. Silly people had exchanged kisses in the moonlight before without precipitating the fall of the Roman Empire. But Grace didn't think of herself as a silly person, but as a sober, conscientious and mature young woman. Even sober, conscientious and mature young women sometimes did silly things.

> Dear Mr Newton,
> Last night, through the long hours, I thought of so many ways of saying this to you. Let me just say it.
> Someone said, 'The report is that Stanley Newton is engaged to an American teacher'. Of course, they don't think it is Miss Alsina.
> Although it is no disgrace to be engaged, I can't bear to be the one who would give people cause to say *untrue* things about you.
> I feel this too, that since this does not touch morals, we need not worry too much. I trust you will never think of stopping coming to Happy Grove, but I think we should take this as a warning and be more careful. It seems to me the thing to leave off is walking home with me.
> That is my thought, though hard to express.
> Sincerely,
> Grace Neville

Stanley took the letter at face value. For weeks, Joubert the carpenter worked at the school without supervision, presents from the farm arrived without a donor, and the tennis net lay tangled under the stairs; the man seemed to have lost all interest in Quakerism.

Grace decided this was a good thing. Let him attend to his own affairs, to his bananas and his coconuts, it was the right thing for him to do. She hated Jamaica, and she began to look forward to going home on leave. The children were obstinate, pig-headed and stupid, and the climate unbearable. He was up to something, he was planning something. There was something calculating and secret about that man, and he was up to something, sitting over there in that strange oblong house that faced the wrong way, sitting over there planning his next move.

Tumpy brought it, climbing the steps to the verandah, dipping one shoulder at each step in order to raise the crippled leg. It was a handsome white envelope with an invitation, engraved and embossed, from Mr and Mrs Alvin Marriott of Port Antonio to attend the wedding of their daughter Cynthia Ann to Mr Harold David Newton at the Holy Cross Church in Kingston. Accompanying the invitation was a note from Stanley, hoping that as the wedding was to be in the Easter holidays she would be able to honour them with her presence, and offering to escort her to Kingston.

Grace replied that she was honoured, but holidays or not, she couldn't possible be away from school for that long. However, she thanked him for his courtesy, and enclosed a note to Harold wishing him all the happiness in the world.

On the morning she knew that the brothers would be leaving for the wedding, she was up and dressed before dawn.

She thought the Newtons would leave early to avoid the worst of the heat, and it was not yet full light when she heard the buggy. She stood at the window to watch them go past along the cliff-top road below her. To her surprise, the buggy stopped at the gate, and she saw Stanley get out and start climbing the path. She didn't want a conversation in front of Alsina, whom she could hear moving about, so she went out onto the verandah, down the steps, and started down the path to meet him.

The sun got up at that moment, catching the Girls' School and her in a bright glare, making her early morning face paler and more anxious, while Stanley, below her, the shadow and the sea behind him, looked darker and more diabolical than ever.

'I hoped you would come with us.'

'I'm sorry.'

'I very much want to see you.'

'You haven't tried very hard recently.'

'I didn't want to embarrass you with the school, and there was a lot of business.'

'Give Harold and Cynthia my best wishes.'

'May I see you when I come back?'

'Nobody is going to stop you, Mr Newton.'

'Next Sunday, we'll go for a drive in the hills. Have you been up to Top Mountain?'

'No.'

'It's a lovely view. It would make me very happy.'

He looked so serious about it all that Grace laughed.

'It doesn't take much to make you happy, Mr Newton.'

'No, not much. Next Sunday then?'

'Next Sunday.'

As the buggy pitched and rolled up the rain-scoured track leading into the hills, Stanley told her about the wedding. 'It was Catholic,' he said, 'there was a priest and Cynthia wore white.'

Harold had been so nervous that he needed either a couple of drinks or a pair of crutches to get him to the altar, so Stanley had been forced to yield him the bottle. Cynthia had started to blub when the sweat showed through her bodice, and her tears, in turn, had ruined her make up, so she had to go back for repairs, which further delayed the whole business. The priest, whom Stanley imitated to the life, had not remembered who they were. The rum had really flowed at the reception, and old Marriott had disgraced himself by going around repeating endlessly, 'One down and three to go,' and giving cigars to all the bachelors and inviting them to come and see him in Port Antonio.

Grace was glad she had not been able to go, but put on her most charitable voice. 'Do you think they'll be happy?'

Stanley paused a moment too long before he said, 'Yes, yes, definitely,' and then lapsed into silence.

He flicked his whip at the mule who leaned into his collar, heaving the buggy over a large, flat-topped stone.

'I don't think you like Cynthia.'

'Well enough. She may not like living in the bush.'

'What about Harold?'

'He's been in the war. He needs time to settle.'

The hillside was steeper now, and the road had begun to double back on itself in a series of hairpin turns, like a boat tacking into the wind. The breeze freshened and the air was cooler.

'It was the schooner Hesperus,' intoned Stanley, looking at the mule, 'that sailed the wintry sea. The skipper had taken his little daughter, to bear him company . . .'

'What made you think of that?'

'Nothing.'

'Do you know any more of it?'

'Yes.'

'Then go on.'

So he recited the whole of *The Wreck of the Hesperus* as the mule slipped and struggled up the hill, and the fresh breeze fluttered the ribbon in Grace's hat and dried the sweat on her face. He had a strong, resonant voice, and it was plain he enjoyed the rhyme and rhythm for their own sakes. 'Lashed to the mast all stiff and stark' was delivered with rich pathos, and the performance ended with an almost professional dying fall.

Grace was impressed, and questioned him about his interest in poetry. He had a whole repertoire, *Hiawatha*, *Horatius at the Bridge*, *The Glove and the Lion*, poems he had memorized at the Titchfield School in Port Antonio, and which he had never forgotten. He had left school when his father died ten years before, because his mother needed him to run the property. Harold had stayed at school, just as Harold had been the one to go to war.

'How old were you when your father died?'

'Seventeen.'

'He must have been quite a young man.'

'No.'

'Then he married late.'

'Yes . . . my father brought his young wife with him from Wales when he came to Jamaica, but she died within six months of malaria. He didn't marry again . . . not for a long time. He took up with my mother late in life.'

'You are fond of your mother?'

'More than that. I'm proud of my mother. A woman of no education or family, she has kept a place in the world for herself, and for her sons.'

By now they were high enough to be cool and to hear in the woods the cooing of pea doves, and the staccato rattle of a woodpecker. The road had flattened out, running along a ridge, with a view down a steep valley to the sea.

Stanley pulled up the buggy where the view was complete. Grace took off her hat to let the breeze through her hair. Below, the steep-sided valley clothed in bush showed here and there more regular patches of cultivation, rows of coconuts, or the flat green tongues of the banana. From that height, the horizon was curved, and the sea was a blue wall encircling the green.

'This is ours,' said Stanley, 'Harold's and mine. My father bought it when he left the church. From here, where we're sitting, over there to the top of that hill, then the line runs across to the clump of bamboos you can see over there, behind that hill down to the river, and the river is the boundary down to the sea. On this side, from the big guango tree down to the valley bottom. On the other side is small people's land, and the village. Up again to that bluff where the john crows are circling, and down past the school to the sea.'

'And he took her to a high place and showed her all the kingdoms of the world . . .' Grace smiled, and with the wind lifting the waves of hair on her forehead, her eyes deep-set and warm, and the little smile at once ironical and tender, she looked most excessively winsome.

'I want you to marry me,' said Stanley.

He took her hand, and she let it lie across his palm, so much paler than the sunburned back of the other, which he then placed upon it, imprisoning her fingers. They both sat still, contemplating this joining of hands, a silent tableau, the mule, the buggy and its two passengers perched on the bluff above the valley that was his, where nothing moved but the shadow of a cloud drifting in from the sea. So they stayed, afraid to move forward, unwilling to move back, until they were separated by the sound of women's voices. Two women came round the corner, carrying pails of water on their heads, barefooted on the sharp gravel, their swathed buttocks swinging in exaggerated motion to compensate for the load. They both seemed to be haranguing each other at the same time, a torrent of words quite unintelligible to Grace, and as they came toward the buggy they added a conversation with the occupants.

'Aaaright, Mass Stanley . . .'
'. . . Howdy do, Teachah . . .'
'Tekking' de cool breeze, ma'm?'
'. . . Busha, you 'ave any wuk fi mi dis week, sar?'
'. . . you mus' need 'oman fi bruk coc'nut . . .'

'Esther, don' talk to me now,' replied Stanley, his accent suddenly broader. 'Come to de yard, Monday.'

'Yes sar, yes sar, I see is important business . . .'

'Im no wa'fi talk to hugly ole s'mady like you now . . .'

And they moved on, cackling like the witches in Macbeth.

Stanley waited until they had turned the corner.

'My question,' he said.

'What question?'

'Will you marry me?'

'Are you taking pity on a spinster?'

'A spinster! Grace, you are young and beautiful.'

'That's what my father said when I told him I was going into the mission field. "So, you intend to be a spinster, Grace," he said. And truthfully I did not expect a proposal of marriage to be my lot in Jamaica.'

'It is. If you like, I am asking the spinster to take pity on me.'

'No, it's impossible. Stanley you are a fine man, but . . .'

'Will you think about it?'

'I don't want to give you any hope, because I do not want to disappoint you. I think too much of you.'

'Too much to deny me out of hand.'

'I'm going home, on leave, for the summer, as you know. I will think about it, for what I might feel here and now I would want to feel when I am at home in Iowa.'

Going home was six days on the banana boat in order to reach the incredible frenzy of New York, and then two more days of the filth and endless clatter of the train to arrive at a small town, and then a dirt road running between cornfields, a shiny mailbox with 'Neville' painted on it, a white clapboard house with maple-shaded grass in front, an orchard and an outhouse at the back and, across the rutted yard, a red barn and a rail fence imprisoning the pigs.

Grace was asked to speak in Meeting about the mission work in Jamaica, and she did. She spoke one Sunday in a small white meeting house on a wave in the prairie, surrounded by buggies and Model-T Fords. There, in the dark interior, she described the Happy Grove School and the Friends' church in the faraway sunlight. She said

Jamaicans were a deeply religious people, anxious for the Word of God. She said that though they worked hard, they were still desperately poor, and needed help. The Iowa farmers were good and generous folk. A collection was taken for the mission. But even as she watched them giving money she had the uneasy feeling that though she had talked earnestly and well their response was automatic, and she had communicated very little.

Afterwards, meeting friends, she thought how different she had become because they all seemed changed. Old Horace Brown was fatter; Agatha had more freckles, and Betty Wedemeyer had taken to wearing spectacles. The Brooks children had shot up like corn. Even folks' characters had changed; she'd never realized how pompous William Carter was, while the Gerhardts were a lot nicer than she remembered, but Alexander Wyatt, who she'd always thought was genial and pleasant, was, when you came right down to it, a blithering fool.

All that didn't explain the difference. It was that she saw them all now from another viewpoint, and they were no longer an absolute, not the sum of humanity, but one small group of it, whose skin and clothes and voices, and whose minds, were local and particular.

The following week, the men came for haymaking. There not being room in the kitchen, Amy, her stepmother, laid a spread for them under the maple trees. She and Grace had cooked for a day or two, ham, chicken, porkchops, and mounds of mashed potatoes, five kinds of salad, and corn on the cob. There were apple pies and blueberry pies and pecan pies, and jugs and jugs of buttermilk.

Grace sat on the porch steps and watched them eat, farmers and farmers' sons, in blue overalls, their white skins tanned, or freckled, or burned, hair blond or brown, wet from the pump and plastered down, but sticking up again already. She observed the serious business of eating, and the little jokes that passed between them, a dig in the ribs, a tease, a piece of good humoured mockery. She looked at their faces in turn, two of them handsome, all of them glowing with health. Good men, good husbands.

'When are you coming home for good, Grace?' Arthur Neville, her father, was sitting on the step beside her.

'I've promised the Mission Board another year.'

'And that'll be that?'

'I suppose.'

'Some people stay on.'

Grace didn't reply.

'You haven't told us about your friends down there. Maybe you don't have any.'

'Yes, I do.'

'Men friends? You don't have a beau down in Jamaica do you?'

Grace looked directly at him. 'I have a good friend.'

'Teacher?'

'He's a farmer. His farm is a lot bigger than this one, though I doubt it gives him a better living.'

'That's interesting. What does he raise?'

'Bananas mostly.'

'Well, I never. Englishman is he?'

'No, he's Jamaican.'

'Jamaican. What colour would he be? Is he black?'

'No, he's brown. His mother is black, but his father was British.'

'That's interesting. Well, you watch your step, Grace. I don't fancy any nigger grandchildren.'

It was said so casually, so off-hand, that Grace was caught off balance, and she paused before she replied in a low voice, 'I'm surprised at you, a religious man and a Friend.'

'Religion's got nothing to do with it. Setting them free is one thing, and educating them another, but there's nothing in the Good Book that says you have to marry them.'

'There's nothing that says you mustn't.'

'Is that what you're planning to do, marry this man?'

'Of course not.'

'Then there's no point in this talk, is there?'

'You started it,' Grace snapped. She picked up his plate and went into the kitchen. She was shaking with rage. She put the plate down on the table, then slowly picked it up again, and smashed it on the rim of the sink. It gave her time to compose herself, picking up the pieces.

Nothing else was said, and the subject was thereafter avoided, but like anything else deliberately ignored it grew in importance, enlarged by silences, defined by sharp exchanges over other matters, totally irrelevant; it altered Arthur's listening, for both he and Amy knew she was no longer mentioning Stanley. This small, dark, unknown man did not attend the summer gatherings, took no part in the feeding of the pigs, the churning of the butter, or the hay-making, but in the long Iowa twilight, as the family, never very talkative, sat on the porch in silence, Arthur whittling, Amy sewing, and Grace, her Bible on her lap, looking past the maple to the yellowing horizon, Stanley could not be ignored. His very absence became palpable and present.

'The unseen guest,' said Grace, out loud.

'What was that?'

'The unseen guest at every meal. Our Lord Jesus Christ.'

Chapter Five

The stately movement of a ship allows time to experience the emotions of arrival in the proper sequence, time to enjoy the swift leap, glide and dive of the flying fish at dawn, to look down at the white foam hissing along the ship's side, to look up in awe at the huge mass of Jamaica rising from the sea, still clear of the rain clouds, all her peaks visible, five, six, seven thousand feet up in the azure air, time to distinguish the red roofs of Port Antonio huddled in the green, a line of white beach, the lighthouse, candy-striped, the brown limestone cliffs, red splashes of poinciana, the tops of the royal palms rising above the houses.

In the channel, the ship slowed, the engines grew quieter, as did the sea, changing from blue to dark green in the shadow of the land. Grace recognized De Roux on the pilot boat as it chugged toward them, small, busy and important. As he came up the side, he saw Grace at the rail, and called out pleasantly.

'Stanley waiting for you on the wharf.'

Grace was thrown into confusion; she could think of no possible reply; she felt herself blushing, a sensation she hated. She turned abruptly and fled to the safety of her cabin and the reassurance of her luggage, packed and ready, neatly organized, all hers, all ordered, in control. Through the porthole she saw the town coming closer, roofs, windows, balconies, trees close enough to distinguish separate leaves, a person watching, and a dog like all Jamaican dogs, half-starved and indolent. She felt ashamed, cowardly, hiding in the cabin. If Stanley had come twenty-five miles, and had given up his day's work in order to meet her, she could at least go up on deck.

Where was he? The edge of the wharf was in bright sunshine, and there were labourers waiting for the warps, ready to make the ship fast. Behind in the shadow of the shed there were other men moving among the great piles of green bananas neatly stacked and wrapped in wet trash, a man in a pith helmet, and a tally clerk in a white shirt. Then Stanley stepped out of the shadows into the sunshine on her left and stood looking at her. He was wearing riding breeches with leather gaiters, a khaki jacket and a tie, and carrying a felt hat in his hand.

Grace lifted her hand, tentatively, and waved.

Stanley smiled, raised the hat and waved it slightly. Grace looked up and down the wharf, but there was no sign of Alsina, or Mr Khadurian, or the school buggy. There was to be no escape.

'Welcome back. We're glad to have you.'

'We, Mr Newton?'

'Yes, all of us.'

'I thought there'd be someone from the school.'

'I had to be in Port Antonio on business anyway, and the school buggy is broken down.'

'How did you manage that?'

'What a thing to say,' he said, all innocence. 'Would I do such a thing?'

'I think you'd be capable of anything if you put your mind to it.'

Stanley went off to find her luggage and make sure it was loaded on the buggy. That accomplished, Grace was eager to set off, but Stanley suggested they should celebrate her return to Jamaica by having lunch at the Titchfield Hotel. Grace decided not to argue. Besides, she was hungry, and that wonderful lassitude of heat and humidity had already begun to take toll of her moral fibre. This, too, was home, she thought, as they clattered through Port Antonio, along its gravelled main street lined with shops, unpainted posts supporting their corrugated iron roofs, the dark shops themselves breathing out the smell of salted fish, brown sugar, and bread, and the street overcrowded as always with people on no special errand, calling out to one another, laughing, leaning on fenceposts, or moving slowly across in front of the buggy with a lazy, indolent swaying of the hips.

They went past the market crammed with women guarding their piles of fruit and vegetables, past the war memorial, a skimpy cenotaph reminding all and sundry that even Port Antonio had contributed her sons to the general butchery in Flanders' fields, past the brick courthouse with the Union Jack flying from the cupola and a policeman in a white jacket and black trousers with broad red seams hanging over the iron balcony smoking a cigarette. They went on up the hill to the middle-class part of town, the residential district where two-storeyed houses sat in their own gardens, and maids swept verandahs, and lighter coloured children played on grassier lawns.

They went through the menu at the Titchfield, from the callaloo soup to the stewed guavas and coconut cream, sitting on the verandah overlooking the harbour entrance.

'Are you glad to be back?' It was a question casually put, but cunningly intended.

Grace reflected on it. 'I'm not sure I've been away. I don't think our hearts and minds are big enough to cope with God's world. Ten days ago I was in Iowa, and that was real, as if it were the only reality, and now Jamaica again, and this is so real. I may have to divide myself in two.'

She smiled. Stanley was listening as to a divine revelation, and concerned at the same time with the curve of her lip, her cheekbones and her hazel eyes. It was embarrassing to be so totally observed.

'You look very prosperous,' she said.

'Oh well, we try to make an impression.'

'Has the farm done well?'

'Not too bad,' replied Stanley. 'We've had good rains, and the banana price is so-so. We're all right if no breeze.'

'If no breeze?'

'Hurricane. It's the season.'

Grace looked past him at the sunlit garden, a pechary hopping on the lawn, a green and yellow coconut frond outlined against the calm, blue sea.

'If no breeze – that doesn't seem real either.'

'Real enough. Mind you, we should have had our share already, but you never know.'

'When was the last?'

'We had one in '17, one in '18 and '19.'

'Were your crops insured?'

Stanley shook his head ruefully. 'In '17, I didn't think about it, in '18 I thought lightning wouldn't strike twice, and by '19 we couldn't afford it. We lost everything. Complete destruction. Harold was very upset. I don't blame him. He felt I'd let him down when he was away fighting for King and Country. I wanted to give up and get a job in a bank, in an office, selling insurance, anything. But I had good friends, people who gave me credit because they knew I was sober and hardworking, and I don't mind telling you, I prayed.'

'How is Harold?' Grace said, 'and Cynthia?'

'Harold's all right, up and down. He's never really settled since he got back from the War. Getting married, of course, is a good thing.'

'They're happy?'

'Oh yes, oh yes.'

'And Cynthia?'

Stanley paused. 'In my opinion, Cynthia needs an interest. You see, my mother runs the house. I'm busy. So if Harold isn't there, time hangs heavy on her hands. She's not used to living in the country.'

'She could work for the church, or for the school.'

'Perhaps you could encourage her.'

'That would be impertinent.'

'A family would help. Starting a family.'

There was a silence as they both reflected on the idea of a family. Grace sat looking at her empty coffee cup. Stanley stirred, pulled his watch out, opened it, and snapped it shut again.

'Oh my,' he said. 'We must be running along.'

They were halfway to the school and the buggy had entered the romantic ravine known as Devil's Elbow, where the road is overhung by ferns and orchids, when Stanley plucked up the courage to break another of their silences.

'Have you had time to think about getting married?'

'It's quite impossible. It's out of the question.'

'Why?'

'Oh, Stanley, please don't ask. If the answer is no the reasons don't matter.'

'You are sure?'

'Yes,' in a low voice.

'I just wanted to know. I can't keep the offer open for ever.'

'Of course not. There are other fish in the sea.'

'Yes.'

They both became absorbed once more in the movements of the mule and the lurching of the buggy.

Stanley said, 'It's not true. I'll wait for you, Grace, until you've done your duty to the school and the Mission.'

'Then I'll go home.'

Stanley addressed the mule, raising his voice to attract the attention of the oracle.

'Do you think she'll go back to Iowa, Marcus?'

Marcus, the sterile product of miscegenation, kept moving, his head nodding, his ludicrous ears flapping to his own rhythm, minding his own business, which was to pull a load of misery up a long uphill slope.

Of course there was more to be said, thought, written and prayed about. Stanley and Grace embarked on a debate that lasted through a summer, two rainy seasons and a hot Christmas. Did they have a relationship, or was it imagined? Should it ripen into friendship, love, or retreat into courtesy? Should it end abruptly, cruelly, mercifully, happily? They were of different nations, different colours, in a world where millions are slaughtered for those differences alone. They wished they had never met, that they could be spared decision or indecision, but such doubts and fears made the touch of hands more exciting, greetings more charged, farewells more poignant, and the strange accents of each other's voices more amusing, wiser, kinder, and more endearing, and gave to the whole weight and presence of each other's bodies a special agony, a stronger passion.

If sexual need is so powerful that when perverted it becomes rape, murder or violation of children, if it can produce self-torture and suicide, then two healthy and high-principled young people can hardly be expected to control it. Stanley and Grace were like two swimmers, caught by an undertow, and becoming aware of it, turning in circles to decide which bank to make for, together or alone, and in that brief circling drifting beyond safety, the current bearing them faster, ever faster, past any point of rescue, rock or tree, or pebble beach, until the swift current, blending with the sound of thunder swept them toward the Niagara of their own desire.

How did he know she was alone in the house, that the girls had gone sea-bathing, that Alsina was at a staff meeting from which she, Grace, had excused herself because of a headache, and that it was Myrtle's afternoon off? He must be having her watched, and all her movements reported by some sinister bush telegraph, 'Boom-de-boom, de-boom. Miss Nebble alone in de 'ouse!'

Well, if not, why was his buggy coming up the hill?

Grace stood back from the window, so she couldn't be seen, and watched the mule struggling up the steep slope. He was looking up toward the window. She moved away, and went back to the desk where she had been writing, this time a letter to her sister in Des Moines, describing her work in Jamaica.

> ... there is so much sickness and death. Sunday I had my first experience of committing a body. All the people concerned were about the most wicked and rude I ever saw. It was a mother leaving five sick, almost naked children. I was just sick at the way the people acted, then I was told they acted unusually well. Why will folk mix the sacred and the vulgar with death so? And oh, the superstition ...

She could hear the buggy now, right at the foot of the stairs! If he left it here, the whole village would see it! He might as well blow a trumpet. She moved to the wooden jalousies overlooking the steps. Mercifully the buggy had moved away. He was going to leave it in the dark shadow of the almond tree. Thank God for small mercies, but did that mean he was intending a long visit?

Stanley was walking back toward the house. Grace decided she wouldn't be trapped inside the house, so she opened the door and stepped out to meet him even as he came up the steps removing the offending helmet. He was handsome, gentle and serious, and she was glad to see him, but he shouldn't have come.

'I was just passing by . . .'

'Didn't you get my letter? I wrote to you yesterday.'

'Yes.'

'I said I couldn't invite you, under the circumstances.'

'I was just passing by. I thought there might be something I could do.'

'That was a kind thought. I admit, Mr Newton that I'm accustomed to talk things over with you, even to ask favours.'

'It's no inconvenience.'

'Perhaps it's not good for me, or even good for the school. We should stand on our own feet.'

'You don't want anything at all from me. Is that it?'

'I didn't say that. Why can't folks who want to understand just understand? Why can't you leave me alone?'

He let go the verandah railing, and turned his palm upwards in a small gesture of helplessness, and let his arm fall by his side. He stood looking at her, mute, loving and determined.

'You'd best come in,' she said. 'There's no tea till next week, but we have fresh limes, and I can make you some lemonade.'

The limes were in a basket in the pantry, which was shuttered and in semi-darkness. The brown sugar was in a safe, screened against cockroaches, and the cool water in the earthenware pot. Grace looked for a knife, found one in a drawer, and began, as he watched, to cut the green limes in half. She squeezed them, holding them between fingers and palm, forcing the juice, which ran down her hand into a pitcher.

'I'm not sure about these limes,' she said. 'They may be too sour. You're the expert.'

'Where did they come from?'

'The yard, I reckon. Tucker brought them.'

'Let's see,' he said, and coming closer, took not a lime but her wet hand with the juice and kissed it, tasting.

'They are good,' he said, and kept her hand imprisoned.

'Let go . . . my hands are sticky . . . please.'

He ignored her, turning her to face him, and drawing her close, letting go, and putting his arms, instead, around her waist. They kissed, lip to lip, twice, tenderly, hearing in the still house, close, the loud beating of their hearts, and far off, the murmur of the sea.

'I love you.'

'Please.'

He held her more tightly, and she pressed her body into his, he eager, hot, she trembling violently. He kissed her till the trembling stopped and she responded with an equal passion, yielding, withholding nothing, answering back, then suddenly, once again, breaking off, pushing him away.

'Please, Stanley. Leave me alone, please.'

'I love you.'

'Then do as I say.'

'No.'

She pushed the hair back from her forehead. 'You have me at your mercy,' she said, bitterly. 'At your mercy.'

Stanley stood, holding her hands, looking into her eyes, and she waited, consenting. But the note of bitterness had been a warning. This is too important, he thought, too important to be wrong.

'When you are ready,' he said, 'and not till then.'

Chapter Six

During the holidays, Grace missed her girls. However much trouble they were, however noisy and giggly, they were better than a silent dormitory. She might have despaired of ever teaching them anything, of getting Chloris to understand algebra or Joy to wash her hands before eating, Ruth to think of anything else but boys and Martha not to squeeze those awful pimples, but their lives, their slow progress toward womanhood, the identification of each talent, however small, was what she was there for, it was her calling. The school with no one in it but the teachers was a travesty.

So she turned her attention to the village. More and more she became involved in the lives of the people, and they, discovering a sympathetic and a helping hand, came more to rely on her. Grace knew nothing about medicine beyond elementary hygiene, what constituted a proper diet and the names of one or two common medicines. But that and her self-assurance qualified her to be both doctor and nurse. She was not a farm girl from Iowa for nothing. Herself unmarried she still knew something about the body of a woman, the problems of pregnancy, childbirth and the rearing of children and, more important, what she did know was not clouded by superstition, so she became both obstetrician and pediatrician to the village. Besides, she loved babies, and there was no shortage of them. In the mornings, under the shade of the almond tree, there were always two or three mothers waiting patiently to talk to her, to show her a baby, or to ask advice. Many an afternoon found her on foot in the village lanes, stopping to talk, looking for the home of one who was sick, or sitting on the step of someone's hut with a baby in her lap.

Jamaicans, she had been told, were simple people, a foolish phrase which, if it meant anything, meant that they laughed and sang and danced, and their reactions were swift and spontaneous. But she was to discover that they were also quick to violence, subject to terrible rages and depressions, prone to madness and to murder. Many a girl beaten by her lover came to Grace with her story, and so she became involved with their relationships and with the men, for she demanded that the guilty man should appear to tell his story. So she became psychologist and marriage counsellor in a world of promiscuity and illegitimacy.

She no longer thought the people strange. Knowing each name and face, each type and feature, she found that their common blackness became the least and not the most important thing about them. Her ear also had been tuned. When she had arrived in Jamaica she thought that people like the Newtons and the teachers spoke English with an accent but that the village spoke another language altogether. Now that language was beginning to make sense. She became accustomed to the village, and the village made her welcome.

Particularly in the holidays, Grace would make long trips in the buggy, which she drove herself, to help service somewhere in the hills, or to be visiting preacher at some other church along the coast,

Baptist or Methodist; and weekday evenings would find her at prayer meetings or choir practice in some stifling hot room lit by one kerosene lamp and full of the stench of sweat and religious ecstasy.

After prayer meetings far from home, she was always escorted back by men of the congregation, two or three of them walking behind the buggy, silent, or muttering to each other in a low tone, black in the blackness, guarding her. At first she was more afraid of her deep-voiced escorts than of the night, but after a while she felt she knew them, each and all, and knew that no one in the green world wished her harm, that she was in the hands of God, and these black guardian angels were her friends.

Stanley was a member of the Kingston Cricket Club. He wasn't rich enough or important enough for the Jamaica Club, which like the best London clubs had no activity except its own existence, he wasn't white enough for the Liguanea Club and didn't play polo, and the Jockey Club was out of the question. Living in the country he had no opportunity to play cricket at Sabina Park, but loved the game, and it was there he met his friends. Some like himself were landowners, others professional men or businessmen; some white, English civil servants, bankers or businessmen posted to Jamaica; some brown, lawyers or merchants or doctors of old Jamaican families; none black.

Netherton and Hurst were in the bar sipping whisky and soda, and they offered Stanley a drink.

'Something soft,' said Stanley, as he always did.

'Sorry, Stanley,' said Netherton. 'Wouldn't have wasted my time offering you a drink. I thought you were your brother.' He turned to the barman, 'You have any lemonade for Mr Newton?' and turning back to Stanley, 'How is life in the bush, man?'

'Struggling along,' said Stanley.

'Not the way I heard it. The stakes Harold was playing for last week you fellows must have a gold mine out there.'

Stanley glanced at Hurst, who was watching him closely.

'He didn't tell you about it?' said Hurst.

'Of course he did,' replied Stanley immediately, and then regretted it. Harold had told him nothing, and he would have liked to know what Harold had won or lost and whose money he was playing with.

They moved on to the verandah of the pavilion overlooking the cricket pitch. Lunch was served on white linen, with silver plate, a hibiscus floating in a bowl of water, and an elderly waiter accustomed to being the butt of the members' humour. The menu would have graced a London club, and while they ate, the ritual of cricket was enacted for their benefit on the sun-browned turf below, the smooth run, the elegant stroke, the white-clad fielders moving in slow motion in the blinding heat. Beyond, over the roofs and tree-tops of Kingston, the afternoon breeze was coming up, bringing white caps to the blue harbour.

The conversation drifted back and forth between the progress of the game, the merits of the players, and the prospects for Jamaica. For centuries the privileged of Kingston have considered themselves threatened, under siege. England was five thousand miles away, the poor discontent were under the floorboards and there was no refuge in the encircling sea. So at lunch, watching the cricket, the conversation was a catalogue of complaint and prophecies of imminent disaster. Even when Hurst offered the tentative opinion that things could be worse, that there was a post-war boom, export prices were good and people were investing in Jamaica, building new hotels and buying land, Stanley hemmed and hawed and Netherton was almost angry.

'You see, man, we are not equipped in Jamaica to handle good times. We have no skills to build anything permanent. A bit of money may be made or lost, or taken out of the island. The one thing constant in Jamaica, good times or bad, is that the people keep on breeding, and every time you turn around there are more mouths to feed.'

'And the lean years shall devour them, kith and kin,' said Stanley.

He excused himself at the tea interval. He was preoccupied with the news of Harold's gambling escapade, and feared the worst. If Harold had won he would have boasted about it and, by the same token, his silence meant that he had lost a lot.

Stanley had half a mind to cut short the trip to Kingston, and go straight home to have it out with Harold. But on the way back to his lodgings he decided that bad news could wait till morning. There was a Gloria Swanson picture at the Palace, and he dearly loved moving pictures. If he went over to Argyll Crescent and called on the Spences, he might persuade Kathleen to go with him. Grace could have no objection, she wanted him to be free, she said so. Kathleen was just twenty and looking for a husband. She was a bit of a flibbertigibbet, and he was afraid that, like Cynthia, country life might not suit her, but she had wicked little eyes, a smile that made you happy, and the smoothest coffee-brown skin in creation.

It didn't work. Kathleen was confined to her room with a mysterious fever, and all he saw of her luscious body was a brown ankle below a crumpled dressing gown. All he heard was the flip-flop of mules as she went into the kitchen, and from time to time her high plaintive voice calling for her mother. Stanley spent the evening on the verandah, listening to Mrs Spence, a huge brown lady firmly anchored in her rocking chair by the weight of her buttocks. She must have been beautiful as her daughter was now, and he imagined she could still be warm, still laugh, still charm. But somewhere along the line the woman had decided that life was a labyrinth of illness and danger, a journey beset by drunken husbands, insane relatives, colds, flu, chills, malaria, rheumatism, and constant dying of impecunious aunts. Her conversation was a rhapsodic moan, a litany of anxiety. Her only safety was where she was, on her own verandah, in her rocking chair. She sat, in slippers, her fat thighs slightly spread showing the rolled stocking tops just above the knee, her printed dress bulging, a shawl around her shoulders, her wide mouth rouged, her black hair bobbed. Her shrewd but sleepy eyes glanced occasionally at Stanley, to make sure that he was listening, but most of the time they were fixed on the encircling darkness, on the potential dangers of the night, while the eternal melody of complaint flowed from her into the garden, like the warble of a lugubrious nightingale.

My God, thought Stanley, suppose Kathleen turned out to be like that.

Once a week, Aunt Mary, the oldest missionary, made a voyage to church. The meeting house was fifty yards away down the muddy lane lined by royal palms, but it was still an expedition. Her servant, Loraleen, supported her on one side, and Grace, who was visiting, and who was going to preach, assisted her on the other. Isaac waited at the gate with a dray, drawn by a donkey. On the back of the dray was a neatly folded krukus bag, for comfort and for cleanliness. Isaac helped to lift her on to the dray, where she sat, facing backwards, her legs dangling. All this may have been galling to one who as a young woman had walked the Rio Grande valleys and crossed the Blue Mountains on a mule, but it did not seem so. Isaac urged, the donkey pulled, Grace and Loraleen walked on either side, and Aunt Mary on the dray journeyed joyously toward God.

The meeting house was a one-room wooden building. Pulpit and lectern were the same. Only one bench had a back, and that was reserved for the old lady. The narrow windows were rendered ecclesiastical by panes of red, yellow or frosted glass, and the doors stayed open to the squelchy yard. The congregation numbered fifteen, most of them East Indians, but Isaac, his woman, and a young man in a high collar and a blue serge suit were black. Aunt Mary and Grace were white. There was a small piano, out of tune but lovingly polished, and Grace accompanied the hymns. They sang 'Breathe on me, Breath of God' and 'Brightest and Best.' There was a period of silent prayer. Grace preached, the one about the ninety and nine who safely lay in the shelter of the fold, and the rejoicing occasioned by the return of the lost sheep. It was a theme much on her mind at the time, but she delivered it in a version abbreviated to the size of the congregation and the state of Aunt Mary's bladder.

Yet, after the service, Aunt Mary stayed on her bench. She declined the assistance of Loraleen, asking her to wait outside, and when Grace had said goodbye to the worshippers, and they had all passed through the gate in the hibiscus hedge, she summoned Grace to sit beside her.

'I hear that you are courting.'

Grace's reply was firm, unhesitating, the voice of decision and determination. 'No, that's over.'

Aunt Mary looked directly at her, the pale blue eyes as innocent as a child's.

'I have a letter from the Board of Missions asking me to counsel you against this marriage.'

'Well, there's no need, but how impertinent,' said Grace, and there was real anger in her voice.

Aunt Mary smiled. 'They mean well.'

'So do Alsina, Ruby, Bob Steere and Wilma, all of them mean well. But that's not it, Aunt Mary. It would kill my father.'

'Does he say so? Dying is not so easy. Grace, until you came to Jamaica, I was afraid of dying. Now I can die in peace because when you came, I knew that I had seen the one whose shoes I was not worthy to unloose. I gave a helping hand to Jamaica, you will give your heart as well.'

'No, I'm going back to Iowa.'

Aunt Mary plucked at a fold of her dress, and stirred. Her jaw moved, but no words came, and there was a silence between them, the young woman and the old, sitting together in the empty church. Outside, it was beginning to rain. Aunt Mary seemed to have forgotten what they were talking about, or had remembered something else, her childhood, or the dinner that Loraleen was keeping warm. But she had not forgotten, she was merely gathering herself, and when she spoke the quavering of age had gone.

'Grace, if your love be pure and honest, it cannot be denied because of the colour of your skin, or his, for that would blaspheme against the God who made you both. Let us pray.'

Aunt Mary folded her freckled, blue-veined hands in her lap, closed her eyes and lifted her face to the light.

That night, back at the Girls' School, Grace lay in bed watching the fireflies on the ceiling, a brief glow of greenish light, going out, then another, and another. She was quite unable to sleep.

What a difference it made, the word of one old lady. Everyone else had spoken against it, or been silently against it, and the problem, the dreadful anxiety, the moral torment, and the physical longing had remained, had not been swept away by the torrent of contrary opinion. One word, one word from Aunt Mary had brought a measure of peace, and a new excitement. Everyone was against it, that is, everyone on her side of the line. What line? The colour line; the line of foreigners, the line of Christians. Well, good heavens, what sort of Christianity was that? What about the black Christians, the people in the village, the children in the school, Dr Foster, Stanley's mother? Stanley's mother would be her mother-in-law. That would give them something to talk about. Stanley's father was out of it, he was dead. But there was no question of his opinion. Looking at the congregation of the Church of England in Manchioneal, anyone would know that randy old Welshman had fathered not only Stanley and Harold but half of them as well. The old reprobate. Was Stanley like him? Would he be faithful, steadfast, and a friend?

Stanley. Yes, he was quiet and dependable, but that wasn't all. There was a devil in the man, a wicked devil, and that devil had set his cap for her. He was hiding behind Stanley the Christian, Stanley the gentleman, Stanley the trustworthy and sober. He was a wicked, ambitious devil who meant to possess her, and destroy her. Grace smiled in the darkness. She had a devil of her own. The isle was full of devils.

Mr Hoffman, the headmaster, a slim, black Cupid with a starched collar and pink fingernails, presided over Sunday tea on his verandah. After service that morning, Grace had surprised him by saying suddenly, 'Montclair, will you invite Stanley and myself to tea? I want to talk to him.' He had invited no one else, as he had no instruction to do so. Now, his two guests were ignoring him, and, it seemed, each other as well, for only the wind in the coconuts and the sea below the cliffs were audible. Clearly, Cupid's job was done, and he was not needed as chaperone, so he bethought himself of other duties.

'Algebra,' Mr Hoffman said, and departed.

Stanley was fascinated by a butterfly on a stone. Grace pushed a wisp of hair back from her forehead. It was, as usual, hot.

'Montclair said you wanted to talk to me,' said Stanley, taking the plunge.

Grace took a deep breath, then sighed, then started again. 'I don't want to give you too much hope, Mr Newton,' she said, 'but I will allow you to see me again.'

Stanley abandoned his contemplation of the butterfly and turned to her. Their eyes met, giving and receiving the same challenge, the same promise. She put her hand in his. Stanley, looking at her, saw her eyes fill with tears, and when the first one fell, he wiped it away. He moved closer, and she rested her head on his shoulder, his arm around her waist. So they stayed, in a torment of touching, while Grace wept.

Joy and sorrow have a common language: tears. The tears of joy come silently. We weep for dying, and for loving, for love is a kind of death. It is the death of a self, proud, frightened and alone, a self dying into union with one other, and so into a union with all others, the world around, above, within. In tears we are helpless, we surrender, understanding that this all-important self is nothing, and will die. In tears we are ready to die, peacefully, and there is no harm or hurt in dying, only a return to the great womb of life.

'Are you comfortable?' Grace said.

'My shoulder's a bit stiff.'

'I'm sorry.'

He kissed her.

Then he rose, and stood in front of her. Taking both her hands he helped her to her feet. He was on the grass, she on the step, so she looked down at him. She was his goddess, hazel-eyed and wise, he her dark devil, mocking and amused.

'Shall we stop crying and be happy now?' he asked.

'Yes,' she said, and smiled.

Chapter Seven

Seaside church, as the Friends' church was called, was never full in the holidays, so Grace's wedding party fitted easily into a dozen benches at the front. On the groom's side there were Harold, Cynthia, Stanley's mother in pale blue satin with a white hat, Mr Warren, the bookkeeper from Williamsfield, Dimsey the foreman, who looked too much like the Newtons, Garvey, the manager of the bank in Morant Bay, the Pitters from Retreat, and Burstall, the United Fruit Company's agent at Long Bay. For some of these, being in church at all was an unaccustomed purgation, and they sat sweating in their sober suits while their wives smiled and fluttered their fans at each other.

On the bride's side, the Quaker contingent, at home with God, were white and smiling. No disappointment showed, no fear, and looking on the bright side they were aware that Grace might be the bridge to the community, that the sacrifice of her body might close the gap between the ministers and those to whom they ministered, a gap that, despite all care and concern, had never been closed before. Behind them sat the local pillars of the church, farmers and tradesmen, black, respectable, with wives genteelly dressed, small sons in suits and little girls with plaited hair, washed, brushed and starched, clad in pink, yellow and white, carrying little posies of flowers.

Stanley's suit, tailored for him by Charles Dyer of King Street, emphasized how slim he was, and how small. Grace had set out to make her own wedding dress, and given up; she could not cut or pin without bursting into tears. Just the sight of the material had made her think of her dead mother and her father marrying that Amy woman, and summer evenings in Iowa, long summer evenings when she had sat on the porch and looked out over the cornfield to the line of willows along the creek, watching the day and the greenness fade to black, just sitting there until it was time to light a lamp in the parlour. Life was unbearable, unutterably and inevitably doomed to misery. Mabel had come in from the village and helped her. The result was a credit to Grace's tears and Mabel's stitching. It was simple, a fitted bodice, long sleeves and a full skirt, with a little bonnet and veil, like a maid's cap, demure and roguish.

The reception was at the Mission Home, with tea and cakes under the poinciana, and lemonade for the children. Everyone said what a nice occasion it was, and how lucky Stanley was, and how Grace had made such a good choice, and how Jamaica and America were now united in a loving bond.

In the midst of this came the big surprise. Stanley had hired a car for the honeymoon. This strange object, a Model-T, had been hidden behind the Mission Home, and there was a burst of laughter and applause as it appeared with Harold, wearing goggles, at the wheel and the luggage strapped to the back. Grace and Stanley came out of the Mission Home, pelted with stinging rice. Grace tossed her bouquet neatly to the plainest of the Marriott girls, and Harold put the car in gear and drove off. The men pretended the car needed to be pushed, and the women laughed. Harold pulled out the throttle and the car shot through the gate and across the church yard, heading for the road. Children ran after it, keeping up as long as possible, and calling out farewells.

Then, as there was no drink, the planters drifted toward their buggies, and the villagers, seeing that those who came from far were going, paid their respects to the missionaries, and made for the path that led up to the village, to their cottages hidden in the trees.

Because there were now two couples living in the old Williamsfield house, it was agreed that another servant was necessary, so Grace engaged one. She had noticed the girl first in Sunday School, and later when she joined the choir. She was a tiny thing, but wiry, energetic, and of unfailing good humour. She had high cheekbones, and very bright eyes in a very black face. She smiled often, a dazzlingly white smile of pure joy, and when she laughed it was as if she were dancing, swaying from the hip with her arms dangling and her head thrown back. Her real name was something else, but everybody called her Sunshine.

Sunshine knew nothing, nothing about cooking, sewing or ironing, nothing about serving at table. Grace set herself to teach her. As a young bride, a young Christian, and a farmer's daughter, Grace would have preferred to do these chores herself, but she had learned that in Jamaica it was not possible without overturning the structure of society; she was a mistress, and mistress she should be. Besides, Sunshine needed the work, and the shilling a week wages, and she was very good company.

They were together in the yard behind the kitchen where the ironing board was set out, and Grace was showing Sunshine how to lay out a shirt sleeve, how to sprinkle it, and how to test the iron, when Tumpy came back from the post office with the letter.

It was from America, with an Iowa postmark, Grace had been expecting to hear from her father, but it was not his handwriting. She feared the worst.

'Sunshine,' she said, 'leave the shirts until later, just do Mr Stanley's underwear and socks.' Then she moved away, around the corner of the house to read the letter in private. The sea breeze blew the envelope away and ruffled the sheets of paper so that she had to hold them in both hands.

Richland, Iowa
August 15, 1923

Dear Grace,

Your letter telling us of your marriage plans came some weeks ago – can such a thing be called a marriage? Arthur will not write and says he will not speak to you again. I am writing as you must have an answer, and you must know our feelings. Arthur took to his bed for three days, though he is back at work because he must. He speaks to nobody as if he mourned a death, worse than a death, a shame. Tell her he wishes you joy with your nigger husband, he says, but wants you to know you are no more his kith or kin. May God forgive you for what you have done to us, and all respectable folk . . .

Grace was shaking, trembling so violently that she could no longer read or hold the letter. She gasped for breath, trying to control herself, trying not to cry, or scream, and by doing neither trembled all the more. In the warm sunshine, she was very cold. She looked outward, past the oleander blossom to the windruffled waves, and inward at the same instant to her home, to see her father by the pot-bellied stove, his large calloused hands holding her mother's Bible on his knees, and little Amy perched at the writing desk, scratching away at this letter that was meant to kill her.

Sunshine was calling, 'Mrs Newton, Mrs Newton I think I burning Mr Stanley's underpants, ma'm. I mean it singe . . . I'm sorry, ma'm.'

'It's all right, never mind. I'll do this batch. You watch me, and you'll learn.'

'Yes'm. Yes.'

Grace forced herself to finish the ironing, though her hands were shaking, her mouth was dry, and she wanted to be sick.

'I can do it now, mistress, please.'

Grace put the iron back on the coals, turned and ran, ran indoors, ran to the safety of her room, threw herself face downwards on the bed, and cried.

About tea time, Mama Newton, like a black Queen Victoria, banged imperiously on the door. 'Grace, you come out here now, come along. You can carry on and cry, and cry and carry on, but you can't expect other people to listen to you. Come out, do you hear! I'm having my tea on the verandah, and I want you to come sit with me.'

Grace, who had by now achieved a sitting position on the edge of the bed, muttered her assent. She rose, washed her face slowly in the tepid water from the pitcher, dried it, changed her blouse, re-did her hair, and some twenty minutes later took her place by Mama Newton's tea tray on the verandah. Cynthia, pregnant and eager for scandal, drama, or tragedy, had been banished, told by Mama Newton to supervise the cooking of the stew peas for supper because

Madlyn, the cook, had quarrelled with her baby-father and might decide to poison everybody.

'So,' said Mama Newton to Grace, 'somebody dead?'

Grace told her about the letter, '... that Amy is not even my own mother, just a nobody, a little widow woman who darns the old man's socks.'

'Don't speak hard of her, Grace. White people mad sometimes. They don't understand. Don't hackle your mind about it, and don't hold any bitterness in your heart,' she took Grace's hand, 'for one day, sure as fate, they will come to you for forgiveness.'

Mama Newton pursued the ritual of tea, pouring, stirring, nibbling at cookies, but this did not disturb her line of thought, or the seriousness of her manner. 'Grace, there are those who will turn against you, who are not worthy to wash your feet. Remember the words of Ruth in the Holy Bible. "Whither thou goest, I will go, and where thou lodgest, I will lodge. Thy people shall be my people and thy God, my God." If your family forsake you, you have family here.' Mama Newton spread her arms wide in an all-embracing gesture. 'A whole island full of family! Come, give your mother a kiss.'

Grace obeyed. She rose, leaned over the old lady in the rocking chair, and kissed her on the forehead. Mama Newton patted her on the hip, then, as Grace straightened up, something else caught the matriarchal eye.

'Grace, is that Harold coming up the hill? I hope he's walking steady.'

It was, and he wasn't. Harold had climbed the dirt track through the pasture, negotiated the gap in the wall which was the entrance to the yard, and was attempting the last twenty yards of lawn which separated him from the verandah. Having to do this under the watchful eyes of Grace and his mother, one young, one old, one black, one white, both disapproving angels, was almost impossible. He paused to wipe his brow.

'Having tea?' said Harold.

There was no reply, so Harold continued his approach, but as he lifted his leg to touch the bottom step, Mama Newton's anger stopped him like a bullet.

'Harold! I can smell the rum from here! Nobody comes through my front door in that condition. Go round the back, and Harold ... bathe off the stinking rum sweat before you come to supper!'

Harold did not come to supper at all. He was waiting, he said, for his mother to apologize to him, an idea which made Mama Newton laugh. Stanley was at supper. Back from the fields at last light, he was clean and shining in a freshly ironed shirt, his damp hair neatly brushed. He sat opposite Grace, with Mama Newton between them. Cynthia, sulking, was at the other end. Sunshine had gone home, so Madlyn herself served the stew peas and rice with an air of conscious martyrdom. Cynthia took a plate in to Harold, which was meant as a kindness but produced a violent outburst which echoed through the house. Cynthia replied in kind, and Harold got as good as he gave. The words were not distinguishable, only the sense, the music, the tenor and soprano of it, which mounted to the crescendo of a slap, and fell away to whimpering.

The audience at the supper table sat through the performance in silence. It was a hot night, made hotter by the kerosene lamp on the table, the glass shade of which was emblazoned with the motto 'Home Sweet Home'. Small reddish brown bugs hurtled through the window to crash against the lamp, and fall on their backs on the white tablecloth, paddling their legs helplessly. Grace spent the meal flipping them over with her fork, so they could crawl or fly away. Mama Newton sat stony-faced, like a Buddha in the lamplight. This left Stanley, and only Stanley, to appreciate Madlyn's cooking. He was hungry; he had been on his mule all day, riding the wet banana fields. The quarrel in the next room did not slow his knife and fork. Even so, he was aware that Grace, opposite him, had been crying. What about? he wondered. He would have to deal with that after supper.

After supper, they went for a walk, to get away from the house where the battle of Harold and Cynthia still dragged on, and from the verandah and the slow creak of Mama Newton's rocking chair. They went through the gap in the wall, keeping the house in sight, but hidden from it in the black shade of the almond tree. There they kissed, he with the passion of health, she with the desperate longing of misery and despair.

'What's the matter, darling?'

'Nothing. Harold and Cynthia, I guess. Living so close.'

She did not tell him about Amy's letter. What, she thought, was the use? Why should he bear that burden? The letter said he was less than a man, a thing to be ashamed of. He should not have to answer such a charge. He should not be made to feel guilty simply for being what he was, warm, loving, thoughtful and tender. It was her burden, her family, and the terrible pain of their rejection, and the awful knowledge that had come to her with Amy's letter, that somewhere in a small corner of her heart, a part of her agreed with them. How, with her upbringing, could it be otherwise? That, she decided, was to be her secret, and her shame, her need to be forgiven, unconfessed.

Stanley came home from Port Antonio one day with an architect's drawing of the house he was going to build on the bush-covered hill between the Williamsfield house and the church. He unrolled it proudly on the dining table for Grace to see.

'Who did this?' asked Grace.

'It's just a sketch. Livingstone drew it for me. I told him what I wanted.'

'A castle?'

'I told him I wanted a residence for the first family of the parish, for that is what we are, and that is what we are going to be.'

Grace was staring at the drawing, at the two round towers which dominated the facade, topped with conical roofs like witches' hats.

'Stanley, what are these?'

'That's the style,' said Stanley, 'like a French chateau. There's only one other house in Jamaica like it, old man Lewis' place in St James.'

'I won't have it,' said Grace, 'I won't set foot in it. Stanley, if I wanted to live in a French chateau, I'd have turned Catholic and gone to France. It's not magnificent, it's pretentious.'

'I don't see why Jamaica shouldn't have beautiful architecture like Europe and the States. We don't have to live in huts.'

'And what will it cost?'

'It won't cost any more. I'm building it all with local labour.'

'It's pretentious and that's that. It's not Quakerly.'

'Don't bring religion into this, Grace, please.'

'Stanley, it's ugly and I'm not living in it, and that's that.'

So Stanley put the plans away, and set about designing the house himself. His tools were a tape measure coiled in a leather case like a discus, pegs, string and a carpenter's square. The bush was cleared by machete, and the plan of the house laid out on the earth. Stanley, in his khaki riding breeches, cotton shirt, braces and felt hat, supervised Joubert, the carpenter, and Adams, the mason, hopping about among the pieces of string to determine the position and size of the rooms.

Grace had to visit the site and give her approval before a spade could be turned. Instead of the towers, a verandah was to run on three sides of the house. Within, a living room, dining room, and an office. A guest bedroom faced the sea. Their own bedroom was to be on the eastern side, overlooking the church, and behind it a room Stanley called the nursery. There was to be a bathroom at the back, with running water piped from a storage tank in the yard. The kitchen and servants' quarters were to be separate, in the back yard. Grace suggested that they be connected to the house by a covered way, 'to keep the rain out of the soup'.

The walls and foundations were to be cut stone, the floors of cedar, the interior walls of rendered concrete, the roof a series of A-frames bolted to the walls and covered in native shingle. Grace, remembering the frame houses of her childhood, objected to the weight of stone and concrete, but Stanley protested that he was not building something for hurricanes to blow away. Lightness would come from the large sash windows, pairs of them, two dozen panes for every room.

'It's too big,' said Grace.

'When there's family, it won't be big enough.' And two weeks later, unbeknown to Grace, the house already started to grow. Stanley heard that a furniture factory in the next parish was closing down, and there were bargains to be had, so he got into the buggy and hurried over there. He found a set of solid mahogany doors, seven foot six by three foot six, ordered for a merchant's mansion in Kingston and cancelled by his bankruptcy, going cheap. To use them he had to push the bedrooms further to the east, and make a central corridor opening, by these splendid doors, to all the rooms.

At this time, Stanley was a happy man, for happiness to him was total absorption; absorption in the planning of things, the making of things, the doing of things.

Grace, on the other hand, was idle, and hated idleness. Sunshine and Madlyn handled the house between them. Tumpy took care of the yard and the flower beds. Mama Newton, in the manner of the old, seemed to care only about food, living from one meal to the next, and filling the intervals with worry about draughts, about being cold, or hot, or feeling real or imagined pains in shoulder, leg, stomach, back, head, neck, finger or toe. Cynthia was absorbed in her pregnancy, which she spoke of as unmitigated disaster, complaining about what the damn little thing was doing to her looks. Her skin was getting coarse, she said, her ankles swelling; she had totally lost her appetite, something an impartial observer would not have noticed; she would never recover her figure, and the sheer pain and worry of childbirth would wrinkle her face forever. She wept at the horror of it all, then cheered herself up with memories of parties, dancing, flirtations under the moon, wonderful times, wonderful things that would never come again.

So Grace escaped Mama Newton's ailments and Cynthia's tears by a renewed interest in the school. Mr Hoffman, chronically short of teachers, was only too glad to have her. She tutored, filling in for teachers ill or absent. To this she added Sunday school, and Wednesday prayer meeting, and Tuesday choir practice. When Cynthia complained that only her pregnancy kept her idle, Grace refrained from pointing out that she also was pregnant.

Time heals no wounds, but they are bandaged and obscured, pushed from the forefront of the mind by new activity. The walls of Stone Haven were rising and its naked roof beams were silhouetted against the rain clouds. The church, the school, Stanley himself and the new life inside her obscured the pain of Amy's letter, so much so that when it came to mind, suddenly, without warning, waking, or walking to work, in the middle of a meal or a prayer, Grace sought her own company and her own tears. If at such times Stanley found her weeping, she could say she wept because she loved him, and was happy, which was also true.

Grace was at the Boys' School when she got the news about Mama Newton. She was in the library, tutoring an East Indian boy about the career of Oliver Cromwell, when Tumpy rapped on the window sill.

'Miss Grace, mam, is Mama Newton, mam. She fall down on de verandah, an' it look like she gwine dead. Miss Cynthia bawlin' and she say you mus' come.'

Grace knew that Stanley was away on banana business, but she thought Harold was home, or at Sammy Ying's drinking.

'Where's Mr Harold?'

'Gone to Kingston, mam. He gone this mawnin'. Miss Cynthia say you mus' come.'

Mama Newton had had a heart attack, and hovered for days between death and life. When she recovered, she maintained that she had died, and gone to heaven. Jesus had sent her back, but not before she had seen her husband, Morgan, singing in the heavenly choir. The celestial visit had taken away her greed and petulance, purged her of petty cares. She no longer worried about her aches and pains, her failing functions or her appetite. She was bedridden, and bore it with a patient sweetness.

Grace spent many hours at her bedside, reading to her, praying with her, and listening to the old woman talk, talking about the precious past as if by doing so she could possess it once again.

'Morgan,' she would say, 'Mor . . . gan, the Reverend Mor . . . gan, lovely man, as sweet as sugar. I don't come from around here, you know, Grace. My family come from Fairy Hill, and we used was to go to the Baptist Church at Long Bay. But one night, that church burned down, so we all voyage down to the stone church at Manchioneal, built by the Reverend Morgan. That's how I meet him.

'Morgan! When Morgan was in the pulpit preaching there was angels flying round the rafters and devils diving into the ground. When Morgan look down at the girls in the congregation they just naturally press their knees together. I was wearing a little white dress and a hat with flowers, and sitting in the front row, and as Morgan's eyes pass over me, he draw breath, and I shiver. Not only me, Grace, he was a devil. He was determined to turn all Jamaica into Christians, and if he couldn't convert them, he was going to breed them.

'When he come to Jamaica first, he had a little Welsh wife with him, but she was sickly, and she didn't last long. Poor soul.'

'So then you married him?' said Grace.

'Married. Married don't come into it. I had was to drive off the opposition first, because every ugly white woman in Kingston was coming to country for tea, and every black girl who could shake her backside was shaking it at Morgan. So I make up my mind they was not going to get him, and I pick myself up, and walk into his house, and Grace, I was one damn good-looking woman, and I said, "Reverend, I come to keep house for you."

'Morgan. I used to call him my bull of many colours. His hair was black, face red, hands brown, eyes blue, his body white as milk, except for his black grasspiece and his pink and white whatyoucallit. Morgan!'

'Then you married him.'

'Well, no, Grace, that's what I'm trying to tell you. Morgan didn't want to married again. He had me, and any other gal he wanted in the district, and the bishop didn't want any black Mrs Parson in the diocese. Housekeeper was all right, and bastard pickney was all right, but wife! No, sir! So Stanley born bastard. Understand? Grace, I was actually nursing Stanley one Sunday morning with Morgan standing there in his black clothes, watching me, when he said, "Love, we are going to marry. I'm going to leave the church, and buy a farm."

'Morgan leave the church for me, but God took him back.'

'And Harold?' said Grace.

'Harold born after we married. So, by law, the property belong only to Harold. You should know that. Harold is the only boy legitimate. Stanley don't own nothing. You should know that!'

When Mama Newton died, Grace was alone in the house. Harold was off on one of his mysterious visits to Kingston. Cynthia had gone to her mother's in Port Antonio to await the birth of her baby. Stanley was not far away, supervising the building of the house on the next hill. Grace came in with a mid-morning cup of tea for Mama Newton, and found her lying on her side, her eyes open staring out of the window, seeing nothing.

There was no sign of struggle or convulsion. She seemed only to have turned to look, or listen, to a vision or a voice. She was hardly cold, and Grace could lay her straight and close her eyes, murmuring a prayer, confident as Mama Newton herself had been that Morgan and God would joyfully receive her.

Chapter Eight

'So what's the problem?'

Stanley told him, and Hurst listened attentively, nodding once or twice as if he had heard it all before. He had. George Hurst was a white man, he was Jamaica born, and the second generation of the legal firm of Hurst and Clark, so the vagaries of the island's social life were not strange to him.

'Morgan left no will?'

'I haven't found one.'

'Jamaicans are a brute,' said Hurst, digressing to give himself time to think. 'I'm trying to buy a little piece of land up in St Andrew, to build a cottage or something like that. Every time I go up there, this little old woman comes out of the bush, claims she owns it, but can't sell it.' He affected her dialect, '"Is not me alone hown it, sar," she says. "Seben a we, two gawn a Panama, two a New Yahk, one dead an' one lawse." "You 'ave papah seh so?" I ask her. "Papah! Papah, sah! Pshaw!"'

Stanley tried to smile, and managed a rueful twitch. He did not care for the comparison between the old woman's dilemma and his own.

'Your case is not so bad. But Stanley, why haven't you done something about this before?'

Stanley paused before replying. 'I let sleeping dogs lie, but now Harold has a son, and I'm also married, and my wife is pregnant. Things are different. I must look to the future.'

Hurst smiled. 'You could ask Harold to make you a gift of your share, but you run the risk of him saying no.'

'I don't think he would – but I don't know about his wife. She's not likely to give anything away.'

'You can buy it.'

'I'm not going to buy what's mine, even if I could afford it.'

'You're a damn fool, Stanley, to have done nothing about this thing until the woman has a son.'

'But is there anything I can do now?'

'Oh, yes. The attorney general will recognize a claim to the property based on use and occupation.'

'That would do, that would certainly do!' exclaimed Stanley.

Hurst's expression told him that his relief was premature. 'It takes time. If you now, at this late date, file a claim to your share of your father's property, as his natural son, based also on use and occupation, that claim must remain undisputed for seven years. During that time you may not lease, or sell, you may not even leave the property for more than so many days at a time, I'm not sure of the number, I'll look it up for you.'

'Seven years.'

'From the time of the filing of the claim. It's reasonable. This island is full of bastards. Everybody would be claiming property right and left and centre.'

'So Mrs Newton and I are at the mercy of my brother and his wife for seven years.'

'Yes, he can throw you off at any time. I'll draw up the papers for you, right away.' He rose. 'Don't worry about it. Where you having lunch? I'm going to Sabina Park, and watch some cricket.'

'Not today,' said Stanley, 'I have some more business to do.'

Hurst came round the desk to show him the door. Hurst was white, he was wearing a club tie, and he was five inches taller than Stanley. Stanley felt a friendly pat on the shoulder.

'I'll have the papers ready by Friday.'

Stanley went out into the blinding sunshine of Duke Street. He had no other business, but he could not face the club, not that day. The reason why he had done nothing all these years was simply to avoid what he had just been forced to do, admit to Hurst, to the club, and to all Kingston that he, Stanley Newton, banana planter, sportsman, pillar of the Anglican church, the man who married the Quaker missionary, was a bastard.

He was walking down the street, toward the Myrtle Bank Hotel, but he changed his mind, and started up again. There was a restaurant on the top floor of a Chinese grocery on East Queen Street, and though it was rumoured that they used dog meat in the patties, it would do well enough, for bastards.

*

Grace was determined to have her baby in her own bed. The women of her family had been pioneers, who gave birth where the wagon stopped or the house was built. The idea of going to a hospital appalled her. Besides, the four-poster Stanley had picked up cheap when the furniture company went bankrupt was a lot more comfortable than anything she'd find in a nursing home.

Stanley made what preparations he could. A distant cousin of Sunshine's, a woman called Naomi, who had attended so many births that she was called a midwife, was moved into the servants' quarters. The mule was tethered at night just outside Tumpy's room. It was a busy time for Stanley. If a banana boat was in Port Antonio he often went without sleep for two nights on end. Harold tried to help, foregoing his urgent business in Kingston, his domestic evenings with Cynthia, and his afternoons at Sammy Ying's. Stanley was grateful, but even so he was not able to rest, nor able to sit at home and wait for a baby when there was work to be done.

He was close to home when it finally happened. He had been moving cattle to a fresh pasture, and came home for midday dinner as usual. Coming up the steps, he noticed Cynthia and Naomi chatting away in the kitchen; he saw that the dining table was laid for two; but there was no sign of Grace. He found her in a corner of the bedroom, sitting in the rocking chair. She was sweating and pale.

'What's the matter, Grace? You started?'

'I don't know.'

'Have you sent for Doctor Foster?'

'I don't want to trouble him with a false alarm.'

Even as she spoke, she caught her breath.

Stanley turned and ran, across the hall, and through the dining room.

'Naomi! Come! Come! Just attend to Mrs Newton. Where is that boy with the mule?'

'The mule out back, sar, but I send de boy to Spring Bottom for water as the yabba is low . . .'

'I said he was not to leave the yard! Go see about Mrs Newton. Go on!'

Sunshine and Naomi, abashed, hurried past him into the house. Stanley went out into the yard, calling for Tumpy, but there was no sign of him. He found the mule's halter on the ground under the logwood tree, and went into the pasture to look for the animal. For an agonizing moment he thought the mule had strayed, but then he saw it, asleep standing up, in the black shade of a clump of bamboo. He caught it, and dragged the dozing animal back toward the house. As he got there, Tumpy appeared with a five gallon tin of fresh spring water balanced on his head.

'Boy, I told you not to leave the yard.'

'Busha, Naomi say . . .'

'Never mind that. Get up now, and go for Doctor Foster, you hear . . . where you going now?'

'Pick a switch, sar. Dis mule lazy, sar.'

Tumpy cut a switch from the guava bush, clambered on to the mule with a folded krukus bag as a saddle, and with the halter rope in one hand and the switch in the other, and by dint of energetic kicking with his bare heels, persuaded the creature to amble out of the yard.

'Dinner ready, sar.'

Sunshine was at his elbow.

'What?'

'Dinner ready, busha. Miss Grace say she not eatin', but you mus' have you dinner.'

'Is she all right?'

'Yes, busha, yes. Naomi very experience', sar. Not to worry busha. I can serve dinner when you ready.'

There was nothing else to do. Stanley sat alone at the head of the table being served a three-course meal, pepperpot soup, beef and dumplings, and baked bananas with coconut cream. Just behind him, two closed doors away, he could hear the reassuring murmur of Naomi's voice, punctuated with increasing frequency by the sound of a woman in pain, his wife. After lunch, he went out on the verandah to look out for Dr Foster.

Meanwhile, on the high four-poster, Naomi had arranged Grace to her satisfaction. She wore her best nightie, pulled up around her waist, her legs and stomach bare, pillows under her knees. There were layers of clean towels under her to catch the breaking of the waters. Sunshine brought a glass of fresh water, and from time to time Naomi sponged her forehead and neck with a wet linen towel. In the second hour the contractions came faster and faster, tearing convulsions that made Grace stiffen her frame and bite her hands to prevent herself from screaming.

'Missis,' said Naomi, taking her hand, 'you close up, you fightin' it, baby try to bawn, you hol' 'im een. Push 'im hout, push 'im hout! When de pain come nex', squeeze, squeeze, squeeze 'im hout . . .'

Grace tried. When the pain came back, when she was being cut in half by a fiery sword, she pushed mightily, she braced herself against the headboard, forgetting to suffer, forgetting she must die with dignity, fighting back against it, pushing . . . pushing . . .

'Yes, man, yes. You bulgin' hout, 'im in de channel. A'right, ah see de likkle 'ead.'

Sunshine was smiling down at her. Grace took her arms. Then she moaned again, and her nails bit deep into Sunshine's flesh. Her teeth were bared, her eyes unseeing, fighting back at the terrible pain.

'Yes, ma'm, yes, ma'm, yes . . .'

Naomi's hand was supporting a slimy purple hairy little head, and a forefinger of her other hand found purchase under a tiny armpit. She eased the baby's body into the light.

'Sunshine, fetch de knife, de cord mus' cut. Dis baby in haste, eh. 'Im can't wait fe doctor.'

Stanley heard Sunshine running through the house, and dared not look, or question her. At the same time, he saw Dr Foster's buggy making the turn out of the valley, and coming along the white gravel road between the cricket ground and the coconut palms along the edge of the cliff. Then he heard a baby cry.

In the room, Naomi assured herself that the baby was well. A boy, she said, and kissed his little cock for luck.

'Sunshine, wrap up de baby, then go tell Mass Stanley he does have a boy child.'

Dr Foster arrived in time to neaten up the navel, to congratulate Naomi, and to clean up Grace. Stanley was not allowed in until all trace of blood and battle had been removed. Grace's hair was brushed, and her face washed. When Stanley first saw him, his son was wrapped and sponged and clean, lying in the crook of his mother's arm, his little pink face wrinkled and puckered, his eyes squeezed shut like a puppy's.

Tumpy was sent into the pasture with a spade to bury the caul under a trumpet tree, as was the custom, so the child would prosper, and to keep it from the john crows which were already circling.

In the couple of weeks before John's birth, Stanley had slept in the room next door, the nursery, on a low iron bed next to the waiting crib and a chest of drawers filled with baby clothes and nappies. Every morning, Mabel, the cook, had come to the back step as he was putting on his boots, bringing a mug of cocoa and a hunk of hard-dough bread.

On the morning after the birth of his son, Stanley was not there when she arrived. Mabel knocked, called out to him, and left the tray on the step. It stayed there, gathering ants, for Stanley could not get out of bed; he was paralysed. From where he lay, he watched the eastern sky flush with sunrise, turn pale blue and brighten with the day. He saw white cumulus appear, and the top branches of the quickstick wave in the morning breeze, but he could not sit up or move.

He listened to the activities of the women in the next room. Sunshine brought Grace some tea. The baby cried on waking, screamed in protest when it was changed, almost strangling itself with fury, and snuffled and guzzled when it was fed. He heard Grace ask if he had gone out, and Sunshine's footsteps on the wooden floors as she went in search of Mabel. He heard their faraway voices in excited conference, and then Mabel again, knocking on the back door.

'Busha.'

'Come in, Mabel,' he said.

Mabel came in to see him lying in bed, in his red and yellow striped pyjamas, the sheet up to his waist.

'You don't eat your breakfast, busha, you sick?'

'No, no. Just help me up.'

Mabel leaned over the bed, got an arm around his shoulders, and tried to raise him. When she felt the limp weight, she let go.

'Busha, you know I has a bad back. I'll just call Naomi.'

Grace, in bed with the baby, heard some of this, indistinctly, and called out. Sunshine came in from Grace's room, and Naomi from the yard. Together, they got Stanley to his feet, but his knees buckled, and he complained of fiery pain in his joints. There was nothing for it but to lay him down again, and put the sheet back over him.

Naomi sent Mabel to send Tumpy into the bush to look for some leaf to make a herbal tea, and she told Sunshine to stay with Mass Stanley while she went in to explain it all to Grace.

'Nothin' no wrong wid 'im, mam. Is ongle cares an' worries. Him tek all de labour, him tek all de pain, an' him jus' exhaus'. De birt', de birt' exhaus' 'im. Some men do dat. I know one man, Mistress Grace, I know one man when 'oman 'ave baby fe' 'im, mek milk outa 'im own ches'. Nothin' no wrong wid Busha, nothin' no wrong.'

'I hope he's not making milk,' said Grace.

Dr Foster's diagnosis was not quite so picturesque. Stanley had been working too hard, and was suffering from rheumatism. He recommended a cure at the mineral springs at Bath in St Thomas in the East.

A valise was packed for Stanley, Mabel dressed him and wrapped him in a blanket, and Harold and Tumpy lifted him into the buggy. Harold drove the buggy down the newly completed driveway, which he pointed out to Stanley was as rough as a river bottom, and joined the main road at the foot of the hill. This road led past the school and through the village. Along the way, men who had heard the stories of Stanley's collapse removed their hats as the buggy went by, just in case.

Some hot and dusty miles on, they came to the top of Quaw Hill, where the road overlooks the lush valley of the Plantain Garden River. They paused to rest the mule, enjoying the breeze, and admire the miles and miles of sugar cane on the flat alluvial soil.

'That's what I want,' said the sick man, wrapped in a blanket, 'a piece of that valley, and that's what I'm going to get.'

'It's hell down there, Stanley. Mosquito. I wouldn't work there for any money. Malaria. You see people down there beating themselves with bush to kill mosquito, walking with a black cloud around them, man.'

'They wouldn't touch you, Harold.'

'Why not?'

'Your blood is too full of rum.'

'Mosquito! They love rum. No, Stanley, you don't want anything to do with that valley.'

'I do. There are ten thousand acres down there, going to waste, with no drainage, gone sour, wasted on second class sugar cane, thrown out as pasture. Harold, it's a crying shame.'

'We still have land we haven't developed.'

'Not land like that.'

Harold paused.

'Why did you go to see Hurst?'

Stanley was silent.

'You think I don't know,' Harold went on. 'I know the legal position – Stanley, you're my brother! You think I would ever run you off the place? It's share and share alike, isn't that so? Law should not come between brothers. If we want to talk about legal position, we should talk together. Not with Hurst. You are my brother, I would never run you off the property, so help me God.'

This last was said in a voice hushed and sacred, implying an oath, a lifelong contract between them. Stanley considered it.

'No, I don't think you would, but would you give me legal title to my half of the property?'

Harold managed to look both embarrassed and sincere. 'Stanley, we've had no trouble in the past, and as long as we are sharing the proceeds, half and half, we don't have to worry about title. I never quarrel with your management, and look at the house you've built. It's better than mine. I made no objection to that.'

'All right, let's talk about the house. Would you give me title to that, so in case something happened to me, my wife and children would have something of their own?'

'It's the curse of Jamaica, you know, cutting up land into little pieces. Nothing is going to happen to you. When you get better we'll talk about it again.'

Chapter Nine

Mr Khadurian had a camera, not just a box with a blank eye but a German camera, a Zeiss, that had been sent to him by his cousin, an Armenian refugee who had found work in Zurich. He was very careful of the camera, worried that the salt air might ruin the lens, and it lived in a green baize bag in his chest of drawers with his handkerchiefs and socks. The camera came out for special occasions and for special people. As the Newtons were, in his opinion, the most photogenic in the community, it always appeared when Mr Khadurian was invited to tea.

There is a portrait of John, taken in the drawing room. He is sitting in a wicker and mahogany wing chair, his little feet up on the seat, hands between his knees, his head tilted to one side, a quizzical expression on his face; he has long curls to his shoulders, ringlets his mother would not cut till he was four. There is another on the front steps when he had learned to walk; Grace is sitting on a cushion; Stanley is in the shadow of the verandah behind her; John, in rompers or short overalls, has a hand on her knee, looking up at her face. There is another, still later, with Sunshine and a new arrival, baby sister Miriam, taken on the lawn. John is in short pants and shirt, bare-footed, squinting at the light; Sunshine is sitting on a stool with the baby Miriam on her lap.

Pictures of Grace, with her Bible and wide-brimmed hat on the way to church, or with Mabel on breadmaking day, their arms covered in flour, Grace's hair loose about her face, show a woman still beautiful, but thinner, tired, and without the mischief or gaiety of earlier days. The heat shows, and the strain. She is too young and pretty to be a mother, teacher, pastor and pioneer – one or two of those perhaps, but not all at once. Far away as she is, she looks like so many of her sisters who were enduring the hardships of the depression in the Midwest in the early thirties.

The photographs of herself and her children were sent off to America, regularly. Her father was not speaking to her, but she was still speaking to him. She told him how the farm was doing, how many bananas, how many coconuts, the births and deaths of cattle and pets, the hiring and firing of servants and teachers. She recorded the small achievements of her offspring at running, climbing, swimming and saying of prayers. She told him how John had kneeled by his bed one night and said, 'Dear Heavenly Father which art in Ioway,' and how Sunshine had corrected him, 'No Mass John, you Father is in Heaven, is you grandfather in Ioway.'

When, in 1931, a letter arrived from America, it was not from her father, nor from Amy, but from her younger sister, Alice, who had married and moved to Oregon.

> Dear Grace,
> Gilbert and I have been to Iowa for Thanksgiving, and I promised myself to write to you the minute I got home, which is some weeks ago now, but I want to give you news of Pa and Amy.
> Pa's hair is snow-white now, but he is still working just the same, boasting he can pitch as much hay as any man in Fairfield County. Sometimes though he talks of retirement and Charles encourages him in this. There was talk of a hardware store. Amy favors a diner, for she is so proud of her pancakes, and the drivers would be company for Pa . . .

There followed a lot of news about Charles' job in Portland, Oregon, which he was lucky to have in such hard times, and of three beautiful children, a boy and two girls, whom Grace had never seen. Then the letter went on:

> . . . well, Grace, Pa does not speak of you much, but we know better. Keep your letters coming for they mean a lot to him. He knows what days they come, and the chores are always done before the postman passes. There is a picture of you and your children in the corner of his mirror . . .

There was more, followed by various blessings and recommendations to the Almighty, which Grace could not read for her eyes were blurred with tears.

Stanley was loyal to his father's church, the Church of England, and the Church of England was, of course, the Church of Jamaica. It might allow beachheads by Catholics, who helped educate the urban middle class, by Baptists and Methodists who staked an early claim by their struggle against slavery, or even poaching raids by such Johnny-come-latelies as Adventists, Christian Scientists, or Jehovah's Witnesses; it might even have closed a benign eye to the presence of Muslims, Jews, Hindus and whatever it was that the Chinese were, but the Church of England was still the Church of Jamaica as far as Stanley was concerned. Miriam and John were baptized in the

Anglican church, but that safely accomplished, he felt his patriarchal duty done, and handed them over to Grace and the Quakers for their actual religious upbringing. So, on Sundays, Grace and the children went to Seaside, Stanley to Manchioneal while Cynthia stayed at home waiting for a passing priest, and Harold went to Sammy Ying's to play dominoes.

Grace felt widowed, always worshipping without a husband, and she tried to involve him in the Seaside church. He resisted. Two churches, like two wives, leaves a man no time for business. Grace persisted, until she found a way; her annual pageant. There was something of the actor in Stanley; he had a fine, declamatory voice, and had even been invited by the great Marcus Garvey himself to recite on his platform, which he did until Garvey defaulted on his promise of expenses. Rehearsals brought him to her church, and brought them together, learning his lines by lamplight after the children had gone to sleep. So Stanley, in robes like mattress ticking and wearing a cardboard crown, brought a long line of Old Testament heroes to the boards of the Seaside church. He suffered as Job; as Aaron struck water from the rocks; he wept for Babylon; and escaped from Egypt. But his supreme achievement was Nehemiah, building a city out of painted boxes: steps and streets, houses, domes and minarets to heaven.

It was much appreciated in the district, and so was Stanley's cricket team, for which he supplied the ground, the roller, the stumps, the whitewash, pads, bats, ball, and a small scoreboard. Each season the pavilion was reconstructed out of bamboo poles and thatched with coconut. The whole neighbourhood turned out to watch. The girls swayed slowly past the players, or ran, teasing and laughing, into the pavilion. Men played draughts, or slept in the shade. Visiting teams came from as far away as Fairy Hill or Priestman's River, on foot, on donkey back, or in a cart, and, later, brought their own supporters in a truck, whose singing echoed up and down the valleys.

Stanley did not insist on shoes, but all his team saved up for whites, and the cricket ground looked as smart as any green in England. Both brothers played; Harold was a fast bowler, and a slogger; Stanley, an opening bat, dapper and quick, playing mostly off the back foot, with wristy cuts and glances.

Grace did not attend the cricket matches because Stanley allowed rum in the pavilion. Church was church, Stanley argued, but cricket was cricket, and his players simply would not turn up if Saturday afternoon meant drinking lemonade. He could frown on it, but certainly not ban it. So Grace sent down sandwiches and cakes for the interval but watched Stanley's innings from the safety of her hilltop verandah, four hundred yards away. John and his cousin William watched, sitting on white-washed boundary stones, eating snowballs, shaved ice doused in pink syrup, or played their own matches with the village boys behind the pavilion, using coconut bats and green Seville oranges. At close of play, the boys were sent home.

Stanley stayed until the music started, and the rhythm of the mento drowned all conversation. After that, no one would miss him. He reminded Harold that Cynthia would be waiting, and departed, but he always knew that Harold would stay on through the moonlit, dancing night, till the bottles all were empty and the skirts all raised.

'There is no money in the account, Mr Newton.'

Stanley, in the act of opening his briefcase, paused to look at Mr Pike, white shirt and tie, rimless glasses, and a view of the Canadian Rockies on the calendar behind him. Stanley knew there was money, enough to buy a truck. There was two hundred and seventy pounds, ten shillings and threepence. He had done his sums the night before, working, as he always did on these important matters, in elaborate copperplate on the back of an envelope.

'Unless you've made a deposit this morning,' the white man said, his accent Canadian, nasal, alien and hateful.

'No, no, I haven't,' Stanley muttered.

Pike looked at the file, lowering his head so Stanley could count the hairs on his bald, red pate, bald like a john crow.

'There's a cheque here for three hundred pounds, cashed in Kingston last week.'

'Cashed?'

'Didn't you know about it?'

'Yes, yes, of course I did. Harold's cheque, wasn't it? It slipped my mind for a minute. Yes, yes. I was thinking of buying this vehicle on overdraft...'

A girl came in, her waistband riding high above her pregnancy, her slippers slapping the wooden floor. She was carrying a tray with two glasses of fresh water; a beaded cloth covered each one to prevent flies from landing on the rim. Pike helped himself, but Stanley declined, raising a pale palm.

'. . . that's really why I came, to explain the situation.'

It was a good recovery, but Pike was not fooled.

'Stanley, you can't run your business like this. There's a very simple solution. All cheques drawn on the estate account should bear both signatures. Don't you own the place together, equally?'

Stanley nodded. 'Yes, of course. Of course.'

It was not so. Of the Biblical seven years, there was still a year to run, a year and thirteen days. Stanley had never wanted a direct conflict with his brother, so he had tried to control his expenditure by persuasion or tacit disapproval. Harold was a grown man, father of a family, and could not be treated like a child. But three hundred in a week! And he, Stanley, having to suffer the humiliation of coming into Pike's office without even knowing about it.

'Why not have two signatures on every cheque?' queried Mr Pike.

'No, no,' said Stanley. 'Harold wouldn't agree to it.'

'You could say it was a request of the bank.'

'No, no. I'm sure there's a reasonable explanation for the expenditure in question. Harold and I can't be expected to consult on everything, and it would cause ill-feeling if we weren't free to draw cheques. It's gone very well in the past . . . I'll speak to him . . .'

Stanley realized he was mumbling again, and stopped. Pike was looking at him closely, trying to understand. He could not tell Pike that he had no power to control Harold; that he, Stanley, owned nothing at all; that all his life, and for another year to come, he lived by his younger brother's grace and favour.

'Let's leave it at that,' Stanley said, 'for the time being.'

Cynthia, who hardly ever left her house, came over to Stone Haven for coffee with Grace. For the journey, short in time and distance but long in significance, she made careful preparation. She wore white high-heeled shoes, stockings, a large-flowered print, and a white hat. She put on rouge, lipstick and powder. Grace, who never wore make-up, acknowledged the importance of the visit by having Sunshine serve coffee in the drawing room, on a tray, with home-made cookies. Their two chairs were by the window and the net curtains blew inward, waving gently. Grace enquired if Cynthia minded the draught, and Cynthia assured her that the breeze was pleasant and cooling. She admired the new piano, made in Germany, a gift from Stanley. Grace admitted that she practised regularly, and told Cynthia that John was already playing scales and could pick out 'Breathe on me, breath of God' with one finger. She offered to teach William as well, but Cynthia thought it would be a waste of time for a boy.

'I don't know what to do, Grace,' Cynthia said suddenly. 'I've come to the end of my patience. I don't know what to do!'

Grace waited, looking understanding.

'About Harold, about our marriage, about his gambling and drinking.'

'The only thing you can do is make a Christian home for him.'

'You're saying I don't?'

'I'm not making any judgment.'

'Sounded like a judgment to me. He's always welcome at home, but all he wants to do is drink and gamble.'

'I know.'

'Well, what do you expect me to do about it? I love him, you know, and we have good times...' Cynthia seemed about to burst into tears, but recovered quickly. 'One little quarrel and he's gone! I don't know what do, Grace.'

'Why do you quarrel?'

'We don't quarrel. But I get vexed sometimes when he calls me greedy for money, or says I don't look after myself. Look at me. I'm a good-looking woman.'

Grace admitted that she was. Cynthia had coarsened a little, and her hips were heftier, but she was still attractive.

'No, I think he just picks a fight with me as an excuse. He is wanting to do something, to go off and do some damn foolishness, so he turns on me.'

'Yes.'

Cynthia caught the note of sympathy and understanding in Grace's voice, and sprang to the attack.

'But listen to me, Grace, you and Stanley can't be holy about it, and so God-damn righteous, holy and righteous. Because the trouble starts with Stanley. Harold is the younger brother. Stanley says Harold is not responsible. How does he know that? He gives him no responsibility, and then complains about him. You see, it started long ago when Harold went to war and put himself in jeopardy for King and Country. It's hard to come back to little Jamaica after . . .'

'That's no excuse.'

'Excuse! I'm not making any excuse. Perhaps he had too good a time in England. I don't know, but what I'm saying is when Harold was away, Stanley took all the reins of the property in his hand, and he is not going to let them go. Your Stanley, Mr Perfect Stanley, he means to push his brother out. He does everything, he leaves nothing for Harold to do, and then complains that Harold is not responsible.'

John, six years old, with black, curly hair, soft brown eyes and skin tanned a golden brown, was standing in the doorway. William was thirsty, he said, and they wanted some lemonade. Grace told him to ask Mabel whether there were any limes. John passed through the drawing room, bare-footed, hitching up his short trousers as he went.

John's passage had given Grace time to think. She so strongly detested both Harold and Cynthia, that she wanted to be sure she herself was blameless.

'If you think it's Stanley's fault, I'll speak to Stanley, of course. If they could come to a clear agreement about Harold's duties, perhaps that would help.'

Stanley resented Cynthia's suggestion that he wanted to push Harold out. Cynthia's problem, said Stanley, was that she was idle. She sat over there on that verandah like an old obeah woman, bad-mouthing people and stirring curses in a pot. Nevertheless, he promised, he would speak to Harold.

He found his brother in the works yard the next morning, joking with the old hags who shelled coconut. Harold was a great favourite of theirs, for though most of them were grandmothers he treated them like pretty young girls and made them shriek with laughter. Stanley, looking serious, drew him away from this scene of merriment and Harold, sensing drama, was immediately sober and thoughtful.

He agreed that he was gambling too much. He was mortified to think that he was losing money that belonged to Stanley, and therefore to Grace. He promised to stop. He swore on a stack of Bibles. He went further. He said he would not set foot in Kingston until he had paid off all his debts. He wanted to stay home; he had been neglecting Cynthia, who was a marvellous woman; he wanted desperately to feel that he was pulling his weight. He thought Stanley's idea of carefully defined spheres of authority was absolutely the right thing, and wondered why they had not made the arrangement before.

Stanley proposed that he would continue to look after the banana cultivation, and the purchasing of supplies. Harold would take over the coconuts, including the drying of copra, the cattle, the citrus, and the rolling stock. He felt that would be a fair distribution, and Harold agreed enthusiastically. He confessed that he had never liked bananas; they were more trouble than they were worth, and if he had his way the whole place would be in cattle and coconuts anyway. Harold was willing to bet that the crops in his care would show a bigger profit per acre than Stanley's bananas.

Stanley declined the bet.

The transformation of Harold was something to behold. Every morning he was out before sunrise; he walked every yard of his coconut fields; he knew the cattle all by name, and he and Vishy, the Indian cattleman, became close friends. He developed an ambitious plan for planting grapefruit, and he envisaged forests of mahogany and teak crowning the property. He marked out a site for a hotel (when they could raise the money) and dreamed of buying a trawler for fishing in the deep sea. Then he was struck by a series of mishaps: a calf was born blind, his grapefruit seedlings, left unshaded, shrivelled and died, and a whole load of coconuts was stolen because his headman had forgotten to send the cart for them, and they had lain temptingly by the roadside for three days.

When Stanley heard bad news, he used to make a little clucking sound with his tongue on the roof of his mouth and shake his head sadly. Then, with a sigh, he would address himself to the problem. He set off to find Harold, who was not in the works yard, nor in the copra shed, nor in the cattle pen. Vishy told him that Mass Harold had gone to Sammy Ying's.

Stanley walked along the gravel road to the shop, avoiding puddles left from the morning rain. A man, Zebedee, came down the track from the village perched on the hindquarters of his donkey. They wished each other good morning. Another man, Thomas, in patchy pants, machete in hand, stood on the cement porch of the shop, leaning against a post. He was waiting for the rum shop, a small zinc annex with a signboard announcing its liquor licence, to open. Thomas watched Stanley approach, expressionless. Stanley said, 'Morning, Thomas' and after a while Thomas stirred, and replied, enigmatically, 'Yes, busha.'

Stanley went on into the dark shop. It smelled of salted fish, flour and brown sugar, but mostly of salted fish. Mrs Ying was behind the counter, serving two bony-legged black children.

'Mass Harold is here?'

'Yes, Mr Newton.'

Stanley lifted the flap in the counter, and passed through a beaded doorway into the back room. In the middle of this was a bare table, stained with damp and visited by flies, and a number of wooden stools. A window, made of wood inside and zinc outside, and held open by a prop, gave onto a view of the sea. A door led into a dirt yard with a high fence, full of chickens and Chinese children without pants.

Sammy Ying, in trousers and singlet, welcomed Stanley. Harold was sitting there, facing him, and there were two others, Adams, the mason, and Cunningham, a small settler whose land was up in the mountains. The social club was in session.

Stanley seldom attended as he did not drink, but neither Adams nor Cunningham nor Sammy Ying held that against him. On the contrary, Sammy treated him with a respect bordering on affection. He double washed a tumbler that had been standing on the window sill, opened a bottle of cream soda, and persuaded Stanley to sit down. His English, Jamaican in a Chinese accent, was incomprehensible, so he smiled a lot. Stanley replied to him in pidgin, and occasionally a word or two from one or the other would break through, and then there would be more nodding and smiling. Though Stanley did not frequent the place, Grace sent there for all her groceries and, every Friday, Stanley gave Sammy a cheque in exchange for all his cash which he used to pay the labourers, who promptly returned it to Sammy, a fiscal merry-go-round of extreme simplicity and mutual benefit. It meant that coins circulated in the district almost indefinitely, and many a florin or half crown with Queen Victoria's image smoothed by time and dented by testing teeth served and survived in the village.

One such coin lay on the table, for Harold, generous as ever, was paying. He faced Stanley in silence, protected by the presence of Adams and Cunningham. The men talked about the rain that morning, and the possibility of a breeze; they lamented the high cost of things; agreed that George V was a good king and George Headley a great batsman. Then Harold asked Sammy for another rum. Adams and Cunningham, knowing that Stanley had not come there for a drink, begged off, and departed with slow and melodious goodbyes. Sammy disappeared into the yard.

'You've come to give me hell, I suppose,' said Harold.

'I don't think there's much point in that. But if this is how you're going to spend your time, how can I give you responsibility for half the property?'

'Stanley, you're a hard man. One or two little bits of bad luck and you're down on me.'

'You're down on yourself. What are you doing drinking at this hour of the morning? If this is how you spend your time . . .'

'Coconut don't need me to grow. They grow if I watch, and they grow if I don't watch.'

'But the labourers will not work if they know you're idle.'

'What do you mean idle? I only stopped off to say howdy to the boys. I'm just waiting for Vishy to bring in a bull calf that we have to cut. You look as if I'm planning to stay here all day, but I'm not . . .'

Harold rose and, with a theatrical gesture, poured the rum out of the window, and walked through the front of the shop. Sammy Ying reappeared.

'Missah Newton, sah, wan' tawk . . . bredda come . . . buy lan' . . . bredda shop . . . pickney, pickney . . .'

'I'll talk to you about it another day, Sammy.'

'A'right, a'right, Mass Stanley, tek sweetie fi you pickney, sah.'

Stanley accepted the paradise plums for Miriam and John, and Sammy nodded and smiled. There would be time to talk to Newton again about a piece of roadside land on which to build a shop for his brother, newly arrived from China, and Harold would be back to replace the rum so dramatically wasted.

Chapter Ten

Harold returned a few days later, and with increasing frequency, until the back room came to be known as 'Mass 'Arol' hoffice'. He drank all day, steadily, and lost ha'pennies and farthings to horny-handed village men at dice, or dominoes, or blackjack. Meanwhile his son William spent all day and every day at Stone Haven with his cousin, John. How Cynthia passed the long hot hours until he weaved his way slowly home to a lamplit supper Harold did not know and did not care. He was not even much surprised or much disturbed when one night Cynthia was not there. The girl, Ruby, told him that she had gone to Port Antonio, and Mass William was at Stone Haven with Missis Grace.

'When she coming back?'

'A don' know, sar. She say, jus' to say, she gawn to her moddah.'

Harold made a noise, halfway between a sigh and a murmur of assent.

A week or so later, Grace, at her desk, heard the most tremendous quarrel coming across the gully from Harold's yard. It was a man and a woman. The woman was Harold's cook, the man was not Harold. The words were indistinguishable, the voices high-pitched, sometimes one, then the other, sometimes both at once, breaking into outbursts of anguish and anger, of threatened violence and screaming terror, dying away and starting again, a long sustained babble of denunciation and defiance.

Grace called Sunshine from the kitchen, and asked her if she knew what was going on.

'Ruby man beatin' 'im, missis. 'Im seh 'im tek up wid Mass 'Arol'.'

'Is it true?'

'Me no know, missis. De gal seh 'im don' do nuttin', an' 'im seh 'im mus' lef Mass Arol' yard, an' 'im seh 'im nah leave, 'cause is de ongle money 'im got, an' 'im seh 'im gwine kill 'im, but 'im is all mout', 'im na kill nobody.'

Grace's ear was tuned, but she still had trouble with Jamaican pronouns that showed no differentiation of sex, but she persisted until she had winkled out the whole tale of jealousy and despair. She complained to Stanley, and begged him to speak to Harold. If it were true that Harold had taken the girl as a concubine and that her man knew about it and had broadcast it to the whole village by threatening to kill her, then Stanley's own reputation, and theirs, and the position of the whole family was at risk. By association, the authority of the church, even the reputation of the school, were threatened, as these institutions were so intricately involved with the behaviour of the Newtons.

Stanley was evasive. He did not want another brush with Harold, and though he disapproved he believed the only thing to do about sexual immorality was to ignore it, and then, if necessary, to accept the results. But he promised to speak to Harold.

He elected to broach the subject while they were watching Vishy and his sons branding cattle, the conversation covered by the bawling of calves and the attention of the Indians distracted by smoke and the smell of scorching hide.

'What's the name of that girl that works for you?'

'Ruby.'

'Her man is complaining in the village.'

'Stanley, it's none of your business, hear.'

'Yes and no. I don't care . . .'

'Then who cares?'

Stanley could not admit he was representing church, state, and his wife's opinion, so he was silent.

'It's nobody's damn business you hear!' Harold said hotly, and his anger angered Stanley.

'It is. We live in a small community and you are supposed to set an example.'

'Example, my rass! Just because you join the missionaries, don't come and preach to me. You want to become a white man, become a white man! You're into property and morality and all o' that. I know you jus' waiting for your letter to come, your claim to be recognized. It comin' soon, eh? You watch out, Stanley. You vex me and I'll run you off, before dat letter come, you an' you blasted wife!'

*

It was getting to the point where Stanley could hardly talk to Harold, and hated to look him in the face, something Harold was also reluctant to do, so their conversations were muttered, looking away from each other. Perhaps both of them still hoped for a word, or a moment that might bring them together, allow them to smile, to look each other full in the face, acknowledging their fraternity. They might have hoped, but it did not happen.

What happened, Stanley thought bitterly, was that he was raising Harold's son, running Harold's farm, even sometimes, though Harold didn't know this, sending money to Harold's wife, while Harold, in the old house on the other hill, was drinking rum and misbehaving with his cook.

Stanley watched him from a distance, a slim figure in khaki coming down the path from the old house, or leaning on the rail of the cattle pen, or meandering toward the rum shop, drifting through life, a passenger. Stanley wondered where and when it had all gone wrong for Harold. Was it because he was the younger, and therefore doomed to be the rebel? Had he himself been too hard on Harold, too much the disciplinary elder brother, or had it all gone sour in England, when Harold, a young, landed gentleman from the colonies, a cricket-playing, blazer-wearing gentleman from the West Indies, gone to fight for King and Country, found out that he wasn't a hero, and never could be a hero, because in the eyes of his fellow soldiers he was only a nigger?

At breakfast, one hot morning, in the turning of the wind, when the sea-breeze was still a far-off ruffle on the sea, the letter arrived. Tumpy brought it up the hill and gave it to Sunshine, who offered it to Stanley.

'Leave it on the sideboard, Sunshine,' he reminded her. He never read his mail at table, though a glance had told him what it was, or might be. He finished his own breakfast, and sat waiting while the children cleaned their plates, asked to be excused, and departed scraping chairs and with a thumping of bare feet.

'Is that it?' Grace asked, after Stanley, deliberately and carefully, had slit the envelope with a paper-knife. Stanley, with an expression of the utmost gravity, read the letter and handed it to her. He looked as if he had just seen a writ of execution.

'There's really no need for this performance,' Grace said sharply. 'Read it to me.'

It was from Hurst. The seven years had passed. Stanley's claim to half the property of his father was recognized. Bastard or not, half the estate was his, and he, Morgan's eldest son, was finally his heir, and his own son would one day inherit.

'You'd best go tell Harold about it. We don't want it said that you kept any secrets from him.'

There was time enough to tell Harold when he ran into him in the course of the day, Stanley protested, but Grace was insistent.

'He won't have left for the rum shop yet, and he has to know. Go now.'

So Stanley put the letter in his breast pocket, put on his old felt hat, and headed down from his yard into the gully, and up again to the Williamsfield house.

Harold was at breakfast, alone. He was wearing pyjama trousers; he was barefoot, bare-chested and unshaven. His lean, yellowish body, hairless, was surmounted by a darker face, made darker again by stubble. He was eating a plate of pickled mackerel and green banana, and drinking coffee from a white enamel mug.

'Ruby, get some coffee for Mass Stanley, hear?'

Stanley felt uncomfortably aware of his neatly ironed field clothes, his clean hands and his clean boots. He perched on the windowsill to avoid the table.

'Stanley, you blocking my breeze.'

Stanley sat down. Ruby came in with a mug of hot coffee which smelled delicious.

'What happen?' asked Harold, his cheeks full of green banana.

'The letter has come. My claim has been recognized.' Stanley touched the brown envelope in his breast pocket. 'You want to see it?'

'I don't need to see it.'

'I thought I should let you know.'

'Well, Brother Stanley, congratulations.'

'At least that's out of the way.'

'Right.'

Harold returned to his meal, and Stanley sat, sipping coffee, watching him. Then he looked up toward the wall above the china cabinet where a sepia portrait of the Reverend Morgan hung in an oval frame.

'Right. Nothing's changed.'

'Nothing's changed.'

'I'll be running along.' Stanley rose, patted his brother's bare shoulder, and moved away. At the door, he turned. Harold was still intent on his food. 'You working today?'

'No,' said Harold. 'I'm going to Kingston.'

This once, Stanley decided not to worry about it, for worry would accomplish nothing. He sent word to the overseer to have a couple of mules saddled, and by mid-morning they were riding the boundaries of his estate. It had always been his, it was always going to be his, but that morning he seemed to be seeing it for the first time, the beauty of it. He had not noticed before the splendid views of valley, hill, and sea, the exquisite texture of a banana leaf, the tiny flower on the Spanish needle, or the crayfish skittering under stones when the mule's hoof muddied their crystal pool. By noon, such romantic visions had merged with more common concerns. Six Acre needed weeding, the trenches in Matty's Piece were choked, and there were two cases of Panama disease needing burning. And he saw things he had never seen before, possibilities. It had never occurred to him that Patoo Ground, planted in guinea grass, might support a small herd, that coconuts would thrive in the sandy soil of the headland, and that all his back lands, all his creepered and bird-haunted bush, was crying out for cutlass, fork, and pick-axe, waiting for banana.

Harold had other problems. He had played out two sevens, and a jack. Yap Sing was showing three kings. Harold had the other two sevens in his hand. What did the Chinaman have? Ferdy, Thomson, and Mass Albert had all folded. The Chinaman bet a hundred. Harold raised him again. Yap Sing turned up an ace and Harold another seven. They were both playing the same game now, showing threes, which might be all there was, or bluffing a full house, or bluffing fours. But Harold wasn't bluffing, he had the other seven, he had four of a kind. He wasn't bluffing this time, though they'd all remember the day he'd scared off Mass Albert with the I.O.U.

Yap Sing didn't look scared, but he never did. Win or lose, he looked the same. But he was bluffing, Harold was sure of it. He might even have the full house, but not fours, never fours!

It was Yap Sing to bet.

'Another hundred,' he said.

'Thomson, you have a piece of paper?' asked Harold.

Thomson supplied one, and Harold wrote on it, 'I.O.U. £500, on the surety of Williamsfield Estate'. Doing so, he remembered for a moment the brown envelope in Stanley's breast pocket, but putting that out of his mind, he signed it, 'Harold Newton'.

'Five hundred,' he said.

The Chinaman stood up so he could reach into all his pockets, and pulled out a roll of bills from one trouser pocket, another from the pocket of his white linen jacket, and a third from his hip pocket.

'All right, Mass Harold, show me.'

Harold turned up the fourth seven, but did not reach for the pot, for in that instant he knew, he knew without seeing it, that the Chinaman had the fourth king.

'Eight thousand,' Stanley said, announcing doom.

'Eight!' said Mr Pike. 'It must have been some poker game.'

'Apparently, it went on for a week.'

'How much do you think your property is worth, Mr Newton? If you were buying, what would you have to pay for it?'

'I haven't had a valuation.'

'Twenty thousand?'

'More or less.'

Pike looked up at the Rockies for inspiration, fiddled with his pencil, made a note, used the eraser end to scratch his ear, then settled back in his chair and looked directly at Stanley with all the accumulated innocence of the Bank of Nova Scotia.

'Suppose I offer you a mortgage loan of ten thousand at six per cent, which would pay off Harold's obligation, and give a little capital for development.'

'It would solve my problem.'

'In the short term, but I would make it a condition that you use the money to buy out your brother.'

'I couldn't do that,' muttered Stanley, quickly.

Pike went on as if he had not heard him. 'Your brother is a charming man, and I like him. He's a gentleman, and he's good company, but he has never impressed me as keen on farming, and he has a weakness . . .'

'We all do,' said Stanley, gallantly.

'Surely. I like a drink myself, and a game of cards on a Saturday night, but my problem is I could not justify the loan to head office if I had to tell them that the whole thing could end up at the wrong end of a royal flush. Think about it, Stanley.'

'It would be a turnaround, wouldn't it,' Grace said, 'to start off owning nothing, and end up with all of it?'

'How could I do that to my brother?'

'How can you avoid it?'

This, on the verandah having tea, watching the boys play Chevy-chase with some others from the village who had become regulars.

At night, they returned to it. Grace was in bed, and Stanley, as was his habit, perched on the windowsill, letting the night breeze cool him, interposing his own silhouette between Grace and her view of the church tower with the silvered sea behind it.

'The trouble is, Harold doesn't care about the property at all.'

'Didn't you know that?'

'Yes. No. I thought that however foolish he may be from time to time, he has to care about it. It's ours, it's our life.'

'Yours. You can't spend your life paying his gambling debts. There'll come a time when you have to buy him out to protect ourselves, and the children, or he will drag us down, Stanley.'

'Yes,' said Stanley, 'but if I let him go, he'll sink.'

Stanley moved from the windowsill to sit on the edge of the bed, and his hand reached out in the dark to touch his wife.

'You tell me, Grace, what is the Christian thing to do?'

Grace sat up. 'Darling, I don't know. I pray about it, and I argue with myself constantly. What can we do, more than we do? Yet the Bible says we must always go the second mile.'

'I've done all the miles I can travel.'

'There is this to consider, Stanley. You say that the property is your life, but Harold would say it is his prison. Maybe Harold was not meant to be a farmer. If you buy him out, you might be doing him a kindness. He would make an excellent salesman, a travelling man. He is a town person by nature. If he lived in town, instead of going there on a spree, he could settle down, find his own feet. You could have done him a great harm by protecting him so long.'

Stanley's mind had moved on already. 'It's a big mortgage, and I've only just got title.'

The battle was won. 'Where I come from,' Grace said, 'every farmer gets a mortgage with his first pair of overalls.'

Harold was delighted with the idea. It was of course, the answer to all his problems. The trouble all along, he told Stanley, was that he had been a fish out of water. He wasn't suited to farming, and there wasn't room for two at the head of affairs. He thought the price was fair, very fair. His debts would all be paid and he would have two thousand pounds to get started in a business. He fancied opening a sporting goods store, because in Kingston sporting goods were in great demand and handled only through department stores. A specialty shop would soon attract the business. He might go to England to get exclusive contracts with some of the sporting goods manufacturers, Slazenger rackets, exclusive to Jamaica. If that didn't work, he might go into radio. A radio shop. Wireless, as they called it back in Britain. If he could find a technical chap as a partner, radio might be even better than sporting goods. Harold suggested they have a drink on it, and discuss the details.

They adjourned to Sammy's back room with a rum for Harold and a reluctant cream soda for Stanley.

'It was Pike's idea, was it?'

'That doesn't matter.'

'Of course not. If you hadn't thought of it yourself, you should have,' said Harold, smiling.

'What will you do about young William?'

'As soon as I get my eye in, he'll come to Kingston, but for the time being he can stay with you, if Grace don't mind. I want to keep the Williamsfield house. If you remember, Stanley, I did the same for you. I want to keep the house, and the land in front as far as the sea.'

Stanley paused. 'I'm not sure about that.' He had hoped that the purchase would mean the complete evacuation of Harold and his family.

'Cynthia would never agree unless we can keep the house and land.'

'Cynthia? I thought she was out of it.'

'No, sir. She's just visiting her mother, that's all. Cynthia always said you wanted to get rid of me, and I must never let go the house. If all else fails, she said, she is the mother of my son, and she wants a roof over her head.'

'All right,' said Stanley, 'but I thought she hated the place.'

'She does, my brother, but she doesn't want you to have it. Let's settle it that way for the time being. As soon as I can get properly started, as soon as I see my way clear, and the family are back together, she'll forget all about it. Though it would be nice to drive out from time to time for a weekend in the country.'

Stanley said nothing. Harold finished his rum.

'The trouble with cream soda,' he said, 'is that nobody in his right mind would want a second one. Sammy! Bring the rum bottle, hear?'

Sammy heard, and obliged.

It was six months before they heard any more about Harold, six months before the noon bus brought him home from Kingston.

Grace sensed that something was wrong when she heard it stop at the bottom of the Stone Haven drive. It usually stopped in Hector's River, and not again until Manchioneal. She watched Harold coming up the hill. At first, she thought it might be Stanley. They were, after all, brothers, though she couldn't imagine what Stanley might be doing on the bus, which had now disappeared, leaving its dust and the sound of its engine. She was sure it was Harold when he paused halfway up the hill to dab the sweat from his forehead. Grace retreated into the house. She decided that Harold would find her at work, an implied rebuke, and if there was no work, at least writing a letter.

So she was at her desk, pen in hand, when Harold darkened the doorway. He was still in his coat and tie, his shirt still buttoned at the neck though his collar was wet with sweat. His face was slim, brown and handsome, and his teeth were white as he smiled. He looked as if he had lost weight, and he was sober.

'Grace, how are you? Working as usual, eh. Stanley not here?'

'No. He's in the field.'

'Well, of course. I'll just come in for a while.'

'Would you like coffee?'

'Coffee? Yes. Thank you,' he smiled.

They had coffee on the front verandah. Harold had washed his face, and the sea breeze cooled him. It was so much cooler than Kingston. William came to say hello to his father, John and Miriam to pay their respects. Then the boys padded off again to play and Harold took Miriam on his knee, where she sat bolt upright, frightened and puzzled by the attention of this stranger.

Grace had no news of Cynthia, but presumed that she was well. Harold said he would have to go and see her, and Grace hoped they would get together again. Harold said it was his fondest wish. They sat in silence for a while. Miriam stirred restlessly, so Harold put her down, and she ran off in search of the boys.

Harold sighed, and Grace, looking directly at him, waited.

'Grace, I want you to put in a word for me, with Stanley, I mean. I'm in a spot of trouble, and I need a job.'

'I thought you were going into business.'

'Yes, of course. No problem about that. I'm going into business, but it takes a while to get stock, have the premises fitted out . . .'

'What happened to the money?'

Harold blinked. His mouth began to tremble, and his whole face crumpled into childhood, into the face of a small, spoiled boy, about to whimper and to wail. It was awful, and Grace, embarrassed, looked away, giving Harold time to compose himself, smile, and resume the façade of the old soldier, the jolly British chap.

'Money's gone west, I'm afraid,' he said. 'I had a bit of bad luck.'

'So,' Grace thought, 'they'll be here forever.'

Meanwhile, the children played. Ignorant of the miseries of their elders, they inhabited their own imagined Eden.

John was the prince of Stone Haven. William, anxious to escape the squabbling of his parents, and his mother's predilection for worming him, had come earlier every morning and left later every night, until, after Cynthia's departure, he never left at all. Miriam could run like the wind and climb like a cat. Though younger and smaller than the boys, she would not be left behind. She sometimes annoyed William, but John was proud of her, though he was too embarrassed ever to say so.

They had a monkey game, played in the quickstick trees. The trees had started life as fenceposts bordering the yard. They had sprouted and grown to form a giant hedge, only briefly bare and blossoming at Easter time. The game was to climb the tree at one end of the fence and negotiate the whole row without touching the ground again. As the children got heavier, the trees got stronger, so despite Grace's fears none of them ever fell on the rusted barbed wire permanently embedded in the quickstick trunks.

They gathered their own toys. From the rocks behind the cow pasture they picked the leaf of life. Mabel used it for curing colds, but they had another use. Its branched and purple stems made tiny soldiers to man the walls of castles on the beach. The guava bushes in the gully made supple bows, and catapults for hunting lizards. Coconut husks made boats, with bamboo masts and almond leaves for sails.

On the jagged cliffs, they sat on blowholes to feel the sea breathe on their backsides, threatening to draw them down, then puffing them away with a salty exhalation. There was a place among the cliffs where the waves flooded into a rocky cove in which there was a sinkhole at the water level. The boys stood thirty feet above it, watching the waves cascade into the cove, fill the hole to overflowing, and recede. Then the hole sucked in the remaining water like a liquid breath, exposing its rocky rim, the jaws of a giant trap. One day, watching this, the regular filling, overflowing and sucking in, mesmerized by the swirling of the water, John grew dizzy, and swayed, with one arm waving in the wind. William, crouched behind him, grabbed his wrist and pulled him back.

'You were gone boy,' said William.

'No, man, not as bad as that.'

'You were falling to your death, and I saved your life,' said William firmly, converting doubt into history.

In the bay, they played paddling games, pushing a log out toward the reef, daring each other to go further out, then suddenly terrified, kicking back toward the shore in fear of shark, barracuda, or conger eel.

The bush above Stone Haven was the place for stalking games, games of jungle warfare featuring death on sight, and endless periods of captivity in caves.

In cricket season, and in football season, a little group of village boys, Tucker, Son-son, Herschell and Monkeyback could be found waiting in the shade of the garage where Stanley kept his truck. Though stumps were made of quickstick, and goal posts coconut husks, only John and William in all the district had a football made of leather, a cricket ball of cork, and an English cricket bat.

Teacher's name was Miss Balfour. She was a thin, black girl in her twenties who wore lipstick and nail polish. She was a graduate of a teacher training college and she was very conscientious and precise. She read movie magazines, and straightened her hair to look like a movie star. She had a lovely smile, and beautiful teeth. John was immediately in love with her, a love encouraged by her coming into the nursery at night to sit on the broad windowsill in the moonlight and look out at the sea. Sometimes she would sing love songs very softly, or just sigh, looking at the moonrise. The boys were filled with hopeless longing as they drifted off to sleep. It was months before Grace told them that Teacher was in love with Mr Grant, a teacher at Happy Grove. She was not looking out to sea, but at the Boy's School, and their siren did not sing for them, and never would.

The boys, jilted, resented this, and took to teasing her, which, being young and all alone, was wounding to her. Her discipline grew strict, and their rebellion simmered. One day, William made a mess of his sums, and Teacher told him he was idle. John called her a name which he had learned from Monkeyback. In ordinary circumstances, he would have been sent to Grace, who would have washed out his mouth with laundry soap, but Grace was in Kingston and Stanley on banana business. Teacher had to deal with the matter herself. She told

John to hold out his hand, and prepared to beat his open palm with the ruler. John refused. She grabbed him. William moved in and punched her in the kidney. There was a flurry of fisticuffs with Teacher giving as good as she got, and sobbing at the same time. Miriam jumped up from the table and joined in, stabbing Teacher with a copy pen, and drawing blood from her forearm.

'I'm going to kill her,' muttered John. 'I'm going to kill her dead.'

He jumped through the window and ran to the woodpile where Tumpy had been chopping wood for the stove. Seizing the axe, he headed back toward the schoolroom, dragging it behind him.

This was the scene that greeted Stanley as his truck rattled up the drive: in the schoolroom, a beleaguered woman fighting for her life, and one young maniac trying to get through the window with an axe.

He slammed on his brakes, unbalancing the sidemen, who thought he'd run over the dog, and ran for John, catching him with one leg over the windowsill. Stanley lifted him by the scruff of the neck, holding him in the air like a puppy.

'What you doing, John? What you doing, boy?'

'I goin' kill her,' said John, struggling. 'I goin' kill de bitch.'

Stanley put him down gently.

'You just put the axe back where you got it from.'

Without waiting to see whether he was obeyed, Stanley moved into the classroom. The war was over. Teacher was weeping and examining the wound in her arm, ink mixing with blood. Miriam, defiant, had resumed her work, blood mixing with ink. William, sweating and dishevelled, looked guiltily at his uncle.

'Teacher, you better go wash the hand and ask Sunshine to bandage it for you.'

As Teacher departed, Stanley unbuckled his belt, pulled it off, wrapped the buckle end round his fist, put John over his knee and thrashed his backside. John endured his punishment in silence, and got extra for his pains, the slap of the belt sounding round the yard, producing high-pitched comment from the kitchen window where Mabel leaned out to watch the sport. Stanley looked round for William, but he was gone, headed for the hills. Miriam was watching him, her little face set and hateful, vowing never to repent.

'I'll let your mother deal with you,' he said.

The sidemen were sent to look for William. They crossed the cow pasture, went down by the bamboo grove and over the hill into the cultivation. They reached the river and went up as far as the drinking-water spring, but there was no sign of him.

'Mass William, come back! Duppy de deh!'

'Ghos'! Night time ghos' tek you, bwoy!'

William heard, but did not move. He knew there were fearful things in the bush, rattling chains and rolling calves. Mabel had told him about the Old Higue that sheds her skin and flies in fire, and the three-legged horse from hell that snorted steam, but he was not coming down from his refuge in the breadfruit tree. He would show them he could die bravely. He stayed till it was dark but when he heard the duppies walking in the woods, he climbed down and ran, and got back in time for supper, which was cocoa and bread.

Teacher left, to John's eternal sorrow, for he loved her deeply.

Chapter Eleven

'I'm not going,' Grace declared, 'unless you come with me. That's final.'

Stanley was nibbling on a Saltine cracker, and sipping a cup of tea on the verandah. It had been a hot day, like most days, but in the cool of Pear Tree Bottom he had seen a banana with fourteen hands.

'Not going to the Five Years Meeting, or not going home?'

'Not going home.'

'That would hurt their feelings.'

'That's their responsibility.'

Stanley sighed. 'Darling, I don't want to rake all that up again.'

'Nor do I. I was hoping to heal the breach. My father has never seen the children.'

'Children make a lot of difference,' agreed Stanley, 'but I'm not sure I could get away.'

He avoided looking at Grace, interested in something going on near his left shoe. A crumb had fallen on the green and white patterned tile and a party of ants had surrounded it, holding it with their forelegs, carrying it, presumably to their nest. But they couldn't seem to decide which way that was as the crumb was moving around like a circus safety net held by clowns, or by Keystone Cops catching a suicide.

'You mean you don't want to go.'

'It's a long way, a trip to the States. It would take a couple of months.'

'The overseer is very reliable.'

'And it would be very expensive.'

'You said you could easily afford my going.'

Stanley gave up on the ants. They were no help.

'We'll see. I haven't been invited yet.'

> ... Pa would have written himself but for his arthritis. He says little gadgets like fountain pens are too fiddly for him. He says, "Tell Grace to come, and bring the children." Stanley is also welcome ...'

The separation indicated a pause, or a prompting, or a question forcing the issue, something like: 'Pa, you've got to say, one way or the other. Grace has to make her plans,' and a 'What do you think, Amy?' followed by a long stare through the window at the snowbound land, and then, finally, 'He'd better come, I guess.'

Stanley tried to sympathize with the old man's dilemma. Grace's family were simple folk; their only acquaintance with negroes was through the pages of *Uncle Tom's Cabin*, or, with luck, *Huckleberry Finn*; they were proud of the fact that Quakers had organized the Underground Railway and led the fight against slavery in America, but they still wouldn't be sure whether or not the colour came off on the sheets.

He tried to sympathize – but why should it be incumbent on him to change the old man's view of the world? There was a simple answer to that: he had married his daughter. Yet Stanley hesitated. He was safe in Jamaica, which is not to say that prejudice did not exist there, but it was subtle, and many-sided, and in Jamaica he knew the rules. His existence was not measured by his colour but by his position, his ability, his money, his charm, his friendships, interests, and all the other thousand things that make a man an individual. He was the father of a family, a property owner, a Justice of the Peace, a member of the Anglican synod and the Kingston Cricket Club. Hats came off when he passed his labourers on the road, and when he went to town very important people slapped him on the back and called him 'Mass Stanley'. To go to America, and have the sum total of Stanley Newton reduced by one brutal equation to the mere element, his blackness, was not a prospect he enjoyed, or a reality he could accept.

'You go, Grace,' he said, 'I have a lot of things to do. It's enough that he said I was welcome.'

'I won't go unless you come with me, Stanley, and that's that.'

'It's the next farm,' she said. 'On the right.'

Stanley could see it; the barn, red, the orchard, newly green, the farmhouse, white under the maple tree, and the little silver blob which was the mailbox and marked the entrance to the Neville place. He glanced sideways at the field running away from him down to the line of the creek, the corn sprouting in neat rows, green and glossy.

'Richland,' he said. 'Rich by name and rich by nature.'

Arthur Neville, repairing a fence that did not need repairing but commanded a good view of the road, looked up to see them coming. 'That'll be Grace,' he said to himself. It could hardly be anyone else. The milkman and the mailman had come and gone, and Stewart's red pick-up usually went the other way. He moved back toward the house, pausing to put the hammer away in the tool shed, timing his arrival with theirs.

The Plymouth came slowly to a stop, Stanley manoeuvring it so that he avoided the lawn, and brought Grace opposite her father. She got out, ran to him, and embraced him.

'Pa.'

'Grace.'

They hugged each other, and kissed, looked at each other's faces, and embraced again. The intensity of their embrace surprised them both, for neither was given to displays of emotion. The long years of absence, of guilt, distress and resentment were swept away by their physical presence, by the seeing and the touching. This was her father, unchanged, she thought, white haired but still slim and straight and strong, with the same quizzical eye and secret smile. This was his daughter, completely changed, a woman now, a woman with an air of authority, capable, accustomed to challenge, a touch of grey in her hair, but still beautiful, still Grace, the one who'd sat on his knee, whose forehead he had kissed a thousand times and wished so many sweet good nights.

Then the man came round the front end of his swank car, neat, in a brown suit and city shoes, wearing a necktie. He was brown all over, with a flattish nose, short black hair parted and slicked down, and big ears. He, Arthur, had made no concessions to their meeting. He was wearing his rubber boots, his overalls and a red flannel shirt.

'Pa, this is Stanley.'

'Howdy-do, sir,' said Stanley, and offered his hand. The old man took it, and thought, this man is supposed to be a farmer, but his hands are soft. He was overcome with disgust, and turned away from the handshake toward the children who were climbing out of the dicky seat, John in short pants and a sweater, Miriam in a new cardigan, skirt and button shoes.

'John, Miriam, shake hands with your grandpa.'

They did so, calling him 'sir', as their father had done, in strangely accented voices. They had curly hair too, but no curlier than Curtis Knight's, and he was no nigger. They were brown, but they'd been in the sun, and no browner than that French Canadian in Fairfield. And they looked like Grace, you could see the resemblance.

'Miriam, John,' he said, putting an arm on the shoulder of each, 'come meet Amy,' and he led them toward the house. Stanley followed.

Amy came out on the porch, a spidery little person in a cotton frock and mud-coloured cotton stockings emerging from little boots, birdlike, high voiced.

'Welcome, come on in, you must be tired. Howdy, Grace. Hi, kids. Isn't she the cutest thing? And Mr Newton, how do you do?'

'Very well, ta. I'll just go get the suitcases.'

Arthur paused, good manners at war with prejudice. 'Go on, Grace, you go on in. I'll help Stanley with the baggage.'

He caught up with Stanley as the suitcases were unloaded on to the lawn.

'That's a swell car. I haven't seen one of them before. I guess it goes lickety-split.'

'Don't know yet, I'm still running it in. It's very comfortable.'

'I'll bet. Well now, what are we going to do with it? I'll take my jalopy out of the barn, and you can put it in there.'

'Oh no. It can stay here, as long as it's out of the way.'

'You leave it right there. The neighbours will think I've struck an oil well. Mine's a '32 Chevy.'

'They're very good.'

'Does the job. Gets me to church on Sunday, and as far as Fairfield, and every once in a while to a funeral somewheres. The folks we know are too old for weddings and christenings, so it's mostly funerals. Come on in.'

Later, when Grace was helping Amy in the kitchen and the children had gone to explore the magic barn, Arthur showed Stanley round the farm. Stanley had discarded his coat and tie, put on a sweater, and borrowed a pair of Arthur's boots which were much too big for him. They surveyed the orchard, the vegetable patch, the state of the corn, and the clover, the cows in the pasture, the pigs in the pen. Stanley admired everything, particularly the two grey draught horses.

'Do they work for a living?'

'Sure. All my hauling, all my ploughing. Some people around here have gone in for tractors but the horses will see me out.'

'Handsome-looking fellows. Lovely quarters.'

'Yes, they're fine boys. Do you use horses?'

'No. Cows.'

Arthur looked at him in amazement. The man used milch cows for ploughing!

'Cattle,' Stanley corrected himself. 'Steers, longhorned Brahmin cattle. We use mules for the light work and steers for the heavy work.'

'I've seen pictures of them. They've got humps.'

'Yes.'

'The yoke sitting right on their necks between the horns and the hump.'

'Yes.'

'Well, it's better'n tractors. By my way of thinking tractors are no good for the soil. They tear up the fields.'

Stanley agreed. 'They'll do the job quicker, but they put people out of work, and in the long run, it's my feeling, they will be more expensive. As soon as everyone's got tractors, when you've got rid of your horses, and I've got rid of my Brahmin steers, they'll raise the price of oil and gas, and raise the price of tyres and spare parts, and we will have destroyed our fields, and made ourselves bankrupt into the bargain.'

Arthur took another look at the little brown man. He was no fool. Maybe there was something to him after all. He smiled. 'Milch cows. I thought you pulled your plough with milch cows. Let's go see what Amy's got for us.'

That evening, after Amy's dinner had been eaten and praised, they moved into the parlour. In deference to his cold-blooded visitors, Arthur had lit the pot-bellied stove to warm the room. He had the wing chair, Stanley the easy chair; Amy and Grace sat on straight chairs; the kids on the rug in front of the stove. Amy found a box of family photographs, which were passed around. Some of them were already faded and mottled brown beyond recognition, but among them were good ones of Grace at her graduation, the mortar board over her youthful brow, and of Grace's mother, as a bride, in a lace dress with a tiny waist. Some were of Grace's sister Alice and her family, others of farm boys long grown and long forgotten.

The heat from the stove had made Arthur sleepy, and visitors or not, the chores had to be done in the morning, but before retiring, he felt he had to mark Grace's return and the presence of her family.

'Let us pray,' he said.

Grace and Amy bowed their heads. Stanley, who was leaning back, sat forward, put an elbow on his thigh and rested his head on his hand. The visiting children sat on their heels, and dropped their chins into their chests.

'Heavenly Father,' murmured Arthur, 'look down in thy infinite mercy on this our family, united in thy love and care. We thank thee for Grace, her husband and her children, and for bringing us together again, after so many years. We thank thee for thy tender mercies, for the gifts bestowed upon us so bountifully, and the good things of the earth. Lead us in the paths of righteousness, and bring us at last to thy eternal peace.'

They all said 'Amen'.

Chapter Twelve

Stanley's Plymouth, now a battle-hardened veteran, splashed along a mile of puddles and potholes, turned ninety degrees left, bounced for another half a mile and entered Holland, where the road was worse. There was no gateway, only a barbed wire fence separating the two estates and a star-apple tree by the roadside. The works yard, dressed with ruins and heaps of coconut husks, was in the centre of the property, at the junction of the canals that gave the place its name. On the far side, over a hump-backed bridge, was the great house, mouldering stone, with a weathered tin roof and a double staircase leading to the entrance on the first floor. A wooden office had been built on the landing in recent times, and behind it was the house proper, a maze of rooms and corridors made dark by screens and louvres, with some mysterious rooms that had no light at all.

Mr Briscoe, the overseer, was waiting for Stanley, and there were two mules saddled, dozing under the big mango tree. Seeing the Plymouth turn into the yard, he came down the stairs to greet his visitor. Briscoe was a big man, of a reddish colour, dressed in khaki and riding boots. His eyes were bleary with incipient cataracts, and his hands shook so much he could no longer sign his name. All evidence to the contrary, rum was not the cause of the shaking hands: that was the malaria, for which rum and quinine were the only antidotes. He had served his English owners for thirty years, remitting them money in the good years and excuses in the bad. They had ignored his constant pleas to keep some of the profit for development or repair, and he accepted their silence as a reply. He took nothing for himself but rum. Rum was his accommodation to an intolerable job in an intolerable place; it kept him sweet, and functioning.

Stanley declined his offer of a starter, and an invitation to look at the books. He said he would do that after he had seen the fields, so Briscoe climbed the stairs again to get his pith helmet.

They set off down the road, more like a wide ditch, between the labourers' barracks. These were huts of four rooms each, sharing a common verandah. Each room was meant for one man, but housed a family. The doors had gone for firewood. As the barracks belonged to the estate, the families were not supposed to be there, so Mr Briscoe when he passed looked straight ahead. Stanley's labourers at Williamsfield came from their own homes in the village, but here in the valley there was no village, and barracks had to be provided. Stanley looked, and his eye was met by sullen women, by naked children, pot-bellied, by a man with a machete across his lap, resting, swishing with a green bush at the mosquitoes which plagued him. Stanley bade them all a cheerful good morning. Only one man replied. He made a mental note that something would have to be done about the barracks.

They rode one side of the property in the morning, the other in the afternoon. They started side by side, but as the ride went on, Briscoe's mule tired under his weight, ignored the whip, and fell behind. Stanley rode on in front, looking at each and every field. The drainage canals were blocked with water lilies and wild ginger. The cane needed replanting, there was Panama disease in the bananas, the coconuts were too old for bearing, the pastures choked and full of deadly nightshade. Mosquitoes followed in a cloud. Stanley, with his sleeves buttoned at the wrist and his shirt tight at the neck, abandoned his face and hands to them, but occasionally slapped the withers of the mule and looked at his hand, red with the beast's blood and speckled black with dead insects.

At the old mouth of the river, he saw alligators, only their heads visible, moving so slowly through the still water that they left no ripple. At the sea shore, where the coconuts stopped and the soil was only sand covered by creeping grass, Stanley paused, gaining some relief from the mosquitoes which could not fly against the sea wind. Briscoe joined him.

'Have I seen it all?'

'Yes, sir. Tell you the truth, Mr Newton, I've seen some parts of this property today I haven't seen for years.'

'I can believe it. The place is in a disgraceful condition.'

'Yes, sir,' said Mr Briscoe and offered no excuse.

At Briscoe's office, over a cup of tea sweetened with condensed milk, Stanley had a look at the books, the pay bills and the production figures presented to him by Briscoe's bookkeeper, a meticulous young Indian who smelled of hair oil. They matched what he had seen.

'You going to buy, Mr Newton?' Briscoe asked, when the book-keeper had departed.

'Perhaps. I can't be sure.'

'I had some other people come to look at the place last week, a man named Kirkstone, and some gentlemen from Kingston. White people, sir, jacket and tie. They spent a while with the books, and the map over yonder, but they didn't see more of the property than they could see through the car window.'

'They might suit you better. You're accustomed to having your owners leave you alone.'

'Maybe so, sir. But it might be nice to have a change – there are things I've had in mind for this property, many years now.'

He looked across at the rum bottle on the window sill, and then back at Stanley who was watching him intently. 'I'm not begging you, Mr Newton, but if you buy, I would like to stay. After what you've seen today, I wouldn't blame you if you wanted another man. As you say, the property is in a disgraceful condition. I have ten years to go before I retire, and I would like the chance to put it right.'

Driving home, Stanley briefly considered Mr Briscoe's plight. It may be that in the circumstances he could have done no better, or it could be that, like Harold, Briscoe was always turning over a new leaf but was unable to find the book. Grace would insist that he be given a chance, but only one. Mr Briscoe's future, however, was not his problem: that was finding the money.

He drove slowly, one hand on the wheel, eyes on the road but mind elsewhere. They wanted thirty-five thousand pounds. He had nothing. He was still paying back the money Pike had loaned him to buy Harold out, and the property was mortgaged to cover it. But that was only a matter of time. If, and the figures revolved in his head, if Holland were producing what it could produce – he made a mental calculation of each crop, deducting labour, development cost and loan interest – if there were no hurricane, it could pay for itself in ten years. He would be able to sit back and enjoy life. Where could he find thirty-five thousand pounds, and find it fast?

As he came round the semicircle of the Stone Haven driveway, he saw that there was a tea party on the verandah. Mr Hoffman's Austin

Seven was parked by the steps and he recognized Hoffman, and Grace, but not the others. He drove round the house and came in the back way as usual, leaving his riding boots to be cleaned. He padded across the dining room and the drawing room to the double doors to the verandah to pay his respects. There was his old friend, Hoffman, and the Reverend Walters who had replaced the Reverend Steere, Mrs Walters, Grace, and a new person. She was introduced as Esther Simms who had just arrived from Boston to take over the Girls' School. Grace had told him she was coming, but he had forgotten.

Stanley excused himself, needing to freshen up. In the bathroom at the end of the hall he washed his hands, face, neck and ears, sponged his chest and shoulders, changed his shirt, and brushed his hair. All this tea-partying was a nuisance. He wanted to talk to Grace about Holland, but he had to do his duty by the Quakers. The new one was quite attractive. He returned to the verandah.

They were still there, and so were his children. John, now eleven, was required to come to tea, but still avoided the ultimate horror of sitting in a chair by sprawling on the steps, facing the sea. Miriam, seven, was employed in passing cookies. On Stanley's arrival, Sunshine appeared with fresh hot water for the teapot.

The new one, Miss Simms, was describing her reactions to Jamaica. She found it beautiful and exciting, which was not surprising, but she also found it sinister, and she could see why the native religion, pocomania, was a religion of fear, mystery and devil worship. Saying so, she glanced at Stanley, as if she were afraid she might have offended him. Stanley was considering her, not her opinions. Tinted, metal-rimmed glasses disguised the expression in her eyes. She had an over-prominent jaw, and a large mole low on her cheek, which, depending on how you looked at it, was either blemish or beauty spot. But she had a good figure, she was young, and she was white.

The Reverend Walters was agreeing with Esther. He pointed out that Jamaica had a history of violence, cruelty and rebellion, and that the memory of these things was instinct in the people, but, thank God, enlightenment was coming to the island, and one day one might create a society to match the beauty of nature. Mr Hoffman said he hoped so, and hoped indeed that the school might make some contribution. Miriam said boys were wicked, and everybody laughed. Then Esther Simms asked Stanley his opinion, but he wasn't listening.

He was looking over John's head at the sea, at the bright horizon, thinking about ways of raising money.

'What do you think, Stanley Newton?' she repeated, not going as far as 'thee', but avoiding 'Mister'.

'About the future of Jamaica?'

'Why, yes.'

'We need the strong hand of Great Britain to steady us,' he said. 'We have a fertile land, but a multitude of poor and unemployed. Some of us are trying, but this problem will get worse, not better. We must educate our leaders, and we need the strong hand of Britain.'

'There are those,' Mr Hoffman said, 'advocating independence, and universal suffrage.'

'Madmen,' said Stanley, firmly.

'What's the name of that fellow who has founded a trade union on the south coast?'

'Bustamante.'

'Troublemaker.'

'Nonsense. He's an opportunist and a demagogue.'

Esther nodded approval of Stanley's astuteness. As she leaned forward to replace her cup on the tray, Stanley considered her again. She was wearing a short-sleeved dress of pale yellow cotton, embroidered, open at the neck. The bodice was tight enough to reveal the shape of small, high breasts. The skirt was full, but under Stanley's gaze she adjusted it to make sure it covered her knees, revealing in the process a glimpse of what she was supposed to be hiding.

The Reverend Walters said it was late, and Mr Hoffman agreed. Stanley told them not to hurry, but to stay as long as they could. Nevertheless, he asked to be excused again as he wanted to start the light plant for it was getting dark. It wasn't, but he was proud of his new Delco generator, and wanted to show off the electric light.

'John, come along.'

John glanced briefly at his father and then back out to sea. From where he sat, below her on the steps, he had been enjoying a more intimate view of Miss Simms than anyone else and he wasn't moving.

So Stanley called Tumpy from the kitchen, and together they went into the vegetable garden where the generator had been installed in its own concrete shed. Under Stanley's eye, Tumpy went through the drill and pressed the starter button. The old generator had needed a crank handle, and it always broke down during supper, but this one started itself and ran continuously until it was switched off at nine o'clock. A wire had been stretched across the gully to give light to Harold and Cynthia, together again in the Williamsfield house.

When Stanley got back to the verandah, the Friends were saying their farewells. He switched on the verandah light, and Mr Hoffman, one foot on the running board, paused to admire it.

'One of these days,' he said, 'we shall have one for the school.'

'I hope so,' said Esther, looking at Stanley, 'I'm a little bit afraid of the dark.'

The good people drove away, leaving Stanley, Grace and the children on the steps.

'If she's afraid of the dark,' Grace commented tartly, 'why did she come to Jamaica?' She turned to John, 'You can switch off the light now, John. It'll only attract moths.'

'It's not the dark,' little Miriam said. 'It's the duppies that hide in the dark. Miss Simms is afraid of ghosts.'

Grace was against the whole idea of buying Holland. She was conditioned to believe that any farmer who got too big for his boots spent the rest of his life in debt. Their life was good, she argued, simple, but they had enough of everything and the opportunity to be of service. Stanley listened, but he did not hear, for his mind was already made up. She was pregnant again, he reminded her; they would have three children, probably more, God willing. He wanted them all to go to university abroad, something he had not been able to do; he wanted to give them a start in life. She, Grace, was the first lady of the parish, whether she wanted to be or not. He was proud of her, and of his family, and wanted them to number among the names of Jamaica. He wanted them to be spoken of in the same breath as the Pringles, the Jacksons, and the Sharps. He didn't count men in Kingston like Issa or Matalon, who were making fortunes in trade. The families of Jamaica, like the families of England, were landed, and he wanted Newton to be of that number.

Grace was bothered by all this, and perplexed. For her, ambition was a two-edged sword; success, good in itself, led to vanity; worldly goods, enjoyable in themselves, led to a forgetting of Christ. It was easier, she reminded him, for a camel to pass through a needle's eye than for a rich man to enter into the kingdom of heaven. Stanley muttered that he wasn't rich yet and not ready for heaven; he wanted to use unused land, provide work for people, and send John and Miriam to university.

Stanley got assurances of credit from the hardware stores and suppliers of agricultural machinery, but that was neither here nor there. After four days, he had reached the bottom of the well. As he walked along Harbour Street, still sanguine as ever, it occurred to him that there might be, even in a place as small as Jamaica, a financial institution that he had not heard of. In the reference section of the Institute, in the red-bound edition of something called *The Handbook of Jamaica*, he found a listing for the Westmoreland Benefit Building Society with headquarters in Savanna-la-Mar. Its chairman, managing director, and principal trustee was a Major A.G. Benson. He remembered the name. He remembered writing it in the scorebook, 'Major Benson's XI'. Five years before, the Major had brought a team from Westmoreland on a round-the-island tour in an open truck, playing matches in a different place every other day. They had played a match at Hector's River and Stanley had entertained them.

Major Benson himself, Stanley recalled, was a thickset man with skin freckled like a ripe banana and copper-coloured curly hair. He had kept his team in order like the martinet he was, for the 'Major' part was real. He had fought in France. After the war he had left England, come to Jamaica to live on a cocoa plantation his grandfather had established in the hills of Westmoreland. Stanley sent a telegram to Benson saying he was coming to see him, and another to Grace to say he would be home in a few days, and set out for the other end of the island. It took a day and a half for he had the May Day mountains to cross, and after that the Santa Cruz range where the road was no more than a cart track in the red dirt.

Benson's house, when he finally got there, was a plantation house, but as far as possible in feeling from the stone fortresses of the sugar plantations. It was a wooden bungalow, set on a grassy knoll, its lawns adorned with flowering hibiscus, and the house itself surrounded by royal palms. Cocoa was planted in the wet valleys behind and, in front, red Devon cattle grazed in light green fields of guinea grass.

Benson would not talk business. Anybody who had come all the way from Kingston to see him was a serious man, and deserved, first of all, hospitality. Stanley must dine with him, and stay the night. They would talk business in the morning. So they sat on the verandah in wicker chairs, the Major with a glass of fifty-year-old rum and Stanley with a lemonade, and talked about Bradman and Learie Constantine, and breeding cattle suitable for Jamaica, and the necessity to get away from dependence on sugar, and the general concept of cooperatives and building societies, and even of trade unions. To Stanley's surprise, Benson was in favour of the latter. They were, he said, the only safeguard against the return of slavery. They were living, he said, in the age of the demagogue. Nation states could fall into the hands of fanatical lunatics, and poor little Jamaica might not escape this. Therefore, he said, any democratic institution, trade union, cooperative, or cricket club, anything that could mobilize against fascism should be supported. Stanley listened with respect. Benson had suffered in the war, he lived alone, he was an educated man, he was entitled to his opinion, and besides, he had money to lend.

They dined well, on roast pork and all the Jamaican vegetables, and talked again afterwards. As he was showing Stanley to his room, Benson said, 'I've put a book by your bedside if you want to look at it, now or in the morning. *Lady Nugent's Journal*. Have you read it?'

'No.'

'You'll be interested in her trip around the island in 1805, I think it was. She spent a day on Holland Estate. Good night.'

He already knows, thought Stanley. Has he made up his mind? There was no point in worrying about it now. Propped up in bed, leaning toward the lamp, he read the *Journal*. The scenes Lady Nugent described came vividly to life for him. He knew the steps on which the peacocks strutted, the rooms in which the planters, the Governor, and his wife had feasted, and the inner chambers where, in the middle of a long hot day, the ladies loosened their stays and removed their dresses to rest between one gargantuan meal and the next. They were the same rooms in which old man Briscoe sat now to eat his salted fish and yellow yam off an enamel plate.

Stanley slept well, in fresh sheets, and woke to the whirr of hummingbirds in the oleanders.

'How much?' the Major asked.

'Thirty-five thousand.'

'I'll lend you twenty, and you offer them a mortgage of fifteen.'

'They won't do that.'

'They will. The interest on that is more than they've been getting from that property, and Kirkstone and his friends have offered less.'

Stanley looked at him in surprise.

'Do you think that because we're out here in the bush we don't know what is going on? Can you pay six and a half percent?'

'Yes.'

'Are you sure?'

'It only depends on how quickly I can develop the place. The restoration of the drainage system is first priority. I'll replant the best of the cane, put in bananas as a cash crop, and cover the place in coconuts. The people in the district need work, and because the sugar estates are seasonal, and I'm not seasonal, I'll have no trouble with labour.'

'You have it all worked out, except for what are uncharitably called the acts of God, death, disease, war . . .'

'. . . or hurricane. Major, I haven't read *Lady Nugent's Journal*, but I have made it my business to study the Jamaican weather from the time when records were first kept. A hurricane strikes this island, not all of the island but some part of it, once every seven years, on average.'

'They say the hurricane belt has moved north.'

'I won't take that chance. I think we are due, and coconut insurance is cheap.'

'Well, Mr Newton, if you are ready, we'll go into the office and meet the other directors. There is no point in saying everything twice.'

The Major offered his hand, and Stanley took it. Shaking hands, he became a different creature, he became a man in debt, a power in the land, and the founder of a family.

Chapter Thirteen

Esther unbuttoned the shirt front of her dress, and slipped it off her shoulders, wriggling to free her arms. This was as cool as she could get without actually disrobing in the middle of the afternoon. There was still a breath of wind off the sea coming into the little office on the top floor of the Girls' School. From the window, she looked down at the white cliff-top road and the blue waves hurrying in to strike the rocks at the base of the cliff, out of sight.

She knew that Stanley might be coming by, but she wasn't watching for him. She was thinking of Lambert, the blind man who had come begging the week before, then walked down the hill, through the gate, across the road and straight over the cliff to his death. She could not understand how it had happened. He must have felt with his bare feet the surface change from grass to gravel, and the incline cease. He must have known he could turn right or left to safety. Instead, he walked on, across the road, and straight over the cliff. What had he thought or felt as he plummeted to his death in the warm waves? Such a sensation it must have been to be blind and flying, still holding the staff, and knowing that a welcome waited, an end to darkness in a greater darkness, peace. He couldn't have just missed his way, dreaming in the heat, and died in an air-filled rush of panic, screaming until he felt the hard slap of the sea, which from that height would strike as hard as a flat rock.

At least, she thought, he was dead now. The blind man had nothing to live for, and he was well out of it.

She raised the front of her skirt lying in her lap and fanned herself, first her thighs and then her face, then let the skirt fall again. She contemplated the pile of grey, ink- and sweat-stained exercise books in front of her, thinking about them with a kind of dispassionate disgust. Their owners were all sea bathing at the Newton's beach. She was alone with the blind man. But she would not jump off the cliff. She would just not be there any more. It was a recurring fantasy with her, that she might simply disappear. There were times when she thought she was invisible.

She was looking at a black book, lying on its side on the shelf above her desk, just at eye-level. The gold letters said *Holy Bible*. She reached out for it and put it in front of her. She would read something, the parable of the talents, or the fifty-second Psalm. No, she would read what God had told her to read, because his Word would keep her sane and safe through this terrible penance, this exile in Jamaica. The book opened at Numbers, chapter thirty-three, and she began to read, slowly, aloud, the list of journeys undertaken by the Israelites.

Out of the corner of her eye she saw Stanley's Plymouth turn into the gate and start the semicircular ascent of the hill. She closed the book, and stood up, letting her skirt fall back into place, put her arms back into her sleeves and did up all the buttons. Then she went into the bedroom, ran a comb through her bobbed hair, and returned to admit her visitor. He had come from the field, in riding breeches and a khaki shirt open at the neck with a notebook in his breast pocket. He courteously removed the stained felt hat he wore.

'I was just passing,' he said, stupidly.

She looked up at him through her round spectacles, wondering whether she was visible to him, or invisible. She found a voice, calm and authoritative.

'How is it getting on? I mean the development of Holland, for I know that is your principal concern.'

'Coming to come,' he said, 'coming along. The water table is dropping.'

She decided she did not want to know about the water table. 'Sit down. Can you stay?'

'A short while,' he replied. 'I just wanted to see you, to see how you're getting on, whether you need anything.'

'Nothing at all,' she said.

'I rode out to East End today. There's a beach there. It must be nearly a mile of white sand, a lovely place for a picnic. As there is no river mouth nearby, the sea water is clean and clear.'

'It sounds swell, but I have to be careful, my skin is too fair.' She showed her arm, as white as milk. 'And,' she continued, 'Grace being so pregnant, I expect picnics will have to wait.'

'I only mentioned it, thinking you might like a little relaxation. You should see more of Jamaica than the inside of the school.'

'I saw Lambert going down the hill.'

'That was dreadful, dreadful.'

'I didn't see him fall,' she added quickly. 'I was doing something else by then. I won't do that.'

'Of course not.'

'Why of course not?'

'You can see.'

She removed her spectacles. 'Not very well. I can still see you.' She reached out and touched his face. 'You look even better, brown and blurry.'

'I want you to like Jamaica.'

'You sound as if Jamaica were all yours.'

'In a way, yes. I'm proud of it.'

'You think I don't?'

'It's a lonely place. That is, it can be lonely, but you'll get into the swing of it, meet some more people after a while.'

'Yes.'

'You might find a husband.'

'Not me.'

'Why not?'

'I don't want one. It's too late for all that. Shall we talk about something else?' She put her spectacles back on.

This time, he removed them, and caressed her face, lightly.

'Leave me alone, Stanley,' she said, turning away from him.

'Why?'

'You know why.'

'No one will know.'

'Because I'm an old maid, and ugly, and I don't want anybody to touch me, ever, ever.'

Grace, so pregnant she felt she was working at arm's length, was writing a letter to the Friends at Buff Bay. It was one of her duties as Clerk of the Jamaica Yearly Meeting to keep in touch with all branches of the Quaker family on the island, to inform them of each other's doings, to help, to advise, and to encourage. Without presuming to compare herself to St Paul, she felt, when she read the epistles, jealous of him and his ability to communicate with the far-flung Christians on such a high poetic plane, confining himself to theology, philosophy, and moral exhortation. She, in contrast, found her own letters inexpressibly mundane, so preoccupied with finance, with employment, with examinations, ill-health and moral backsliding. Paul saw the world as idea, she as fact; perhaps that was why Paul was a saint, and she wasn't.

The children were on the little back verandah just outside the library door. John, cross-legged on the tiles with a reel of cotton and a pot of glue, was making a Chinese kite out of shaved bamboo and coloured tissue paper. Miriam, on the window ledge, was reciting her nine-times table, which her mother corrected automatically as she worked.

'Nine sevens are sixty-three. John, go see if your father's car is still at the Girls' School.'

John did not move, or even look up.

'When it leaves, you can tell Mabel to put the kettle on for tea.'

'I'm right in the middle of this thing, Mamma.'

'I'll go,' Miriam offered.

'No.'

Grace leaned sideways at her desk, so she could look through the door and John could see as well as hear her.

'You go, John. I asked you.'

The Plymouth was clearly visible from the front verandah, across the valley, beyond the church and the Boys' School and the Mission Home, there on the next hill on the seaward side of the Girls' School, shaded by it from the weltering sun. John wished Daddy would hurry up. He was hungry. The tea-tray, with buns, sandwiches, Saltine crackers, guava jelly and fruit cake, was already laid and waiting in the pantry.

'Come on, Daddy,' he muttered, and stamped his foot.

As if at his command, a dark figure, diminished by distance, came round the corner of the building and blended with the car. After a moment the Plymouth began to move silently down the hill toward the main road.

*

'I don't think,' John said, spooning more sugar into his tea, 'I don't think she's very good looking.'

'What do you think, Mamma?'

Grace was pouring a second cup for Stanley.

'Looks don't matter in the eyes of God.'

'Well, maybe not to God, but to me,' said John cheekily.

'She's so old,' Miriam chimed in, making three or four syllables out of old.

'How old is she, Mamma?'

'Miss Simms is thirty-five or so.'

'Thirty-five and horrible.'

'You don't want a beautiful teacher, much less a beautiful headmistress.'

'Mamma was a teacher, and she was beautiful.'

Grace noticed the past tense, and it hurt. She also noticed that Stanley had not rebuked them for what was, after all, a highly improper and discourteous conversation.

'Can we change the subject?'

'Not until you say whether she's horrible-looking or not.'

'She's plain.'

'Homely,' Stanley volunteered, thinking he should make a contribution, and regretting it instantly.

'What's the difference between plain and homely?'

'That's enough, John,' his mother said. 'Go find William. Run along and play, both of you.'

After the departure of the children, the cups of tea were drunk in silence for a while.

'How is Briscoe?'

'Well,' said Stanley, relieved. 'He's working hard. He's lost weight, and he's drinking less. He seems to have got a new lease on life. Whenever I tell him to do something he still starts off by saying it's impossible, "It can't be done, Mass Stanley," but then to his own surprise, he does it. The coconuts are up to twenty thousand trees.'

'I'm glad he's drinking less. You were a long time at the Girls' School.'

'Yes. She's thinking of going back to America.'

'She should discuss that with me, or with the Reverend Walters.'

'Quite so, but I can't refuse my opinion.'

'What was your opinion?'

'I suggested she give it more time.'

Grace said nothing.

Stanley smiled. 'At least you know where I am, Grace. You can see the car.'

'That's true.'

The remark rankled. Why had he bothered to say it? He always left his car in the shade, as any sensible person would do in Jamaica. At this time of day, the seaward side of the Girls' School, just under Esther's bedroom, was shady. He had done the sensible thing. Why draw attention to it? The Plymouth in front of the building, visible from the main road, visible from Hector's River, visible from Stone Haven, visible to Harold and Cynthia at Williamsfield, visible even to the fishermen at sea in their canoes, said loud and clear that Mr Newton had stopped by the Girls' School to see Miss Simms on legitimate school business. If not, then maximum publicity and complete innocence were the perfect alibi.

Stanley left to spend what remained of the day in his office, but Grace stayed on the verandah, looking out to sea and along the coast to the Girls' School, perched on its hill like a witch's castle. She had lived there when she first came to Jamaica, taught there, learned to love the girls she taught, and the language they spoke. She had been courted there, and won. It would be a bad joke. Nonsense. It wouldn't be a bad joke: it would be a downright insult.

She noticed Miriam, walking the tightrope along the driveway wall, startling the lizards, girl and reptile scaring each other.

Esther. She didn't like the woman, though she had become her best friend. After all, there is no obligation to like your friends, or even your husband. Your friends are yours by happenstance, not choice, by accident of time or place; your husband by the happenstance of love, and you must make the best of it. Esther was her friend because she was the only American woman within twenty miles, not counting the pastor's wife, Amy Walters, who was a very humble soul, with every justification for being so. Esther was the only other person who remembered the Fourth of July, or what a silo was, though come to think of it, Esther, being a New Englander, probably didn't. She didn't like the woman. She was prim, the archetypal schoolmarm, at times withdrawn and introverted, at times firmly opinionated, with an air of impending hysteria, bullying you into doing what she wanted for fear of her unhappiness. Grace reproved herself for these unfair and unchristian thoughts. Esther was a brave and dedicated woman, and a labourer in the vineyard, even though she had come at the eleventh hour.

Grace felt the baby stirring inside her, and decided it was his fault, the baby's fault. It was her pregnancy that was at fault, that laid her open to jealousy, to morbid thoughts and uncontrollable emotions. She thought she was going to be sick, right there on the front verandah, in front of Mabel who had appeared silently to remove the tray. She nodded in response to her request to do so, but did not look at Mabel, looking instead at the slowly darkening sea.

The Plymouth continued to stop at the Girls' School, though not every day, and not necessarily for long. It also stopped from time to time at Mr Hoffman's cottage, or the Mission Home. Stanley, though an Anglican, had been persuaded to sit on the Board of Governors of the School, so such visits were all in the line of duty. Grace saw Esther regularly at church, and in the holidays. Esther came to Sunday lunch and sat at Stanley's right, with Grace herself on his left as he carved the roast beef.

Esther could not be avoided, and the situation, if there were a situation, could not be avoided. She could not ask either of them, ask or accuse, because the very asking would put her into an impossible situation. It would be to admit suspicion, to admit jealousy, and to find out nothing. If they denied it, she would have made herself ridiculous. If they admitted it – but that thought was intolerable.

She found herself not looking at Esther, being in a room with her and never looking in her direction, but there is more to a presence than the sight of a person; she could still be heard, her voice, or the movement of her clothing. The distinct sweat and powder smell of her was there. Grace avoided looking at them when they were together, but that solved nothing either, and it was too contrived. She began to stare at them, interpreting their conversations and their lack of conversations, their courtesies, or as it seemed, their lack of courtesy. When she had to deal with Esther directly, she was correct, if somewhat brusque, and friendly, without warmth. She treated

Stanley with a similar reserve, but with a baffled vulnerability, fearing a pain she knew he would inflict. On the other hand, he treated her with more gentleness, more consideration than ever before. Why should he do so if he were not guilty?

So it might have gone on, for weeks, through the birth of her baby, for months, even for years until whatever happened, or hadn't happened, no longer mattered, rendered irrelevant by the physical decay which overwhelms the faithful and the unfaithful together. So it might have been if Mabel and Sunshine had kept their mouths shut, and the Plymouth had not gone to Seaside church.

Grace herself had stayed at home. She had not wanted to risk the walk to church and back again in the full heat of midday. It was a good mile, and all uphill, too much in her condition. So she stayed home, sending the children off to Sunday school, reading awhile, and playing the piano, just for fun. She wanted to check before the roast went in that Mabel had spiced it properly, pricked the skin and stuffed it with garlic and thyme the way Stanley liked it. Mabel had forgotten the week before, possessed, she explained, by a devil. Grace was halfway through the pantry when she heard the voices in the kitchen, coming clearly along the covered way.

'. . . mi no t'ink so.'

'Eberybody know.'

'Nobody know nuttin', is jus' talk dem talkin'.'

'Don't is Christine tell me, an' she work obah dere.'

'Christine 'im is a liad from way back. Mass Stanley wouldn't do dat.'

'You don' know man ya.'

Grace turned quietly and retraced her steps, through the dining room, the table laid for lunch, across the hall, and into her bedroom. She felt nothing, as if she had lost her body and become a ghost in her own house. She stood in the middle of the room, unable to decide where to go or what to do.

The village knew. Her cook and yard boy knew, and she knew nothing, but of course she had known all along. There was nothing to do, nothing to say.

She took hold of the bedpost to steady herself, and then sat on the edge of the bed with her back to the window. She lay on her back and looked up at the ceiling. It needed repainting already; there were grey spots of fungus and in one corner the beginnings of a wasp's nest, never used.

She closed her eyes and looked at Jacob's ladder, seeing its golden rungs disappearing into cloud.

When the church clock struck twelve, and she heard clear on the sea-breeze the last hymn being sung, 'Dear Lord and Father of mankind...', she sat up, eased herself to her feet, and began to prepare for lunch. She removed her clothing, washed herself, and put on a clean maternity dress, dark-blue, with a small floral pattern in grey and yellow. Her hair was disordered, so she sat at her dressing table to do it again, taking out all the pins and placing them in a little dish, then brushing and brushing her long black hair – there were some streaks of grey in it now – preparing to coil it up once more and re-pin it, neatly.

She was doing this when she heard the Plymouth coming up the drive, and looking out saw that it contained Stanley, driving, Esther beside him, and John and Miriam in the jump seat. She put in the last pin, and sat in front of the mirror, waiting, listening to the noises of their arrival, the sound of Sunday shoes on the wooden floors, their voices demanding dinner.

Stanley came in to wash his hands, removing his jacket to reveal his braces and his sweat-stained armpits.

'Church was hot.'

'Are you carrying on with Esther?'

'What gave you that idea?'

'Never mind. Just answer my question.'

Stanley was always meticulously clean, but now he was washing his hands like Pontius Pilate.

'It's all over.'

'Over! How long ago was it over? How long ago did it begin? If it's all over why are you driving her back from church?'

'I was just passing.'

'Oh. You didn't go to church?'

'I went to Manchioneal.'

'You went just to pick her up?'

'I was passing.'

'In all the years we have been together, you have never come to church to give me a lift home.'

'That's not fair, darling. You forbade it. You said it would not look right for the whole congregation to walk to church and you to be driven in a car.'

'But it looks all right for you to drive away from the church with Esther and my children.'

'Can we talk about this later? They will hear us.'

'Answer my question.'

'I answered it.'

'I didn't hear you.'

'I said it was all over. Yes, there was an incident, shameful and unimportant, but it's all over, I promise.'

'What about her?'

'We discussed it. That it would be unfair to you.'

'Stanley, I do not want your charity, or hers.'

'Grace, please.'

She looked at him, forlorn, and utterly sincere, and hated him.

'I don't expect you to understand.'

'I don't, and I never will. Why, Stanley?'

'Oh, darling, there's no reason for these things.'

'Have I failed you? Have I paid too much attention to mission work? I know I have not been a Jamaican wife and given you the sort of social life your friends expect, but they are always welcome at Stone Haven.'

'You are the best of wives. If I wanted one of those flibbertigibbets I could have . . .'

'Is there not enough love? Have I not been warm and loving?'

He tried to approach her, to touch her, but she drew back, away from him.

'Please Grace, you are killing me, saying these things. I told you, there's no reason, nothing to it, it's all over. Maybe you're too good a woman to understand. Lust has no shame, it does not look to past or future . . .'

'You don't have to give me lectures about lust. I've looked after too many women between here and Belle Castle who don't know where, or even who, is the father of their child. I thought you were better than that, Stanley.'

'I am sorry.'

'Is that it? Another teacher at the school, another old maid. You've made a speciality of it. I'm going to Kingston tomorrow to have this baby, may God protect him. That will leave you here alone with Esther. You can have a good time while I'm away.'

She went to the door. 'I think you should change your shirt.'

Mabel was ready to serve. Grace told Miriam to take her place, and sent John to wash his hands. She found Esther on the front verandah.

'Dinner is ready.'

'Thank you, Grace. You missed a good sermon.'

'Oh, was it? Third Sunday. Zephaniah Cunningham.'

'Yes. Black men are better preachers than white, aren't they, Grace? They're not afraid to call fiercely on the Lord.'

'I think the early Quakers preached with the same passion. Nowadays we are too prim. Too dry. Come to dinner.'

They went in together. Stanley asked John to say grace, which he did, mumbling. Stanley stood up to carve, while Grace served the rice and peas and the gravy. Sunshine handed round the vegetables. Esther was silent, smiling benevolently at the children.

John noticed that his mother was crying. He was puzzled, then frightened, for it was as if her face were dissolving. Her eyes were filled with tears, her nostrils were going red, and her mouth was trembling.

'Mamma, what's the matter, Mamma?'

Then Miriam looked up to see her mother's tears, and reached up to pat her as she would a crying doll or a wounded animal. Grace pushed her chair back, and left the room. She contained her sobs until the bedroom door closed behind her, and then they came, the racking sounds of pain, expelling breath and fighting for it at the same time as if undecided whether to live or die.

Grace's sorrow carried clearly to the dining room, and not knowing what to do the diners did nothing, and pursued their meal in silence.

'It's the baby,' Stanley explained. 'It's a difficult time, and it makes her very emotional.'

No one believed this explanation, but having no choice, they accepted it. Miriam wanted to go to her mother, but her father prevented her, telling her to eat up first, Mamma would be all right. Esther kept her eyes on her plate, eating daintily. Stanley summoned

Sunshine to take Grace's plate away and keep it warm, then he continued with his own meal as if nothing had happened. John, though he himself had finished, was outraged. How could his father eat with such composure when his mother was unhappy?

'May I be excused?'

'Don't you want dessert?'

'No.' This was a sacrifice John felt he could make to prove the point.

'Then run along. Run along and play.'

Grace did not come back to the table, or leave her bedroom all that long Sunday afternoon. When the sobbing ceased, the numbness returned. Truly, she thought, my life is over. The journey that started on an Iowa farm, that had led her across the sea to this place, this room, that journey was over. It was over because it had no meaning, no purpose, no reality. It witnessed nothing to God or man. She had ventured in order to serve, she had married out of love and out of principle. That too was meaningless, and there was no way back. She would be a stranger in her own home.

Her husband had betrayed her, and what would become of her little brown children? There was no way back. Jamaica that had been her personal proving ground of faith had become a prison. It was all meaningless. Perhaps she was being punished for her pride. She had taken pride in her mission, pride in her husband, pride in her children. She had begun to think herself worthy and favoured. But what a punishment! Esther of the lantern jaw, another old maid. Oh, God was vindictive, and she did not like his sense of humour. Yes, she must be proud, to think so of her Creator. Her punishment was just. It was just because it existed, for in Him all things are justified. After a while, she began to pray.

The boys had built hurdles under the quickstick trees, and they were running races when the telegram came from Kingston, announcing another birth, a boy, nine and a quarter pounds, mother and son doing well. His homecoming created a new game: watching the baby.

Owl-eyed and clean, the three other children were allowed into Grace's room to see Paul being bathed. Sunshine would arrive from the kitchen with a kettle and a pitcher and carefully prepare the water in an enamel bath. Meanwhile Grace removed the wet nappy revealing his little pointed cock and wrinkled scrotum. Paul was very white, and his brown baby hair was insubstantial as chicken feathers. When Sunshine, balancing him in both hands, lowered him into the water, Paul screamed and turned bright red, but soon, lathered and caressed, he learned it was all a game.

William and John watched unbelieving as he, supported by Sunshine's guarding hands, swam like a tadpole up and down the bath. Sunshine dried him, Miriam was allowed to shake powder over him; then he was offered back to Grace, and she, holding him on one arm, unbuttoned with the other, presenting him with a breast, large, white, networked with blue veins, with a red-brown nipple enlarged for the little brute's benefit. He was howling for it even as it was thrust into his gaping mouth, forcing him to choose between screaming, drowning, or feeding properly. He fed, sucking and snuffling and beating with his little fingers at the breast, continuing so, noisy and determined, until his eyes began to close, his hands loosened, and he, feeding, fell asleep.

Stanley came in to admire the baby, briefly, and to touch the sleeping thing with a manicured forefinger. Then he went on to his new bedroom to collect a clean handkerchief from the top left-hand drawer of his bureau. For reasons which were neither given nor sought, Paul and his crib had ousted Stanley from Grace's bedroom, and he had been installed in the sewing room, with a narrow bed and a chest of drawers. Stanley did not mind being so confined. His life was in the office, at the table, in the field.

There comes a time when it is more comfortable to sleep alone.

Chapter Fourteen

The two boys crowded into the car with Stanley, William on the outside with his arm over the door, John in the middle trying to stay out of the way of the gear lever. There was a stop at the bottom of the hill to instruct the overseer, a stop at the Post Office to pick up the newspaper, and a stop by Ozzie's truck, loaded with banana suckers. The next was by the pasture gate at Quaw Hill. Man-Man, the East Indian cattleman, was there, dismounted from his mule.

'Just going in here a minute,' said Stanley, switching off the engine and getting out. The boys stayed where they were.

'Come along.'

Dutifully, they followed, pushing through the gate behind Stanley and Man-Man, closing it, and following up the cowtrack toward the drinking pond in its circle of trees.

'Ticks in this pasture,' said John.

'And grass lice. Grass lice are worse,' said William, who knew everything.

John, at the rear, avoided the guinea grass on either side so the grass lice would not jump on him. Stanley and Man-Man stopped on the edge of the shade around the drinking pond. On the far side were two horses with thin backs and big bellies. John knew them. They were mares Stanley put to a jack donkey to breed mules. But beside them now were two yearlings, real horses, rich dark bays with black points and alert, eager heads, ears pricked toward the visitors.

'Horse!'

'Where you get dem from, Man-Man?'

'Bawn 'ere, sah. Dem Daddy is a race'orse. Don't is so, busha?'

Yes, George Metaxas. The best horse ever bred in Jamaica. He won the Jamaica Derby some years back.'

'You looking after them for somebody?'

'In a way. You want one?'

'Me!'

'I want first call on the big gelding to ride the property, but the filly is yours if you want her.'

John went weak at the knees, weak with excitement, and love, and longing; love for this enigmatic father of his, for Man-Man, chuckling with pleasure, and longing for the shining creature regarding him from the other side of the shadowed pond.

'You mean it?'

'Yes.'

'You can tell dem apart, Mass John? De big one a lick him modah wid him 'ead, dat is Kat'leen foal, an' de one wid de star pon him farrid, das de likkle filly. 'Im belongst to de mare dem call Stumble.'

'Can Miriam have one?'

'In due course.'

'What about William?'

William was standing a few paces away, pouting slightly, aware that he was to be excluded except by charity, and hating it.

'He can borrow mine when I'm not using it. How's that, William?'

'Yes, sir. Yes, Uncle Stanley, thank you.'

'De likkle filly gwine fas' as light,' said Man-Man.

'How you know, Man-Man?'

'By de shape. Likkle tiny buil' for speed!'

'When can we ride them?'

'Not for a year yet. It will give you something to look forward to. Come along.'

'Dem mus' name dem, busha. Me mus' know de name fi call dem.'

'I'll tell you next week, Man-Man.'

'A'right, sah.'

Stanley called the big gelding Winston, after Churchill. John called the filly Floating Power.

Almost to the day, a year later, a little man got off the bus at Hordley, and walked into Holland.

He was five feet tall, about fifty years old, and black. He wore riding breeches and boots, a tweed jacket and a flat cap. His name was Green, and he had been a famous jockey.

Green was given a room in the great house, and stables were built across the canal, of bamboo and coconut fronds. A boy was employed to cut guinea grass and bring it in for the horses. The blacksmith came from Golden Grove, and Stanley himself went to Kingston to buy the saddles.

The boys sat on the stone steps of the great house to watch Green breaking in their horses. He talked to them constantly in a cooing patois which might have been horse language for no one else could understand it. He was tough without being cruel, and it was amazing how soon the horses trusted him. One day he was lying across their backs while they looked round in amazement, the next they were wearing saddles. The time after that when the boys returned to Holland, Green was perched on Stanley's Winston, walking round in a circle, and a couple of days later Floating Power was stretching her dainty legs at the trot. When the job was done, Stanley persuaded Green to give the boys a lesson before he left.

Green rode Winston, and John sat on his Floating Power. They went out of the works yard, side by side, and over the humpbacked bridge that crossed the canal, with the filly walking sideways and looking at the water for fear of alligators. Then they took the road toward Pond Mouth. Floating Power had one ear forward, the other tilted back to listen to Green.

'Sit up straight, sir,' said Green. 'When you walking you stay so, see me? De rein in a yu han', so . . . 'ere so . . . an' yu foot in a de stirrup, so, like dis, an you han' talk to de 'orse mout' . . . a'right, trot! Touch 'im . . . hup an' down, hup an' down, yu nah lose yu manhood . . . hup an' down . . . an' de rein, de rein . . . a'right, das how yu does trot . . . touch 'im again, sah, we gwine canter . . . jes' like 'ome in a harm chair . . . See me? See me? See me? Yes, good, sah! Now we gwine gallop. Tek up the rein, tek it up, tek it up, stan 'up in a de stirrup, so, so, see me, jus' like a bud on a pos'.'

Floating Power was no longer touching the ground. Stones and puddles and coconut husks flew past underneath. There was the rush of wind past John's ears, and the black mane whipping his face, the sound of hooves on the dirt road and Green perched beside him, keeping pace, watching him, and talking all the time.

''Im is a good likkle 'orse, eh? Slow down now, sah, slow down, siddung 'pan 'im, tek a wrap, an' bring 'im 'ead dung 'pan 'im chis', slow down, sah, or 'im tek you right in a de alligator pond . . . easy, easy, a'right, easy . . .'

They were walking again.

'Well, sah, das all yu 'as to know, but you 'as to practice.'

The next day, Green walked out to Hordley, carrying his little cardboard suitcase, caught the bus, and went back to Kingston.

Holland that had been a hell hole, became a playground. While Stanley and Mr Briscoe sweated over the paybill, the boys herded cattle over the Rockies, attacked covered wagons that had invaded the lands of the Apache, and crossed the Andes with Bolivar to recapture Bogota. They took the beach road to East End to swim, and watched the calves being clamped and branded. With scraps from Grace's sewing basket, John made racing silks, and they raced along the stretch of turf between the sand and the coconut walk, winning a Derby every day. John took the filly home to Stone Haven so that he could care for her himself, but Grace put her foot down when Floating Power was led onto the verandah for tea.

Stanley's insistence on planting sugar cane in swamps, keeping the canal water sweet and the river mouth open, threatened the other attraction Holland held for the boys. It had begun to limit the domain of the alligator.

In the old days, so the story went, Man-Man had killed one with a pick-axe in front of the great house, but now they were confined to the Pond Mouth and the river mouth, with occasional forays up the canals to hunt for crabs, or dogs, or children. Stanley had shot one in the first flush of ownership, and had toyed with the idea of inviting tourists down for alligator hunting and lunches in the style of Simon Taylor, the first owner, but the real business of farming drove all that out of his head. The skin of his alligator, ten feet long, was rolled up in the hall cupboard with the tennis rackets and the cricket bats, and brought out occasionally to impress visiting missionaries at tea.

John conceived the idea of getting one of his own. His mother would not allow guns in the house, and the .303 his father had used was at Holland, in the back of Mr Briscoe's cupboard, together with a .22 and a pistol for taking pot shots at coconut thieves on moonlight nights – so Mr Briscoe said. John had only to persuade the overseer to lend him the .303 and a few rounds of ammunition. His face a mask of sincerity, his brown eyes warm and honest, he confronted the old man while he was eating his midday meal.

'Daddy says I can have it.'

'To shoot alligator?'

'Yes, sir.'

'Is that true?'

William, hovering in the doorway, shuffled about and muttered that it was absolutely true, cross his heart and hope to die.

'It's absolutely true, Mr Briscoe, sir. Daddy said we could, but we had to promise to be careful.'

'You fired a .303 before?'

'No, sir, only a .22.'

'It kicks. It'll knock your shoulder off if you're not holding it properly.'

'Yes, sir.'

'You know de safety catch?'

'Better show me again, sir.'

Briscoe produced the rifle. It was army issue, of the type that killed so many in the Great War, lovingly cared for.

'Be careful how you carry it, hear. Like so. And only release the catch when you're about to fire.'

Under the humpback stone bridge there was a rowboat used for transporting coconuts along the canals. Being payday, the boat was empty, and its oars lay idle in the bottom. The boys set off, rowing or poling through the lily pads and floating coconut limbs, with crabs and herons and wild duck scuttling and flapping out of their way, past the cultivation to where the canal broadened into the Pond Mouth, and the banks disappeared in forests of wild ginger on one side and mangrove on the other.

'Now slowly and quietly,' said John. 'I'll go up front with the gun.'

The rifle clattered against the side as he went forward. William dipped his oar occasionally, just enough to keep the boat moving on the dark water. The Pond Mouth broadened again into a lake among the mangroves, half a mile long. A blue heron startled them, screeching and taking off, trailing a leg in the water. Way down, where the Pond curved, and a gust of sea-breeze rippled and silvered the water, a tarpon jumped.

'Alligator chase him,' whispered John. 'Dis is a good place. Right on de corner there by the big tree. We can tie up de boat and wait. Alligator live here, man. They mus' come.'

William agreed readily. Sitting out in the middle of the water with the Lord knows what in the murky depths below was not to his taste. He was beginning to feel like the cheese in a rat trap, while John, with the gun in his hand, was all confidence.

They tied up the boat, and waited, watching the blank water and the silent mangroves, occasionally slapping at a mosquito or changing position to relieve a cramp.

'John,' said William after half an hour, 'I'm hungry.'

'Sssh.'

'Alligator don't trouble me. What I want to trouble him for?'

'Sssh!'

Silence returned, but nothing broke the dark grey and shining surface of the Pond.

'John, if an alligator come you goin' to miss him. De boat will rock as you tek aim.'

John decided William was right, and climbed out of the boat onto the dry bank that supported the tree to which they were moored.

William pointed at something a hundred yards away, like a floating log, but moving against the current.

John said, 'Oh Lawd, das a big one.'

'Dat is alligator grandfather.'

You could tell how big he was by the width of his head as he approached, moving slowly, without a ripple, up the Pond toward them. The skin of his back appeared, with the prominent scales like the fins of a shark. He was making for the mangroves just opposite them, infinitely slowly, at alligator cruising speed.

John took position under the tree, prone, the heavy rifle supported on his elbow. The bank was only two feet above the water, and the alligator twenty yards away, so he was giving himself an appalling angle, but the top of the massive head was clear in his sights. John released the safety. William was watching the alligator, who, as if he had heard the faint click of the catch, was beginning to sink. John fired. The loud report scattered the birds among the mangroves. There was a splash of water just beyond the alligator, and he was gone.

'Missed! God damn it! God damn it to hell!'

'He won't give you another chance,' said William.

John said, 'Look.'

In the centre of the widening ripple where the alligator had gone down, two eyes appeared, only the eyes, about eighteen inches apart, staring at them. John reloaded, and the eyes submerged.

'Come,' said John, 'we'll go and get him.'

'What do you mean?'

'If we go over there, he's going to come for us, and then I can't miss him, because he'll be coming straight at the rifle.'

They were both disappointed, both terrified, but John was possessed of a blood lust as he had been when he wanted to kill Teacher. William could not argue with his rage, his conviction, or his hatred of the alligator that he had missed, and who then had stared at him, challenging him.

'Untie de boat, we goin' over dere.'

William hesitated, 'No, sir, not me.'

'Coward.'

William's eyes were black with hate, but he untied the boat, and they paddled slowly over the quiet water toward the thick mangroves where they knew the alligator was hiding.

'His house is down under the bank,' said John. 'Stop.'

The boat drifted and stopped, fifteen feet from the edge of the mangroves, fifteen feet for the alligator to charge. Nothing happened. Nothing moved.

'Come out, you brute,' said John, and fired into the mangroves. 'That will vex him.'

The echoes of the shot died away. The mangrove did not rustle, the water lay unbroken, and the two boys sat in the boat, waiting, motionless.

William's mouth had gone dry. He thought he was going to be sick, or shit his pants.

'John, for Jesus' sake, if de alligator come under de boat and turn us over, him kill de two of we. John, enough is enough.'

John looked at him; he despised William for being weak and boastful and Harold's son. Yet how brave he was to do this foolish thing, to risk his life for fear of being called a coward, and his anger drained away. John realized that he too was frightened, so frightened that if the alligator came now, his hands would shake, and he would be too scared to shoot. But he had dared the beast, honour was satisfied. It was time to get the hell out and go home.

William told his father the story, and Uncle Harold, sober and shaking, came to Stone Haven to complain to Stanley. Mr Briscoe was told that on no account was the .303 to leave his room again. John had the belt on his backside once again, and spent a day in the guest room, nourished on bread and water.

It did not cure him. He had conceived an obsession with alligators. He saw them swimming out to sea. Walking, he heard them rustling in the bush, and he knew his horse would one day step on one. They came under his bed at night, and into his dreams. He persuaded William to go back again, promising no heroics, and so they found themselves once more in the coconut boat, afloat on the dark, brooding water, in search of terror.

This time they had no hope, for the .303 was under lock and key. John had only been able to snitch the .22 and a handful of rounds. Briscoe, being a reasonable man, had not bothered to hide it.

'That thing can only tickle an alligator, man,' said William.

'I'll hit him in the eye,' said John.

'This is the last time,' William declared. He had been ashamed of telling tales, and had only come as a kind of penance, and was regretting it already. 'This is the last time,' he repeated.

They were passing the spot where they'd seen the big one when John spotted another, about forty yards away, a little fellow, crossing at right angles to the movement of the boat. It was an impossible shot, forty yards, standing up in a rowing boat, with a toy rifle. John put the butt to his shoulder, squinted, fired, and the alligator leapt into the air, mortally wounded, flashing its pale underbelly, landing on its back. When they got to it, it was floating on its side, motionless. It was only four of five feet long, but it was a real alligator, and they had shot it. John and William each got an oar under the body, and on the second try they flipped the creature over the gunwale and into the bottom of the boat, where it lay on its stomach, right side up, looking very real indeed.

John looked for the mark of the wound, and found that the little bullet had entered the head just by the right eye, smashing into the bone of the upper jaw.

'We got one.'

They had got one, and were carried along on a tide of elation, chattering, congratulating each other, re-living the moment as they rowed toward the works yard.

The alligator moved, contracting a foreleg, raising his head. 'Jesus Christ,' said William, 'de damn thing don't dead.'

John swallowed hard. Quickly, he jammed the barrel of the gun into the back of the alligator's neck, pressing the barrel into the soft spot just behind the brain. He fired. The alligator twitched, and stopped moving, but the shot, passing through the beast, had also passed through the bottom of the rotting boat, and she began to take in water.

'Row for your life!' yelled John, like Captain Ahab, and they rowed.

Chapter Fifteen

'Oh God, our Heavenly Father, we thank thee for the beauty of this place, and for Thy blessings so bounteously bestowed . . .' Teacher Berry prayed in his rich baritone. The Young Friends listened with heads bowed, reverentially. John, in the back row, leaning against the wooden railing, could study the backs of heads, black girls with hair multi-parted and plaited, East Indian girls with smooth hair combed shoulder length, and the scrubbed clean necks of young men, black and brown, in starched white shirts. He could not quarrel with Teacher Berry's sentiments. The place was beautiful, the food was good and plentiful. Breakfast was to be saltfish and ackee and roast breadfruit. Miriam, sent to spy, had reported that dinner was to be even better; curried chicken and rice and peas. Such blessings made religion palatable.

Fairy Hill had an air of tranquillity unusual even for Jamaica. It was a two storey white frame house in the New England style, once the great house of a spice property, and left by a Connecticut Quaker lady to the Jamaican Friends as a rest home.

Behind John, where he leaned on the wooden railing, was a wild gully, damp and full of tree ferns, and a moss-covered guango hung with wild orchids and vines with leaves like giant jigsaw puzzles. Beyond that, a field of coconuts climbed the low hill that hid the sea. Around the prayer meeting on the verandah, a hibiscus hedge obscured the stone foundations. John watched a doctor bird doing his rounds of the hibiscus, his tail coat drooping, and his wings vibrating swifter than vision, then in the twinkling of an eye, one patient restored, he flitted to the next and paused again, gently administering.

'. . . in the name of the Father, the Son, and the Holy Ghost, Amen.'

This valediction amounted almost to heresy, for Quakers have no truck with the Trinity, but in a multi-religious society, tolerance is the first and last commandment. The Young Friends rose, each shook hands with a neighbour, smiled, and turned to the other neighbour, shook hands again, and smiled again. Round the back, someone struck a cowbell, and the exodus to breakfast began.

John and Miriam ate together on the front steps, plates on their knees. They felt no necessity as they did at school tea-dances to sit apart pretending not to know each other. The Friends, as opposed to their schoolmates, would not tease them, and perhaps were too deferential. Their mother, after all, was the Quaker pope, and their lighter skins, their education, and the certainty of later privilege set them apart. The others were locals, students from an orphanage, elementary school teachers, a tailor's son, a small farmer's son, an Indian grocer's daughter with a violin. The social difference embarrassed the children, and it saddened them, for with these Friends they shared a childhood and, more than the boys and girls at boarding school could ever be, they were their people.

Yet, if John hadn't wanted to please his mother and the Conference had been further away from Stone Haven than seventeen miles, he might have found an excuse to stay away. He had taken against Jesus for enjoining us to be perfect when God had made us manifestly flawed, and he felt that chapel at Munro College, twice a day and three times on Sunday, was enough religion for a lifetime.

A morning dip was scheduled, from which Miriam excused herself, and a small safari of the young, their bathing suits rolled up in towels, made their way through the coconut walk toward the beach. John was looking forward to seeing some of the girls in bathing suits, dreading the sight of Teacher Berry stripped, and the pitiful spectacle of the fraternal delegate from Indiana turning red.

He was to be disappointed; most people decided not to swim. The water, after the smiling morning, had gone grey and choppy. The waves were not running in straight rows toward the beach but colliding, throwing up little pyramids and waterspouts as if the wind and currents quarrelled, but there was no wind. One young man who braved the water reported a heavy undertow, and the sky was clouding over, not with the usual high-piled cumulus but with a thin, grey, sun-obscuring film.

While they were walking back, the wind came up, and by the time they reached the rest home, it was blowing thirty or forty miles an hour. The dry limbs were falling in the coconut walk and the quickstick branches thrashing. A thin rain was borne in the rising wind. John was among the last to return and found an atmosphere of siege. Someone had been to the village and come back post haste to say excitedly that there was a storm warning flying from the post office. Everyone was busy fastening windows, closing doors and pulling furniture around.

It came so suddenly. The note of the wind changed from the screaming of a gale to the deep fearsome bass voice of the hurricane. Through this overwhelming sound, they could hear the rain peppering the walls and windows, the cracking of tree trunks and above their heads the house creaking and groaning, begging for mercy. Looking out, John saw that an almond tree had fallen on the Reverend Vincent's car, so arming himself with a machete, he set out to rescue it, a pointless exercise except to pit himself against the storm.

Raindrops were bullets and the wind knocked him over, but fired by heroism, John crawled across the grass to the stricken automobile and managed to chop away a branch or two, until he was temporarily blinded by a raindrop in the eye. Deciding on discretion he started back toward the house. As he was crawling through the gateway, something struck the post above his head, burying itself in the wood. It was a corrugated iron sheet from the kitchen roof, the flying blade of a guillotine, which would have cut him clean in half.

He reached the safety of the stone steps, and huddled close to the foundations, listening to the awesome thunder of the wind.

More quickly than it came, it ceased. There was a complete stillness. The eye of the hurricane was passing over them. The air was sticky, dense, and weighed on the flesh like water. John climbed onto the verandah where the prayer meeting had been and looked down.

'Oh God, our Heavenly Father, we thank thee for the beauty of this place . . .'

The wondrous gully was gone, a dumping ground for sodden leaves and broken branches. The guango lay upended, soil running from its roots like blood. The coconuts beyond had snapped like matchsticks, at one level, depending on the contour of the hill, slashed by one divine cutlass stroke. Looking up, he saw that the second storey of the house was gone, gone somewhere on the wind.

'Somebody in Cuba got a nice house,' he said to the boy next to him. 'Have you seen my sister?'

'No.'

As if in answer to his question, he heard a piano starting up, under water, out of tune, and Miriam's voice singing. Miriam, who knew the story of the *Titanic*, was leading the female Friends in a rendition of 'Nearer my God to Thee'. John decided not to join in. Miriam had a rather ghoulish sense of humour for one so young. He went instead to look for the dinner, picking his way across the debris of the yard. The bits of the kitchen that had not blown away were collapsed in a pile, and digging through it, he came upon the dinner, cast-iron pots of chicken curry, cooked, and rice and peas.

'... and for thy Blessings bounteously bestowed ...'

The wind came back from another quarter, milder than before, a mere hundred miles an hour, slowly abating as the day wore out. The hurricane destroyed little else, except by flooding, for there was little left to destroy.

The children, huddled together on the roofless verandah, looked out at the desolation of the pasture and the woodland that had been, the broken limbs of trees still helplessly thrashing in the wind and rain.

'You think Stone Haven is all right?' John said.

'Oh, yes man,' Miriam replied confidently.

'This is a big house, but the top floor went.'

'Stone Haven is what it says it is, John. Hurricane proof.'

'The windows could blow in, and the roof lift off.'

'Daddy has storm blinds for all of the windows.'

'I'm going home, just to make sure,' John said.

'All right,' she said, 'I'll come with you. We'll pass the word along the way that everybody is safe.'

'No, Miriam, you stay here and take charge of the girls.'

So Miriam organized the girls, all older than herself, to start clearing up inside, while Teacher Berry and the boys indulged in makeshift carpentry, trying to keep out the rain.

It was a long walk to Stone Haven, seventeen miles into a wind dropping slowly from eighty, through seventy to sixty miles an hour. The road was blocked a thousand times. Small trees meant a scramble through the branches, big ones had to be climbed or crawled under.

John plodded forward, head down against the rain. Around him was a new landscape, bare and skeletal. In places, he could see for miles where previously there had been mere foliage. Shattered villages were visible on the hillside slopes. The coconuts were flat, in rows like dead soldiers. One old pinhead tall had kept standing by offering no resistance, but lost its crown, and a john crow was feasting on its heart. Smashed fruit, breadfruit, mangoes, paw-paw and Tahiti apples littered the road, bashed and broken open. The pigs were in heaven, nosing at this fallen treasure. A house by the roadside was a pile of broken planks with an undamaged sewing machine standing in the rain. Its owner was nowhere in sight for most people were still under cover, waiting for the wrath of God to spend itself. A bamboo hut still stood, but beside it a concrete bungalow had been blown flat.

John, looking at it, feared for Stone Haven.

Along the coast, green sand-filled breakers laced with weed were smashing at the shore. Waterside cottages were washed away. The road was two feet deep in sand, coral and weed from the bottom of the bay. He had to detour by the higher ground and through people's back yards.

'A'right, a'right, where yu comin' from?'
'Fairy Hill.'
'How it stay?'
'Mash up, mash up, but de people okay.'
'Good, sah, good. Struggle on.'
'What a blow, eh? What a blow!'

At Long Road, the Chinaman's shop, lifted off its foundations, but otherwise undamaged, had landed on the road, crosswise, so John went in through the front door. Inside there was no sign of groceries, already looted, or hidden by the Chinaman and his family. He went out the back door, and continued on his way.

It was growing dark, and John, in thin clothing, was cold and tired, and each minute more so. Every step against the driving wind became a greater effort. He was wet and shivering, his lips and fingers blue.

'This is supposed to be a hot country,' he muttered to himself.

Destruction had ceased to be a great adventure and become a biting discomfort and a fear, fear that he might not make it, head down against the rain, looking only at his sodden shoes, moving, and moving.

The idea came to him that Stone Haven itself had been destroyed, the roof carried off into the John Crow Mountains, his parents crushed beneath the walls.

A big tree trunk lay across the road, and he had to get down on his hands and knees to crawl under it. John felt his leg cramp, the muscles, cold and tired, seize up in a knot, and he cried out in pain, unable to get up. There was no one to hear, and no one to help. He managed to roll over, scraping his ribs on the tree trunk, and get his icy hands to his leg to massage the hard knot in his calf. He rubbed and kneaded and cursed until the muscle softened, then slowly, carefully, got to his feet.

'Don't do that again, leg,' he said. 'You and me are going home.'

Rounding the big corner by the cricket ground, he saw a light on the Stone Haven hill. It might be no more than a kerosene lamp, John thought, the one that said 'God is our refuge' round the shade. 'Home, boy, home!'

His parents were huddled in the drawing room. Grace looked up as the boy came in, her face like yellowing parchment in the lamplight. 'John, are you all right?'

'Cold.'

'And Miriam?'

'Miriam is all right, Mamma. Nobody was hurt, only the top of the house blown off.'

'I'll get you some towels, and dry clothes,' she said, and went off with a firm stride, covering her relief by doing something that needed to be done. John looked around. There were various pots and buckets collecting drips from the ceiling. His father was sitting on a dining chair, his trouser legs rolled up like a man at the beach, a tweed cap on his head that he had bought to wear on shipboard.

'I thought this house was hurricane proof,' John said. 'Your roof is leaking.'

'A little water, that's all. Your mother was the general, fighting a rearguard action, like Katsoff against Napoleon. Whenever a window blew in, she opened up the room, and gave it to the hurricane. We lost three rooms that way, but the storm never got in here, never had a chance to build up and lift the main roof.'

Young Paul padded in, barefoot, carrying a chamber pot.

'The church roof gone, you know! What a blow, John, what a blow! You walk home?'

'Couldn't run,' John said and picked him up, chamber pot and all, and hugged him. Paul hugged him back, and they clung together.

'Pshaw, man, put me down. I'm in charge of drip water,' Paul said proudly. He put the chamber pot under a drip in the corner, and padded off again.

Grace returned with dry clothes and a towel.

'Change here. It doesn't matter. Mabel is making you a sandwich and some hot cocoa.'

'Is it as bad as I think?' his father asked.

'Yes, sir. The eye passed right over us. Everything is gone. Boston coconuts are all flat. The same at Darlingford.'

'And Muirton?'

'The bananas all gone.'

'Bananas everywhere. Don't bother to tell me about them.'

'At Long Road and Manchioneal, the houses are all gone, the market, the shop, the roof of the police station . . .'

'Terrible, terrible,' said Stanley, shaking his head sadly. 'Did you see anything of Williamsfield?'

'It was getting dark, but I saw nothing standing.'

'Yes,' Stanley said, 'I can tell without looking. The first bad blow came from the north. There are one or two fields at Moro like Pigeon Valley where there will be some trees left standing. Holland will be blown down. One hundred per cent.'

'Doesn't Quaw Hill protect it from that side?'

'No. There'll be a down draft. It will be as if the hurricane just stamped on the property. One hundred per cent.'

'You were insured?'

Stanley looked up at his son. His face was grey, his eyes blank, seeing only the images in his mind. It seemed he had not heard the question. He was still mourning the loss of his fields, his green and golden fields, and all his care and labour.

'Bananas one hundred per cent. The cane will recover, being only a grass, but we'll lose some of the crop from flooding. The coconuts . . .'

'The coconuts were insured, sir?' John repeated.

'Yes, of course, insured.'

'How much a tree?'

His father did not answer, staring at the black, rain-lashed window panes. John tried again.

'How many trees have we lost?'

'A hundred and twenty thousand – just a guess.'

'Will the insurance pay?'

'Oh yes, they will. It's Lloyds of London.'

'Then you're a rich man,' John said, smiling.

Stanley turned to him. He looked old and tired, and spoke like a man pronouncing his own epitaph.

'Rich enough. Yes, but I would prefer to reap the crops. Do you understand that? We would have made the money in time.'

'Think about the people,' Grace said, 'in Hector's River, Belle Castle and Manchioneal. They've lost everything.'

'It's terrible, terrible.'

'I saw some pretty bad things along the way,' John said.

'Jamaica people are wonderful, you know,' Stanley said, 'country people are wonderful. They've lost everything, but then they didn't have very much. They'll scavenge the things blown down, pick up the pieces of their houses; they'll eat ground provisions and fish. Poor people are wonderful, they'll survive.

Chapter Sixteen

Stanley fought the war in a wicker armchair by the shortwave radio in the drawing room. While the net curtains billowed, obscuring and revealing the verandah, the front lawn and the sea, countries were overrun, swastika and jackboot multiplied, generals surrendered and politicians wept.

Stanley's ear was filled with the mellifluous voices of the BBC and the screen of his mind with sinking ships and blazing guns, with tanks tilting over sand dunes, fighter planes swinging like medals on a ribbon of smoke, and European cities collapsing into clouds of their own dust. There was a six o'clock news, in dressing gown and slippers with tea and Saltine biscuits, a nine o'clock news, attired for the field in riding breeches, a one o'clock news, while Mabel kept the soup warm. There was a four o'clock news, with tea, and just before six he trotted in from the office to mark the end of his day with the exploits of Montgomery or MacArthur, or a simple list of casualties on either side, like the score in a cricket match. Paul, on the sofa, picking the skin between his toes, said he was wasting the battery, for the news was almost always the same. He was told to go away and play.

Grace's war was at her desk, under the mezzotint of Christ crowned with thorns, writing to her son gone overseas. The years had taken the softness from her, and left her hard and angular. The wave of hair above her forehead was already grey, and the cheekbones more prominent. The downward curve of her mouth was more accentuated now, her lips thinner and more compressed. She was still beautiful, but her face expressed the loss of joy, a loss only partially redeemed by faith, and will.

John began his war at a Quaker college in Indiana, and he hated it. Pictures of him standing in the snow looked increasingly forlorn and his letters grew shorter and shorter. He did not know why he was at college or what he was studying to be. The American boys his age were all joining the great crusade. He admired pacifists but did not think he was good enough to be one. No one was surprised when his next letter came from Canada. He had joined the Royal Canadian Air Force.

> ... there are a couple of other Jamaicans in my unit, Charlie Swift, Chin Lee, and D'Aguilar, the one we used to call Slushy.
>
> Looking back, I think I made the right decision. I've nothing against America, and so much of it reminded me of you, making me understand you better and love you better, but it wasn't me. I don't know what I am, but a college sophomore in Iowa is what I'm not. Looking forward, as soon as I get my wings, I suppose we'll go to England. All that will be exciting, and this war must be won, for the more we hear of Hitler ... no I don't want to write about politics, only to say, my personal survival doesn't really matter one way or the other, and I must do my bit, whatever that is, for England, but for Jamaica too.
>
> Slushy says we were mad to join up. He says the bully boys

are fighting over the toffee bars, and we being toffee bars should stay out of it . . .

Grace was distressed: she felt that John had joined up in despair, not for conviction's sake but because he was unhappy. His unhappiness bothered her more than his rejection of her faith. She was more concerned perhaps by his rejection of her background. It made her feel she had lost her own childhood, and to lose one's childhood is to die.

Stanley had visions of Harold in the First World War, setting out on his career as a wastrel. He could not help drawing a parallel, but did not want to accept it. Finally he refused to think about it at all, simply hoping his son would survive, come home, and go to work.

Miriam, small, black-haired, full-figured, spent the war at school, cramming English history. She was determined to win a place at Oxford. How else could she be noticed? She knew her father doted on her and indulged her, granting her every whim. It wasn't good enough. She knew her mother loved her and cast her as her shadow, but she was not her mother's image, and could never be. Who or what she was burned in her spirit and her maturing flesh, and found no expression save in the lives of Tudors and Plantagenets, of ancient lords and ladies who lived by blood and treachery and called it honour.

'Why isn't there a history of Jamaica?' she asked her father.

'There must be.'

'I haven't seen one.'

'Jamaica has a history,' Stanley said. 'We were discovered by Columbus, and the British captured us in 1655.'

'Is that all?'

'Of course not, Miriam, but you don't want to know about the Morant Bay Rebellion or Marcus Garvey.'

'Yes, I do. But there's no Jamaican history at school, not even a book in the library.'

'Then you'll have to write one. It'll give you something to do.'

John wrote from England:

> . . . there are two seasons here, cold, and not so cold. When we were training in Canada, it was really cold, your breath would

freeze and your ears fall off, but it was always snug inside, and dry. In England it is just miserable cold, inside and outside. Your underwear is wet in the morning and your sheets are wet when you get into bed.

I have been adopted by a Mrs Letchworth, who has a brick house with lots of chimneys, not far from the base. She has taken it on herself to mother airmen from the Commonwealth, so we RCAF are on her list for tea. My being Jamaican makes me extra special like a rare stamp. The vicar comes, and a retired tea planter from Ceylon. Mrs Letchworth knits, the needles whizzing like propellor blades, faster than the eye can see, so we live in a slipstream of socks. I give her my chocolate ration, and she squeezes my hand and looks moist, but don't worry, Mamma, her husband was killed in the First War, so she is vintage 1914 and her skirts are covered in cat hair.

So much about Mrs Letchworth. I wonder how you are, and Daddy, and Miriam, and Paul, and I wonder what I am doing here sometimes, though to be honest I never think that when I'm flying. I love to fly. I love the aircraft, and the sky, when you can see it in this benighted country.

There are some black ground crew on the base, boys recruited in Jamaica. One of them comes from Manchioneal, name of Brown, Carlton Brown. His father is Brown, a headman at Retreat. I go and talk to them sometimes, just to hear the accent, and to keep in practice so I don't forget how to speak Jamaican.

As yet, they have not been invited to tea by my good-hearted Mrs Letchworth . . .

'At least he didn't mention cricket,' said Stanley. 'When Harold was over there in the army he wrote about nothing but cricket, and drinking in pubs, and could I send him some money. I don't think they paid the army in the First World War. At least, they didn't pay Harold. He was always short of money, and it was difficult to say no when he was supposedly risking his life for King and Country.'

'Don't get started on Harold,' Grace said curtly, and took John's letter away to put it, with others, in the top left-hand drawer of her dressing table, next to her pillow.

Chapter Seventeen

John went to Waterloo Station to meet his little sister. He admired her suitcases, real leather, brand-new, adorned with Elders and Fyffes stickers, and she offered him a maidenly cheek for his fraternal kiss. They took a taxi across Westminster Bridge, past the Houses of Parliament and up Birdcage Walk to the Rubens Hotel just behind Buckingham Palace. It was a glorious cloudless day, such as only England can afford by being so miserly, all the more miraculous for being rare. As they went up the steps of the hotel, the Household Cavalry rode by, an embodied dream of chivalry.

They had lunch in the hotel, and set off shopping. It transpired that but for the coat she was wearing, made by a Jamaican tailor from a pattern cut from an American magazine, Miriam had no warm clothing. They set off on a tour of Knightsbridge, Oxford Street and Regent Street, searching through war-diminished stocks and pre-war styles for scarves and gloves, a cashmere sweater, and a tweed skirt. John suggested woollen underwear.

'I'd rather die,' Miriam said, 'I swear to God, I'd rather die.'

A street photographer snapped them coming out of Swan and Edgar, the handsome airman with his cap worn at a rakish angle, and the Indian princess on his arm, or perhaps a chilled and shrunken Dorothy Lamour.

They had tea at Lyons Corner House, stuffing their parcels underneath their chairs.

'So what's your college called again?'

'Lady Margaret Hall.'

'Sounds posh.'

'Of course.'

'How did you get in?'

'Influence, my dear. Miss Rainforth at Hampton, you remember, she went to Oxford, and she knows someone who knows someone. Everything in England goes by influence.'

'Distinctions in all your subjects must have had something to do with it.'

'I doubt it,' Miriam said.

'What are you going to study?'

'P.P.E. Philosophy, politics and economics.'

'I thought your subject was history.'

'Was. I want to read something useful.'

'Philosophy! As Daddy would say, philosophy can't buy butter.'

'Politics and economics can. Now the war is over, at least on this side, Britain won't be able to hang on to her colonies. Jamaica will be independent in ten years, mark my words.'

John looked at his little sister with something like surprise. He had expected to talk about clothes or boyfriends, and for her to be looking forward to dances and punting on the river. Miriam was looking across the tea room at an Indian boy, about twenty, in a tweed jacket, grey bags, with a long college scarf wound round his neck. He was sipping tea and talking to an English boy, similarly attired, their perfectly accented voices identical, carrying clearly across the intervening space.

'He's ridiculous,' Miriam said.

'Who?'

'That babu man there, pretending to be English.'

'You don't know him, Miriam.'

'He comes from a culture so much older than England's. Why is he aping it?'

'I'll give you six months, and you'll be more English than he is.'

'*You* haven't lost *your* accent. Well, not entirely.'

'I can't. I have no ear.'

'And neither will I. I shall stay what I am.'

'What's that?'

'Black! A black girl from Jamaica.'

'Miriam, don't talk foolishness. You're not black.'

'I'm not white, and I'm not going to make myself ridiculous like that Indian over there.'

Miriam had raised her voice, and the Indian, who may or may not have heard her, turned to look at her, and smiled, a dazzling white smile.

John lit a cigarette. 'Miriam, when I first went to the States, I landed in Miami, to take the train there for New York. At the station, it was cold, maybe not cold for Miami but cold for me, and I decided to go into the waiting room as I had time to kill. But there were two waiting rooms. One said 'Whites' and the other was for black people. I wasn't going to claim to be what I'm not, and I wasn't going to be told where to go, so I stayed on the platform, in the cold.'

'You were wrong,' Miriam said. 'You are Jamaican, and you are black, and you have to take sides.'

'Is it a war?'

'Maybe.'

'You're just afraid of being put down by the English, so you're putting yourself down first.'

'No, John, I'm claiming equality. I'm claiming pride.'

The Indian, who was very attractive, was smiling at her again, and Miriam, suddenly embarrassed, persuaded John to change places, and changed the subject.

'What about you? You planning to stay in England?'

'No.'

'You got yourself an English girlfriend?'

'No.'

'Then you may be interested. Guess who came up on the boat with me. Mavis. You remember Mavis Arkwright?'

'Yes. What's she doing? Holiday?'

'No, man. She says she's taking a course, a nursing course, something to do with children, at somewhere called Great Oswald Street, or Ormond or something like that. I have it written down somewhere. She said she remembered you, and how handsome you were. There's no accounting for tastes.'

'What is she like now?'

'You're interested?'

'No. Answer a simple question.'

'Very glam. A little too flighty for my taste.'

'A nun would be too flighty for your taste.'

'I'm not criticizing,' said Miriam, 'she's just a bit ... exuberant. And she wears too much make up.'

'You're still your mother's daughter.'

*

Before his next leave, John phoned Mavis at the hospital. She was so excited to hear his voice, she said, but she was on duty and couldn't talk, or she'd catch hell from the Sister, and she'd love to meet him, and see him again, that is, if he were the real John Newton for she couldn't hear any Jamaican accent, at least on the phone. John assured her he was the genuine article, and told her he'd be in London the following Thursday. What a shame, she said, she was busy all day, but they could meet at lunchtime. They settled on the pub in the next street which Mavis said was quaint on the outside and disgusting on the inside, like the rest of the country, but it was nearby.

John was early, and sat nursing a pint in the saloon bar, which stank of stale beer and old cigarettes. He read the ads, and the score in last night's dart game, counted the missing light bulbs in the chandelier, and watched the damp ooze down the Nile green walls. There were three silent customers, and a fat dog with an abscess on his ear who monopolized the fire.

Mavis arrived, trumpeted by Cupids, turning the place into the Tyrrhenian sea, gliding toward him like Venus on the halfshell though demurely wrapped in a black coat with a large fox collar. She was wearing scent.

'I don't smell too strong, do I?' she asked breathlessly. 'I had to put something on so I don't smell of chloroform, you know.'

'What will you drink?'

'What's that? Beer. I don't know how you do it. That stuff is terrible, man. I'll have an orange, I don't really drink. But wait a second,' she said, her fingers lightly touching his sleeve, 'it's that bottled orange. I'd better have something to kill the taste, a bit of gin. Just as long as you don't think I'm a drinker. You have to watch out for Jamaicans, you know. Next thing it'll be all over Kingston.'

She smiled, a big, wide, warm smile, and her eyes smiled too, glowing.

'Lord, it's good to see you. Handsome in the uniform, eh? Still serious and quiet. I bet you're a devil underneath though. It's the quiet ones you have to look out for . . .'

John smiled and listened, hearing the rhythms of her speech, accustomed, half-forgotten rhythms, watching the movements of her hands, her hair tossing from side to side, Mavis emphatic, Mavis pensive, Mavis flirtatious.

'... I really couldn't live in that place, man. Dirty! I couldn't believe it, like some Rasta man squat in Trench Town. My mother wouldn't make her yard boy go in a place like that. Cockroach paradise! And they wanted seventeen and six, b. and b. No, sir. I found another place, has a bay window overlooking an iron railing and a piece of grass where the dogs go pooh-pooh. Costs a little more but I don't think Daddy will begrudge it, and if I stuff the windows with toilet paper and get a two-bar electric I might survive. How you manage with the cold, man?'

She had a second gin, only a small one '... small means small over here, eh. Sometimes you can't tell whether it's gin or just rinse water left in the glass...' and told him about working with the sick children, '... some of them terminal, you know, but so brave. I love them. I'll do anything for them. They are so cute and funny. Sometimes you want to cry for them, and they turn round and make you laugh. I pray to God for them, you know, every night I pray for the little children.'

She was silent for a while, staring at the dog with the abscessed ear and sorrowing for the universe. Then she turned back to John, the smile returning.

'So what do you do for social life in this place? If I see another cup of tea, I will just die, expire, fold my hands and flit.'

'When I get leave again, we'll go dancing. I'll take you to the Café Royal, or the Palais, somewhere like that, if you'd like.'

'Just as long as there's no queue. Queue, queue, queue! I won't go to pictures, because I won't stand in a queue. You queue for an hour and a half in the rain, and when you get in the place is empty. The only queue I'm standing in is the queue to leave the country.'

'You'll get to like it after a while,' John said.

The dancing date was agreed on definitely. An evening out, a restaurant, the works, and John lived in a state of expectation so profound it was doomed to disappointment. When the time came, she couldn't make it. It seemed her father had a relative who lived near Cambridge, and it was the only time she could pay her duty call. She was furious, and worse, distressed that John might think she was putting him off. She wasn't, cross her heart.

At least John could take her to the train. In the taxi, she was silent and nervous, twisting her fingers, and looking out, apparently engrossed in a passing parade of ruins, all for sale, or lease, or rent.

'You're angry with me, John.'

'No, of course not. You can't help it.'

'I wouldn't blame you. If I were you, I'd be angry.'

'I'm disappointed, but there's always another time.'

They walked to the platform in silence. Then she turned to him, and put both hands in his, facing him.

'If you want to kiss me . . .'

He kissed her, and she laughed, a low tremulous laugh, then pulled quickly away, picked up the overnight bag he had been carrying for her, and set off toward the train.

John watched, an ache beginning in his heart that he knew would never be assuaged. No one else could ever walk like that, swaying so easily, in that black coat with that ridiculous fur collar over which her brown hair flowed in profusion. No one else could turn, or smile, or wave like that, a private gesture that meant peace and love.

Love is the difficulty in getting there. Life comes after that.

William did not go to university, or to the war, but he moved away from Williamsfield and Stone Haven, in distance, if not in essence. He worked on one of the large sugar estates on the south side of the island as a bookkeeper, which meant he gave out the work on that part of the farm which was his responsibility, checked it every day, made up the pay bills, and paid the labourers on Friday afternoon.

Much of his time was spent on a mule, a large, ginger-coloured animal, no more willing than the rest of its breed. William kept it moving through the sweltering days by liberal use of the supple jack, the sound of which, striking the mule's backside, and the muttered cursing accompanying this encouragement preceded William round the sugar fields.

He did not see the man until he stepped out in front of the mule, a black man in a dirty grey shirt and patched trousers. He must have been squatting in the shade of the cane leaves leaning over the grassy interval. The man, like all William's labourers, carried a machete, but William was sure he had never seen him before. He was a young fellow, slim and muscular, with hair so short it seemed to have been shaved, and slightly bulging, bloodshot eyes.

'A'right, busha. What you name, sar?'

'My name is Newton.'

'Busha Newton. A'right, sar. Me name Minott. Henry Minott.'

'How de do. What you doing on the property?'

'Me, sar. What me doin? Me talkin' to you.'

'You working here?'

'No, sar. Das what we talkin' 'bout.'

'I don't have any work. All de work give out dis week.'

'Me no care about dat, sar. Me want a job.'

'Sorry. Try somewhere else.'

The man, dismissed, did not move, or look as if he intended to go. He stared at William, directly, his eyes bloodshot.

'I'm sorry,' William repeated. 'You understand me? There is no work. Try de nex' place.'

William put his heels into the mule's ribs, and shook the reins, and the beast took a step forward. The man reached up with his left hand and took hold of the rein.

'I want a job.'

'Leggo de mule.'

'I want a job, and red-face busha can't tell me no.'

'Get off the property,' William said, calmly. 'Leggo de mule and get you rass off de property.'

The man yanked at the rein, and raised the machete threateningly, and William, ducking away from the blade, struck the mule with the supplejack, urging it away, but the man hung on and the mule whipped round, throwing William to the ground. Before he could rise the man was standing over him, machete in hand, the bloodshot eyes fixed on William. He struck with the machete, into the dirt, deliberately missing, but getting closer and closer. As William tried desperately to crawl away, scrambling on his back, the man pursued him, laughing, the machete whistling over William's head, preventing him from rising, and thudding into the ground, closer and closer.

William stopped moving, looking up, defying the crazy man, trying bravely to outface him. The man stopped laughing, and his mouth opened, the dried saliva white on his lips.

'Get off the property,' William said, but it was no more than a whisper, and the machete swung again. William heard it before he felt it, a thud, a crunch at the wrist, a cold shock and the warmth of his flowing blood. He looked down to see his own hand, hanging from his forearm by a wisp of flesh.

'Oh my God! God save me!' William cried, and began to scramble away again, on his back. This time the man did not follow, but stood looking at the machete. He touched the red stain on the blade with his finger, and tasted it. William got to his feet, and ran, the blood spurting from his wrist like that of a decapitated chicken flapping madly round the Stone Haven yard. The man's laughter followed him.

Out of sight, William stopped, gasping for breath and looked at the stump of his arm, his life's blood draining away. Clumsily, he found his handkerchief and, weeping and cursing as he did so, improvised a tourniquet. Then he ran on, stumbling, toward safety.

Under the mezzotint of Christ, Grace was writing to the Yearly Meeting of Friends in Philadelphia.

> ... those poor Japanese women and children, what had they done? Surely we could have invited their Emperor to see for himself the destruction of some barren waste, showed their generals and admirals that we possessed the power to destroy the world, and did not want to use it. I believe my country must carry this dishonour for eternity. They tell me the Japanese had done brutal and terrible things, but 'Vengeance is mine, saith the Lord, I will repay.' Vengeance is the code of criminals, not the law and practice of great nations. I cry shame, shame upon America, eternal shame upon my dear and blessed country ...

From outside, she heard a chorus of low-voiced greetings coming from the mendicants who always waited outside her door, and she knew that someone had arrived who did not need to wait, a man, his heavy tread sounding on the tiled verandah. A figure appeared, silhouetted in the doorway, black against the light, John in his uniform.

John is dead, she thought.

'Mamma, did I frighten you? I'm sorry.'

He moved into the room, changing from ghost to body, clothed, flesh warm and tanned, sweat on his face from walking up the hill, eyes that could see, a smiling mouth.

'Mamma, it's me, John. I've come home.'

He kissed her, embraced her, and she held him firmly, making sure.

'John, you gave me quite a turn.'

'Sorry, sorry. I couldn't tell you I was coming. I hitch-hiked home, you see. The Yanks gave me a lift as far as Washington, then another to Miami, Guantanamo, Kingston. I got in just in time to catch the mail van. If you don't want to be frightened, Mamma, get a telephone. Where's Daddy?'

'Riding Holland.'

'It must be Tuesday.'

'Paul's here somewhere. Are you hungry, or thirsty?'

'One thing at a time,' John said, kissing her again.

Paul came, barefoot, slim and brown with tousled hair, like the boy he, John, had been. John picked him up and hugged him.

'Ouch,' Paul said, 'this uniform uncomfortable, man, like an old krukus bag. Put me down, man. I'm not a baby, you know. You home for good?'

'For good or ill.'

'Best you take that something off and burn it, man,' Paul said disdainfully, and then proceeded to important matters. 'You want to see m'horse?'

Paul took John's hand and led him into the yard, and toward the cow pasture.

'Where's Floating Power?' John asked.

'She gone. When you gone to war, Daddy give her to a coolie man to ride. I'm glad you come back, it's lonely around here.'

John looked across at the Williamsfield House.

'How's William?'

'Nobody tell you?'

'No.'

'A man chop off his hand, wid a machete. And Uncle Harold dead.'

'When? When did he die?'

Paul scratched his head. 'Oh, a couple of months ago now.'

'You know what he died of?'

'TB, they said, and liquor.'

Poor Harold, John thought. Thirty years ago he had returned from a war, a young man with all his life before him. What had he done, or not done, to earn so casual an obituary? And William.

'Have you seen William since?'

'No, he's not here. De ongle one leave is Auntie Cynthia. She workin' at de pos' office. Is ongle she livin' obah dere now. Me! I con' go to dat house, boy! De place is full o' duppy.'

Chapter Eighteen

John, alone on the verandah after tea, needed a smoke. He patted his trouser pockets, and the breast pocket of his safari shirt. The cigarettes were there, but no matches. Before the war, he remembered, matches had been kept in the dining room, in a big, marble-topped sideboard with a mirror above and three cupboards below. The matches were in the one on the right. John went to it, stooped, opened the door and, looking in, recoiled as from a pit of snakes.

Plucking up courage, he tried again. They were still there: a bottle of Appleton Estate Jamaica Rum, unopened, a bottle of Johnnie Walker, a bottle of Gordon's Gin, and, on the shelf below, brown bottles of Red Stripe beer, green bottles of ginger ale, colourless bottles of tonic and soda, and the matches, Beacon matches, made in Jamaica, guaranteed not to ignite. He took a box and returned to the verandah.

Grace came out to sit with him, and watch the daylight fade. In what was left of it, she was embroidering a small garment. John noticed how much thinner she had become, seeing the tendons in her hands, her veins, how bony her elbows looked, and through her cotton dress how prominent were her pelvic bones. His mother was ageing by growing gaunt, his father by getting plump, as if he fed on her.

'What are you sewing?'

'It's for Mrs Parkyn's baby.'

'Mrs Parkyn?'

'From Belle Castle. You remember. You have a good memory for people.'

'Yes. Tall girl with slanting eyes. Deep voice. Good-looking.'

His mother made no comment.

'There's liquor in the dining room cupboard.'

'Yes. I put it there.'

John took a last drag on his cigarette, and dropped the butt among the zinnias.

'I must remember,' Grace commented without lifting her eyes from her embroidery, 'to tell Tumpy to clean up that bed.'

'Sorry,' John said, 'what's the liquor for?'

'I decided that if you were determined to get drunk, I would rather you got drunk here, at home, than spend your time in rum shops like your Uncle Harold.'

'Ah. The bones are rattling again.'

'Only if you hear them.'

'Me! C'mon, Mamma. He rules Daddy's imagination, and yours.'

'That may be, but still unkind. We tried very hard with Harold, and failed.'

'So why do you feel guilty?'

'Because he and your father inherited this place together, and he died with nothing. It doesn't matter whose fault it was, one still feels ... sad. But we tried. Stanley bought him business after business. They all collapsed.'

'Was that when William used to come back with tall tales of marvellous places, steers with horns six feet wide, and carloads of gangsters?'

'Yes. Your father even offered to buy him San San. It was going for six thousand pounds. He made one condition, that Harold give up Williamsfield, and move his family away. Aunt Cynthia refused. Since the tourists have moved in, San San is worth a million pounds.'

'Daddy buys me Darlingford to run. Am I supposed to fail?'

'That's up to you, John.'

John thought about it.

'Mamma, can I put the beer in the refrigerator? It's not very good warm.'

'There are two bottles in the refrigerator already. You can have one now, if you like.'

John smiled. 'After supper, perhaps; thank you.'

John wrote from Jamaica,

> ... this place is a hell-hole, Miriam, but I have nowhere else to go. Sometimes I think I will end by killing myself....

And Miriam in England, crouched by her gas fire, replied fiercely.

> ... then kill yourself, John, but don't talk about it! You're just drawing attention to yourself, and you don't need to. Just look at the people in Seaside Church, or the village of Hector's River. Every single one of them has a better reason for suicide. You should be jolly ashamed, so stop it. I don't want to worry about you. I don't have time.
>
> Love,
> Miriam
>
> P.S. I am writing poetry now. I've decided Jamaica needs a literature of its own, or somebody to recognize what literature there is. If you look at the pattern of consonants in:
> Carry me ackee
> Go a Linstead Market
> Not a quattie wut sell ...
> it's easily as good as Chaucer, more complex, more lyrical. Somebody said, 'a country's literature is important in relation to the size of its army.' So, we need an army too!

There were four rum shops between Stone Haven and Darlingford to be passed every morning, seventeen on the way to Port Antonio. When John agreed to manage Darlingford he made a contract with himself not to touch the stuff during working hours.

He also swore he would not ride a mule. As the property was hilly, and essentially without roads, it meant that John must walk, and walk he did until he knew every field and fence, every change of slope or soil, every airless flat, cool glen or breezy hill. A manager who walked, and sweated, and who stopped to talk, was something of a wonder, but soon the labourers ceased to be surprised when John came into view, in khaki and thick walking shoes, carrying the ironwood walking stick that Grace had given him, the same stick Aunt Mary had used when she walked the Rio Grande in her search for souls.

John took Stanley's advice to heart that ninety-nine per cent of the job was handling labour, and set out to find out who his people were. He discovered that Zekiel, who forked banana fields, suffered mysterious headaches, that Sonny Boy saw ghosts, that Monkeyback had a wife in Manchioneal and two more in Port Antonio, that Miss Matty who broke coconuts and Cowhead who loaded copra trays had had a fight at Christmas when Cowhead knocked out half Miss Matty's teeth and that since then he had paid her a shilling a week compensation. He learned that Mr Mullins, his overseer, had been fired from Agualta Vale for dishonesty, and lied to Stanley to get the job, but John believed that, given his dignity, Mullins would be faithful. He shared his midday meals with him, hot, peppery, greasy, washed down with black coffee brought from Stone Haven in a thermos. He took Mullins' advice on all things agricultural, respected his weaknesses, and Mullins loved him.

Each Friday when the bill was paid, each labourer, man or woman, regular or casual knew that John knew his name and history and, though the paybill itself was strictly business, they also knew that John's salary went out in personal loans because he knew the need: a roof for Matty, a piglet for Carmichael, cough medicine for Lorraine's child, and a bottle of white rum for Watchie, who was slave to it.

One Saturday morning, though it was not a working day, John decided to go over to Darlingford. He wanted to look at a piece of ground behind the copra dryer, the slope, the soil, the drainage, and the ease of fencing it. Although pork was the island's favourite meat, the provision of it was a helter-skelter affair. Pigs roamed the villages like dogs, scavenging, and seemed, though only seemed, to have no owners. The big estates, the large farmers, avoided the pig with Biblical distaste. John had not decided whether to raise them for slaughter or simply to import the best available and provide a stud service to raise the level of pig production in the community. As yet, it was only an idea, to which Stanley was, inevitably, opposed. 'They're nasty, noisy, they smell and they're bound to be stolen,' was his verdict, dismissively delivered.

On the way, John drove into Manchioneal, and parked the Vauxhall in the shade of the post offce. His near-side tyres partially blocked the gutter which after the morning showers was busy bearing tangerine peel, leaves and old cigarette packets out to sea. It was market day, and the place was on active slow. A barefoot boy rolled an iron hoop, a woman with a basket on her head went into the market. From behind the car, a mule was approaching loaded with plantains, coconuts and yams, its owner encouraging it with the flat of his machete. Coming toward John was another boy with a string of fish, snapper and grunt. John climbed the concrete steps to the wicket window, and said good morning to Miss Hallett, a busty young lady with horn rimmed glasses, a graduate of Happy Grove. She smiled shyly, greeted him, and handed him three brown envelopes and a blue air letter with an English imprint.

It was in Mavis' handwriting. John decided to read it in the car. He fumbled with it, getting it wrong as usual so that when he had got it open he found he had torn it in half. Fitted together, it was still legible, closely written, the last few lines going round the margins. Like Mavis, it was rambling, jolly, and sentimental, all about the hospital, her new friends, and her social life, in which someone called Nigel figured prominently. She had been invited to Ascot. 'The clothes were all rented and the accents on loan, and the royal family couldn't make it so they sent their cooks in the carriage,' and Henley, 'If you have manners in this country, you must be lower class.' Nevertheless, she now seemed to be enjoying England. She said she dreaded her return to boring old Jamaica, even though in her heart of hearts there could never be anywhere else, and she missed it, and she missed him, even though they had spent so little time together, and she sent him a kiss.

John tucked the letter in his breast pocket, switched on and started the engine, then switched off again. It was Saturday morning after all. Across the street was Marshall's shop, and behind it, Marshall's back room. Mr Marshall greeted him as he went through, and Mrs Marshall, taking stock with a school notebook and a stub of pencil, said 'Mawnin', Mass John.' The back room was a concrete floor with tables and stools. The roof was held up by unpainted three-by-fours, and the walls were only three feet high, excluding dogs and chickens, admitting breeze. Fifty feet away, the water of the harbour lapped on a little patch of muddy sand, rolling weed and coconut husks back and forth, back and forth, back and forth.

Mr Mullins, John's overseer, was there and a man from Port Antonio he didn't know. Mullins, a little abashed to be discovered off-duty by his employer, and John, a little embarrassed to be seen drinking before noon by his employee, both found refuge in the third man, who was a supervisor in the Public Works Department. John bought them all a beer, and the conversation, stiff at first, found ease in alcohol. By the third drink, when they had switched to rum so as not to put too much strain on the bladder, the jokes were dirtier, the laughter louder, and the political opinions more charged with fervour.

There was a lot to be fervent about at the time. The end of the war against Hitler had brought the release from internment of the trade union organizer, Bustamante, and later the granting of universal suffrage. Jamaica had fallen swiftly into the argumental ecstasy of a two-party system. Bustamante, crafty and charismatic, headed the Labour Party, which was at heart conservative. He was being challenged by the People's National Party, led by his cousin, Norman Manley, an urban socialist, forming his own unions in search of a popular base. Independence was in the air, the end of three hundred years of slavery, racism, and colonialism, and there was a dream of federation, a union of the islands which would make the Caribbean into the Aegean of the future.

These thoughts and passions, mellowed by rum, floated on the warm sea wind. No real anger flowed, only the swearing of antagonists and the laughter of friends, only the making of Utopia out of the ruins of the past, while the waves broke on Marshall's beach, rolling the coconuts up the sand like the severed heads of slaves.

When the sunshine was only visible out on the water, John judged it was time to go. His departure was acknowledged, 'All right, Mass John.' 'Yes, sir.' 'Good, sir.' As he moved through the drinkers, he came face to face with a young black man who was coming in.

'Mr Newton.'

'Yes . . .?'

'You surprise to see me here?'

'Where did I see you before?'

'Brown, sir. Carlton Brown. We serve togeddah in de RAF.'

It all came back, this young black man in a blue uniform, seen through the rainwashed windscreen of a Lancaster. John paused. He could not greet this man and pat him on the shoulder, and move on. They shared a full past and an empty future, and both knew it.

'I'm glad to see you're not moving.'

'Yes, sir.'

'What are you doing with yourself?'

'Nothing much. Nothing much at all. Just come home to see me fader.'

John didn't want another drink. He felt his legs unsteady and his mind unclear.

'You staying in Manchioneal?'

'Might.'

'Come see me on Monday, at Darlingford. That's an order.'

'Okay, sir. Okay.'

'Pigs, Carlton. You know anything about pigs?'

'No, sir.'

They were standing by the copra house, in the blazing sun, looking at the site of John's proposed piggery. Carlton mopped his forehead with a white handkerchief.

'You offering me a job, sir?'

'Not yet. I was thinking about it.'

'Thanks, Mr Newton, but I would not work for you, sir.'

It was said with no animosity, a statement of principle, not personal feeling. John was surprised, and intrigued.

'It wouldn't necessarily have to be pigs, Carlton,' he smiled. 'An ex-serviceman back in Jamaica shouldn't be without a job.'

'That's right, that's right, but I don't want any farm work.'

'What's wrong with it?'

'Because it the lowest of the low, sir. You are a good man, Mr Newton, I believe that, and your father and your mother, and de whole family up there in the big yard. I think you does de best you can, but I would not work for you.'

They moved on across the works yard, picking their way between the piles of coconuts. On Mullins' verandah, Carlton accepted a cigarette, puffing at it appreciatively before resuming.

'Farm labour is the lowest of the low. Why is that? People who dig the ground and grow de food are the least in de kingdom. Why is that? Everybody mus' eat, but if you make a useless t'ing like a plastic propeller on a bamboo stick, and hold it up in de breeze, you get more money than for growing food. The man that sell de sugar, the man dat put de sugar in a bag, the man dat make de sugar into rum is all rich, but de man dat dig the furrow starve to death.'

Carlton Brown was right, but being right doesn't buy butter, as Stanley would say. John spoke a little more firmly.

'If I can't give you a job, how can I help you?'

'I don't know, sir. I must find something for myself, something that is mine. If you do not has something for yourself, others will use you, and den throw you away. My uncle, my grandfather's brother, went from Jamaica to dig the Panama Canal, and when de Canal finish, they say, "T'anks bwoy, go home". I has a cousin pick fruit in Florida. When harvest done, they say "Get out de country, bwoy." You an' me, Mr Newton, go to fight Germany. Now war done, "Goodbye." You're all right, sir, you have land, but de rest of us, nobody want to know about us. "Find yourself another war, bwoy, or another canal to dig. Dere is nutting for you in Jamaica."'

'Do you know any others?'

'You mean ground crew? Yes, sir. I know a couple here in Manchioneal, two more in Fairy Hill, of course, Kingston is full of dem – some in Port Antonio, one in Long Bay – oh, yes. You tell me, sir, what are they to do? There is no work in the country, so we must go to town and scuffle, scuffle or steal, and go to gaol.'

John looked at Carlton, strong, black, resentful, with a resentment justified by history and by circumstance. Carlton was offering him a job, a reason not to kill himself, a chance to do something for his country.

'Carlton, do me a favour. Get me the names of all the old RAF ground-crew between here and Port Antonio. We can have a get-together, talk about old times, and see if there is anything we can do to help one another.'

Carlton thought about it. 'Okay, sir. I'll do that. No harm in it.'

Chapter Nineteen

John's pigs were a failure. As Stanley had predicted, they strayed. They strayed at night, jumping the fence and wandering off into the hills. They strayed into carts or onto the backs of donkeys. One strayed onto the top of a bus and went to Kingston. They turned up in people's back yards and walked right into kitchens. They fell into cooking pots or stretched out over hot coals for a snooze, a smoke, and a sizzle. They enriched the life of the community, but they didn't enrich John. Stanley advised him to stick to the traditional crops or at least to post a ranger by the pig pen. One dead thief, he said, and that would be the end of it. John gave up on the pigs.

With a Hungarian called Laszlo, he pioneered banana chips. Laszlo knew all about food processing. Drinking John's rum on the Stone Haven verandah, he waxed enthusiastic about their prospects. He spoke of the fortunes made out of potato chips and corn flakes. The secret, he said, was to present a cheap ingredient in a different guise and sell it at a high price. John took him into the pantry and they made banana chips in the frying pan, cooled them on the window sill, and tasted them. Laszlo clapped his hands with joy. John warned that making banana chips in a frying pan, and making them in a factory, were two different things, at which Laszlo took offence. He was a professional; he knew the problems. They would experiment; they would perfect the chips before launching them on the world market.

With John's money they secured premises in Port Antonio, and Laszlo began his experiments. He turned up every weekend with samples and an insatiable thirst. The chips were not perfect. Sometimes the bananas were too ripe, sometimes too green. The oil was wrong, or the temperature; the salt went soggy in the humid air. Sometimes the chips came out sticking together; sometimes they were rock hard; they were too thick, too thin, too salt, too sweet, and almost always stuck to the back of the front teeth.

Slowly they got better, good enough, John thought, to try them out on his friends. One night, he arrived at Doc Hart's mosquito-guarded cottage carrying a large plastic bag of banana chips. It was Saturday, and some of the boys from the sugar factory were there, and Jackson and Pixley from Bowden Estate. They were toasting the arrival of Pixley's first born, a blond baby boy with blue eyes, who, considering both his parents were dark, gave cause for country humour.

'Nine months to the day,' Pixley said, 'or I'd have to shoot somebody.'

'What about the parson?' Jackson suggested. 'He had blue eyes.'

Everybody laughed.

They turned their attention to John's banana chips, washing them down with beer. Each had a different criticism, each a different comment, but they all agreed when Doc Hart said that they were edible, saleable, and if put into the hands of school children they could make a significant contribution to the fight against malnutrition in Jamaica. John was on to a good thing, they said, and they toasted the success of the project.

Laszlo was sent to Miami with a banker's draft in his pocket to purchase the machinery he needed. He never returned.

John fared better through his association of RAF veterans. With John's money they bought a truck. It did the property work. In between it did general haulage for the community, transporting goats, chickens, or whole wedding parties in black suits and brilliant frocks, drinking and singing 'O Perfect Love' as the truck rocked and rolled.

Carlton, ex-RAF, was his partner in the truck as driver, mechanic, and business manager, and two other veterans were his sidemen. It didn't matter how often Stanley told John that the RAF were robbing him. John knew; and knew that Carlton knew he knew; but Carlton also knew when to stop. The truck was his road up from agricultural slavery, and he would not abuse it. He made sure John had enough to cover his costs, and a bit more. After that, the RAF did business on the side, and they were all happy.

Another veteran, Walrus by name, while reading a magazine on John's verandah conceived the idea of putting an outboard motor on his father's canoe and going out to the deep in search of fish. John gave Walrus a lift to Port Antonio, introduced him to the bank manager, and stood security for his loan. Walrus' first motorized catch drew a record crowd in Manchioneal, for it was the largest ever seen there; kingfish, dolphin fish, and barracuda.

So everybody had to have an outboard, even those whose canoes were not truly seaworthy – which accounted for the death of Moses Clark, lost in a squall. But catches grew, and there was more fish in Manchioneal than they could eat. Another of the RAF, name of Mervyn, approached John with the idea of buying a Honda motorbike, fitting it with an ice-box, and rushing the fish to market in Kingston.

The village prospered, and John, supported by the RAF, ran for and was elected to the parochial board, on which he was the lightest-skinned member, as Stanley in his day had been the darkest. In the upper room of the old courthouse, he and his fellows sweated over the minutes as Grace and her Friends had sweated over their prayers.

In this capacity, John had an excuse to explore the hinterland of his own country. Away from the coastal road he found another Jamaica that had coexisted with slavery, and outlived it, a Jamaica without plantations, without beaches or tourists, towns or foreign investments. It was a world of hillside subsistence farmers, an independent peasantry, ignorant and superstitious, but wise in their own world, with a dignity not found in cities. In the old days they had been invaded by nonconformist missionaries whose revivalism, blended with African belief and African music, produced the robust religion practised in their little wooden churches. More recently, they had been visited by schoolteachers, by a district nurse, or by some lone policeman in search of a fugitive. Now they were visited by John in his battered Vauxhall, in search of a constituency, giving an old woman a lift to the doctor, reading a letter to an illiterate, talking about a cooperative, or acting as judge in a boundary dispute.

'Those that touch pitch shall be defiled,' was Stanley's first reaction when John announced his intention to run for the House of Representatives. 'Politics is the natural occupation of rogues and thieves,' was his more considered judgment.

Stanley argued that John was asking for trouble, seeking to be humiliated. He was a property owner, a dirty word in the new Jamaica. Bustamante would characterize him as a boss, a bloodsucker. Manley would call him a capitalist, a dodo bird ripe for extinction. John should be building himself a shelter, not standing in the rain.

'Which one will you choose, my boy? Busta, or Manley? Which party are you going to join?'

'I'm running as an independent.'

'Then you'll lose.'

'Maybe so.'

'The people only know the two big men, Busta and Manley. You must choose which coat tail to ride on.'

'Neither of them will choose me, but the people will. I will go find out what they want, and what they need, and represent them. Capitalism and socialism in Portland is alphabet soup. Politics here is people, and problems.'

'You will lose.'

Grace listened without comment. In private, she explained to Stanley that John needed to do it to stay sane, to stay alive. Stone Haven was too small for him. There he was, a grown man, still living in the nursery, with his ribboned uniform collecting cobwebs in the cupboard. John had the itch to serve; he also had ambition. She saw no contradiction in that. Politics, she said, was indeed a profession for rogues, and would be, until good men entered it.

To John, she only said, 'Is it possible to be in politics without drinking?'

'I don't know, Mamma,' he replied. 'I don't know.'

John's Vauxhall was parked across the way from the shop, a shack hanging off the hillside with its rear end on stilts. The car looked like a travelling gramophone, covered in placards, with speakers mounted on the roof.

From it issued a barrage of songs, floating over the plumes of bamboo groves, and the half-furled leaves of trumpet trees, down into hidden yam patches, shaded cocoa trees and coffee bushes, and plantains hidden in the mountain bush. Strange songs they were for this deep valley, songs like 'When Johnny comes Marching Home Again', 'Johnny is my Darling', and one specially composed and performed by the great Lord Spider, 'John Newton is victorious' which contained such rhymes as 'socialism lost at sea' with 'Busta down upon one knee' and 'John reach town triumphallee'.

Counterpointing the music came the complaint of Carlton's engine, audible for miles as he swayed slowly up the road, collecting supporters on their way to hear John speak. John was the only politician who had ever come as high as Mammee Mountain, and no one was going to miss it. On Carlton's truck, by mule or donkey, but for the most part on foot, the audience came out of the bush, the sort who had not emerged for a political occasion since the Morant Bay Rebellion in 1865, or heard a public speech since the American lady with the walking stick had passed through preaching the gospel of the Lord-Jesus-Christ-Amen.

Someone had seen the walking stick in John Newton's hand, and called it the rod of correction. Someone else said it was the stick that Moses used to strike the rock, forgetting it had been made right there on the Rio Grande and given to the old Missionary. Carlton spread the story that it was the walking stick of Balthazar, one of the three wise men who followed the star. Carlton was no fool, for the star was the emblem which was to represent John on the voting paper, and all astronomical associations were to be encouraged. He had painted his truck in stars, and likewise the speakers on the Vauxhall which was summoning the people like a crackle-voiced Pied Piper.

While they gathered, John waited in the rum shop. Very early on he decided that the answer to his mother's question was no, for it was in the rum shop that one met the sober citizens, the movers and the doers. Walker's back room, hanging over the precipice, was the place to do business.

For a politician, John was hopelessly reticent, but he made up for it with an ability to listen. The men of Mammee Mountain were as reticent as he. Though formal opinions were exchanged about agriculture, health, education and so on, it was in the silences between the words that trust was finally established.

Mass Oliver, a tall man with a gnarled face, eyes dull, teeth missing, the veins standing out on his long forearms, wearing a tweed cap on his grey head, a pullover, and khaki trousers tucked into rubber boots, led John out of the shop to meet the people. No one was in a hurry, except John, who had three other meetings that night, but he had to greet each person separately before he spoke, and the sober men had each to speak before he did.

At last it was John's turn, his platform a grassy bank next to the shop, the audience on either side of him, across the way, leaning on the car, or sitting on the wings of Carlton's truck. There was no applause as he faced them, just eyes in black faces, measuring him. John began with greetings, followed by expressions of modesty, even of humility, offering himself for their service. In the middle of this, someone said, 'Yes, das right,' somebody else said, 'True, true,' and somebody said, 'All right, Star Boy.' A murmur of approval, a word of encouragement, emboldened him to speak more positively, to reach out to them, to demand their appreciation, and they gave it to him.

John realized that this was not a speech, but a dialogue. They were willing him to inspire them, asking him for rhetoric he did not even know, and had to find. And so he spoke, carried on the tide of their listening.

He talked about Jamaica and its history, how it had become a nation, soon to be independent. He painted the white wings of Columbus' ships, the Arawaks who had lived in these same mountains and whom the Spaniards slaughtered to the last man. He told of the coming of the British and the days of slavery, the slave revolutions and the fierce Maroons who fought the redcoats from these same mountains, and were never defeated. He told of the coming of the East Indians after Emancipation, and the Chinese later on, of Europeans who came and went, and some who stayed to be Jamaicans. He talked of the slow extension of the vote from a handful of planters until now, in the nineteen-fifties, here, in these same mountains it was the right of every man and woman to choose their leaders, and their rulers. He spoke of the Jamaica to come, one nation out of many races, of many religions worshipping one God, one identity of humour, of tolerance, and of dignity, one nation, free.

Then the gramophone started again, playing 'When Johnny comes Marching Home Again', and the candidate moved among the people, shaking calloused hands, patting children on the head, smiling at the girls, and receiving the blessings of old women. Carlton started the truck, John got into the Vauxhall, and the cavalcade set off for the next stop, a place called Aberdeen.

In the event, as Stanley had predicted, John lost. The Socialists, whose candidate was a teacher called Cookson, won; Labour's Dewdney, a union organizer, was second; and Star Boy John Newton third of three. He did well in the Rio Grande valley, well enough in the villages along the coast, badly on large plantations, except his own, and badly in Port Antonio. He was surprised when Dewdney came to see him, two weeks after the election. Dewdney travelled with three of his supporters in a battered Ford which parked by the front steps, a privilege allowed only to strangers. The visitors sat, polite and uncomfortable on the Stone Haven verandah while Grace served them tea, heard their names and where they lived, facts John already knew. They were the hard core of Dewdney's campaign, a dockworker, a headman, and a civil service clerk. When Grace withdrew, Dewdney came to the purpose.

'Busta want to see you.'

'Any time,' said John, 'I'd be glad to see him.' He wasn't quite sure what to say next. Busta could have written him a letter, telegraphed him, sent word by any other bearer. To give himself time to think, he called the girl to take away the tea, and went himself for a tray of drinks, blessing his mother's conversion.

Dewdney drank beer, the workmen rum, and the civil service clerk drank Scotch. They gossiped about the election, agreed that Cookson was lucky, and laughed about the Rasta who came to vote for Haile Selassie, and had to be dragged away and locked up. All agreed that Port Antonio needed industrial development, the harbour needed dredging, and that Portland had more to offer the tourist than Montego Bay ever had, if it wasn't for the rain.

'So you come to see the monster,' Busta screeched, leading John through the bungalow he still preferred to his official residence, and which he shared with his redoubtable secretary, Miss Gladys.

'I heard the monster wanted to see me,' John replied.

'Yes, yes,' Busta said in his high, fluting, broadly accented voice, 'I want to see you. You are a phenomenon!'

'Why is that, sir?'

'Sir! Don't call me sir, call me Busta. From Governor to dog call me Busta.' He put a hand on John's shoulder as they went through the living room, past glass-fronted cupboards, littered coffee tables, framed photographs, toward a terrace shaded by a grapevine. The terrace, populated by politicians, looked out on a dusty lawn with lignum vitae trees flowering blue. In the far corner of the yard, a policeman was polishing the Chief Ministerial Chrysler.

'You see dis lawn?' declaimed Busta. 'It is de only lawn in St Andrew don't have a sprinkler. De middle classes waste de water dat God provided for de poor. Miss Gladys, dis is John Newton.'

Miss Gladys, brown, round, and imposing, rose to take John's hand. She was dwarfed by Busta who was six feet four, and taller by a mane of grey hair. He, rather than the diminutive Selassie, deserved the title of Lion of Judah. His immense presence was yet informal; he wore sandals, gabardine trousers, and a short-sleeved shirt outside the trousers. With his left hand, he picked up the drink he had been working on when John arrived, and with his right still on John's shoulder he made the introductions.

'You know Hugh?'

Hugh raised a casual hand in salute. This was Shearer, head of the Bustamante Industrial Trades Union, handsome, charismatic, a great organizer, and only incidentally famous for his amorous activities.

'You know Donald?'

Donald rose to shake hands, a city dweller in a brown suit, who could add two and two, and was Minister of Finance.

'You know Isaac? You must, because he is from your part of the bush.'

This was Isaac Barrant, a little man with enormous ears, who had started as a sideman on a truck. He was perhaps the shrewdest politician of them all for, uneducated and a nobody, he had made himself the symbol of the post-imperial age. He was a nobody who was somebody now, and for that he was loved, not envied.

'These fellows are supposed to be running the country, but what are they doing? Sitting here drinking my liquor. Miss Gladys, we have a clean glass for Mr Newton?'

Miss Gladys did the honours.

Busta settled his huge frame into a canvas garden chair.

'You wonder why I want to see you?'

John felt the others watching him, and decided to get it wrong.

'When the general election comes, you want me to withdraw. The votes I got cost you the constituency. Dewdney might have won.'

'Dewdney is a fine fellow, but between you, me, and the gatepost, the man is a rascal. Newton, why didn't you join a party?'

'I did think of joining the PNP.'

Busta leapt to his feet in mock anger. 'Don't talk damn foolishness, man! You're a capitalist! A landowner! How can you be a socialist?'

'I don't necessarily believe,' John said slowly, 'that the present system is the best, and I care for the advancement of the people.'

'That's all I want to know, that's all I want to know! But that is not socialism, that is common sense, and common humanity, which is an uncommon thing! We want it. Manley's son went to school with you, right, and you and he are of the same colour, but he has a name for you, 'land baron'. You have sympathy with socialism, but socialism has no sympathy for you! I will tell you what is wrong with Manley and his party. I know the man, you know, he is my cousin. He want to burn down the kitchen to roast the pig. Listen to me, Newton. There is only a handful of people in this country has the ability to lead. If they are a sideman on a truck, like Isaac here, or a stinking capitalist like you, if the ability is there, I want the man! I want you to join the Jamaica Labour Party.'

'I'll think about it,' said John, flattered.

Busta was walking about the terrace now, enjoying himself and his own high-pitched rhetoric.

'What you mean is, I don't reach your price yet. Come the general election, I want you to run again as a Labour candidate.'

'Only in East Portland.'

'Where else? I'm putting Dewdney to grass. You see, Newton, you are big now in the Rio Grande valley and all the villages of Portland. I know Jamaicans, when they take you to heart, they will not forsake you. They will vote for you from now to kingdom come. I didn't send Dewdney to drink your liquor because he was thirsty. I sent him to find out if he could work with you. Come de election, I will give you Dewdney, and the party vote in Port Antonio, and we shall send Teacher Cookson back to school. You drink liquor?'

John nodded, and held out his glass.

'I have to build a party,' Busta went on, 'that can run this place when Independence comes, and keep Manley in permanent opposition, because if you let loose socialism and this crackbrained scheme of federation – Federation of the West Indies – you know what that means? If a man has two chicken, Mr Manley want to take one and send it to Trinidad.'

Shearer laughed.

'Do you have a time-table for independence?' John asked.

'We have independence now!' Busta cried. 'The day the British put me in gaol was the first day of Jamaican independence. The British were stupid! If Hitler wouldn't shake hands with Jesse Owens why he should shake hands with Bustamante? The British had nuttin' to worry about, but they took fright and lock me up. One day I was a troublemaker and a union leader, but the day they lock me up I was a national hero! The day they lock up Bustamante they lost Jamaica. But don't mistake me, Newton, I am not anti-British. The little Queen is my sweetheart, and I love her!'

Chapter Twenty

Mavis' family lived in an uptown house with lawns, flowerbeds, and a drive with two gateways. John, newly-elected Member of the House of Representatives, parked his car in the shade of a poinciana and walked toward the verandah where Mrs Arkwright, in slacks and a purple blouse, showing a deal of plump neck and upper arm, sat on guard, equipped with a Chinese fan and a copy of *Woman's Home Companion*. John had been to a Chamber of Commerce luncheon, so he was still wearing coat and tie. She watched him approach with suspicion.

'Mrs Arkwright? I don't think we've met. I'm John Newton.'

She brightened visibly. 'Oh yes, Mavis told me. Sit down, sit down. Take your jacket off and have something cool.'

'Thank you.'

'You are the MHR?'

'That's right.'

'But MHR nowadays suppose to be black and ugly. What parish send you?'

'Portland.'

'You know, I have never been out there. It is a part of Jamaica I have never seen.'

'It's bush,' John agreed, politely.

'What can I get for you? Lemonade? Rum and lemonade? Rum and ginger? Tea?'

'Rum and lemonade sounds like a good idea.'

Phyllis came onto the verandah.

'Hello, John.'

The sister's aged, John thought, worrying about Mavis.

Mrs Arkwright waved a hand. 'Phyllis, before you sit down, just get a drink for Mr Newton, eh. Where's Mavis?'

'She's inside.'

'Well, tell her she has a visitor.'

'I think she knows, you know.'

'Rum and lemonade? The rum is on the sideboard.'

'I think she knows that too.'

Phyllis went in.

Mrs Arkwright turned to John once more. 'I don't know what Mavis is doing inside.'

'Giving me a chance to meet you.'

She laughed. 'Poor boy, you didn't come here to see old woman. Tell me about Busta. What ruination is that madman planning for us now?'

John was spared the ordeal of defending the government's record and reputation by the arrival of Mr Arkwright, who came in the other gateway and parked his car on the other side of the verandah. His domed forehead shone, and the white shirt he had started the day with was wrinkled and soggy, but collar and tie were firmly in place, and he carried a bulging briefcase. He boomed a greeting to John, and called for a drink of iced water. John had risen, respectfully.

'You Newton? They offered you a drink? Sit down, man. So tell me. What about this increase in excise duties? How is a man supposed to do business?'

'Well, sir,' John smiled, 'a man of your ability will not be bothered by a little thing like that.'

'All you fellows are rascals. I'm just going to wash. Where's Mavis?'

'Inside.'

Arkwright went in, passing Phyllis coming out, with ice, rum, and glasses. His boom sounded from within, 'Mavis! Somebody come to see you. It's too late to change your face.'

'That's so embarrassing,' Mrs Arkwright moaned.

'Mavis will be vexed now, and she won't come out at all. You just relax, Mr Newton.'

But Mavis did come out, pausing in the doorway to be looked at. Then, instead of approaching John, she flopped into the chair that was furthest away, greeting him off-handedly, almost without interest. He need not have worried. She was a little heavier than he remembered, but prettier, for the Jamaican sun had restored her true colour, setting off her eyes and smile. Her hair was still long. That pleased him. He liked women with long hair and a full figure. Mavis had both, and the quick nervous energy, intelligence, and the gift for the unexpected phrase or action that had delighted him years before. He knew all that the minute she came out onto the verandah; he knew it before she spoke; he knew it instinctively.

They passed the time of day with the family for ten minutes or so, agreeing that Jamaica was hot, the place was going to rack and ruin, England was a cold country, and it was impossible to get good servants any longer. John avoided looking at Mavis, who sat in an impatient and rebellious silence.

She rose, suddenly. 'We're going out.'

'Are you back for supper?'

'I don't know.'

'You're welcome, Mr Newton. There's always something to eat.'

'I don't know, Mum,' Mavis said irritably.

'All right, all right. We'll see you when we see you.'

Safely out of the gate, heading downtown, John turned to her. 'It's good to see you.'

'I could kill my family!' she sulked. 'When you're accustomed to living on your own, families are like fleas.'

'Are you glad to see me?'

'Of course.'

He had to be content with that for she was silent for the rest of the drive. Not until they were installed on the balcony of the Yacht Club, where the afternoon breeze had died, and the harbour was still enough to mirror the boats, and the waiter had brought them rum punch in tall glasses, not until then did they return to the all-important subject: themselves.

'Your letters stopped.'

'So did yours.'

'Well, there wasn't much point, Mavis, in writing letters and never getting a reply.'

'I meant to, but I got busy. I mean, I couldn't expect you, on the basis of a couple of days in London, I couldn't expect you even to remember who I was. They say you're the most eligible bachelor in Jamaica now.'

'Who says?'

'They.'

'Why did you decide to come back?'

'England didn't suit.'

'It suited you for a long time.'

'It didn't suit.'

'I thought by now you'd have married an Englishman.'

'Is that so?'

She seemed to be angry about something, about being questioned perhaps. What she had been doing was her business. Then he thought it might be because she was shy and her brusqueness was mere self-protection. Then he was intrigued by the thought that she was angry with him simply for being interested in her.

They talked about other things. He told her tales of political chicanery, and about his affection for Bustamante, a monster to some, a messiah to others, second father to him. She talked about her reaction to Jamaica. She had noticed more money about, and paradoxically, much more poverty. She spoke of Kingston with an almost physical disgust, and he felt emboldened to comment cheerfully, 'The country parts haven't changed that much.'

'The country,' she said, 'is worse, much worse.'

After dinner they went for a drive in the hills and found a place to park that overlooked Kingston. The city, which in the daytime had been a hot and smoky slum obscured in trees, was at night a carpet of fallen stars. They identified the Half-Way-Tree Road, the Spanish Town Road, the line of the harbour, where Fort Henderson was, and the cement factory. Then they fell silent again. By this time, John knew that Mavis' silences did not last forever, and he waited.

'You don't want to have anything to do with me,' she said suddenly and defiantly. 'Do you hear me? I'm rubbish. You're a nice man, and you're going somewhere. Just leave me out. I quite like you, and John, when I tell you this, that's the end of it. But if I don't, if I don't put you straight, it's not fair to you.'

'You'd better tell me.'

'I was married. I suppose I'm divorced as well.'

'Was he English?'

'What else? One of those men that are middle-aged at twenty-five, old at forty. He was dull, dull, dull. We had a semi-detached in Raynes Park! It might as well have been Wormwood Scrubbs.'

'What went wrong?'

'That went wrong! Don't you understand? I was in a semi-detached cage, with a radio, a vacuum cleaner, a one-bar fire, and an electric oven. You can't put your head in an electric oven. In front was a patch of grass, with a circle of other houses filled with young Mums and Dads, and Donald off to the West End and the office and his squash and his cricket. I was a curiosity. I was Carmen Miranda. I was the tropical exotic our Donald had married, and they all came to listen to my accent and wait for me to tell stories about cannibals. Nothing went wrong! I was just cold and wet and bored, and Donald was so understanding I had to leave, or kill him.'

'Is that all?'

'I went to stay with my cousin, Norma. She has a flat in South Ken. and was into the high life. You know Buchanan, that white Jamaican who made a lot of money in real estate? He has a house on Wilton Place, and we used to go there. Very decadent, my dear, with black walls and mirrors, and purple cushions. There was always a pair of lesbians making out on a sofa, and a lot of old Etonians sucking on the ganja as if those dirty Rastas in the Blue Mountains were messengers of God. That's where I met Jeremy.'

He did not want to hear about Jeremy. It was late at night. He had to be at Darlingford before daybreak, and he needed a drink.

'Jeremy was one of the old Etonians who smoked ganja,' he said, patiently.

'Yes. I went with him for eighteen months, and lived with him for six. I was really happy. Have you ever been really happy?'

'No,' said John.

'I don't think most people ever are, you see. Jeremy was younger, and he was a virgin, at least with women. We did everything, and we went everywhere, from Scotland to St Tropez, Ascot, Henley, all those things. He was pretty, and sort of vague, and I knew one thing, he would never hurt me.'

'But he did.'

'You're right this time. And it was so simple. He was going to meet his mother for tea, at the Ritz. We'd been together for eighteen months, and when he told me, I said, "Lovely, I'd like to meet her," and he said, very gently, you know, very quiet and definite, "I'm afraid that's not possible. I'm sorry, Mavis, it's not possible."'

There were footsteps coming up the road. It sounded like one person, a man. They waited in silence for him to pass, but when he came abreast of the car he stopped, and came toward them. John could just distinguish his figure, wearing a shirt of some light material catching what light there was. He leaned down to look into the car, on Mavis' side.

'Good evening, missis.'

'Good evening, sir,' she said.

'You has a man there?'

'Can I help you?' John said.

'No, sir. Just telling you there are people hereabouts will kill you for what you has in your pocket.'

'Thank you,' John said.

He waited until the footsteps had died away before he started the car.

William was in sole possession of the Stone Haven verandah when John and Mavis arrived. He had found himself a drink, and dropped anchor in the shadiest corner.

Mavis got out of the car, smoothing the creases from her skirt.

'Who's that?' John asked.

'William.'

William came forward to meet them, the drink in his right hand, his left wrist in the trouser pocket.

'This is my cousin, William. Mavis Arkwright.'

'Howdy-do. How was the drive from Kingston?'

'Not bad.'

'It was terrible,' Mavis said. 'Hot and miserable, and John was talking the whole time, showing me Jamaica, as if anybody wants to know. It's all bush and black people as far as I can see.'

'You're right,' William said. 'Auntie Grace and Miriam gone to church. Uncle Stanley, as well. But there's a lot of cooking going on out back.'

John escorted Mavis into the house to show her the bathroom, and came back with a bottle of beer. Knowing his own weakness, he stayed off the hard stuff, at least until noon. William was drinking rum.

'Haven't seen you for a long time.'

'You're an important man now. Member of the House, eh! Big shot.' Envy was skilfully blended with congratulation.

'How you getting on?'

'Well, Mass John, as to that – I'm glad you came before the others. I wanted to have a word with you.'

The church clock was striking twelve, heralding the closing hymn. Soon the congregation, Grace and Miriam among them, would be coming down the concrete steps.

'I'm thinking of coming back this way,' William was saying. 'The south coast is a dead-end place, you know, not much prospect.'

'Not much here either,' John replied, briskly.

'I don't know.'

'What are you looking for?'

'Well, I mean, you're busy at Darlingford, right? And you have your politics. Uncle Stanley is getting on. He really needs a manager for Holland Estate, somebody to help him modernize the place. He is still ploughing with cattle, but this is the age of the Caterpillar.'

'We bought one last week. Have you spoken to him?'

'Not yet. I thought you might like to put in a word. I would live on the estate and would be much closer to my mother.'

'You've thought it all through.'

'It's just an idea. I'm not asking any favours.'

Grace and Miriam came back from church, walking as always through the lane from the village, and slowly, leaning forward, up the last steep slope to the house.

Miriam greeted them curtly, and went past. Grace greeted William, and Mavis made her second entrance, from the house this time, hair freshly brushed, and fresh, bright lipstick.

'I'm so very glad to meet you, Mrs Newton,' Mavis said. 'John, we should have come earlier. We could have gone to church.'

'You didn't miss very much, a very boring sermon, and being school holidays there was hardly anybody there.'

'When two or three are gathered together . . .' William volunteered.

'You would have made four, William,' Grace said tersely.

'Auntie, I came all the way from Monymusk and my car is slow.'

'You had time to start drinking,' Grace said. 'I'll just go and wash my hands.' She was tired of excuses, and of feigned deference. God is not mocked. But she was still gracious. 'John, look after Mavis, please. Welcome, my dear.'

Grace went into the drawing room, a tall, spare, angular figure, in a light cotton frock, with a belt at the waist, her grey hair in a bun at the back, a white, brimmed hat on her head.

'Owner man comin' now,' William announced.

Heads turned to see Stanley's new 1955 Chrysler Imperial, as big as the Chief Minister's, purring up the drive, gliding round the semicircle of the front yard to deposit him at the steps. Then it backed discreetly away, and glided toward the garage. Stanley came up the steps, his grey double-breasted suit buttoned across his paunch, his striped shirt and silk tie from Jermyn Street, his brown face plumper now but his black curly hair, neatly brushed, all in place without a trace of grey.

He greeted Mavis jovially, his conditioned reflex to a pretty girl, and the usual pleasantries began, how hot it was, how bad the sermon, how long a drive from Kingston, and:

'Arkwright . . . I don't know the name.'

'My father is in business.'

'Ah, not a professional man.'

'He has an import agency.'

'Groceries, you mean, dry goods, or machinery?'

'Don't ask me, Mr Newton, I have no interest in his business.'

'Quite right,' said Stanley, unrebuked. 'Girls shouldn't concern themselves with things like that.'

Coffee was served on the verandah, from which William excused himself, explaining he had to see his mother before he started back. John accompanied him to his car, a decrepit turtle, purchased, John knew, with a loan from Stanley. John also knew that William hated them all, that he believed that Stanley had cheated his father out of the land and his cousins were rich on his rightful inheritance. He also knew that William would do nothing about it, except hate, except sulk, except drink.

William's mutilation was another matter; it gave him rights, a lien on the family. It excused his drinking, and guaranteed him a job for life, if he wanted one.

'I'll speak to Daddy about the job.'

'Don't do anything special.'

Stanley would accept the responsibility, while holding William in contempt, for he hated lame ducks, but John, more compassionate, or more guilt-ridden, wanted to get past the bitterness, to recall the best that was in William, because they had been children together, and loved and hated each other with a passion never to return.

'Give my regards to Auntie Cynthia.'

John often met Cynthia on the road, he driving, she walking along under a large straw hat quarrelling with herself. He would give her a lift to the Post Office, or to the bottom of her drive, depending on which way she was going, but he never went up to the house.

'She's mad,' said William. 'Every time I go, she abuses me. Then she abuses my father and Uncle Stanley and Aunt Grace, and then she cries and calls me her little darling, and tells me what to eat and what not to eat. Once in a while is enough.'

'Does she need anything?'

'She has her pay from the Post Office.'

'I should really go and visit her.'

'Don't bother.'

'I haven't been over there for fifteen years. We always used to have Christmas dinner at Stone Haven, Boxing Day at Williamsfield. Turkey one day, suckling pig the next.'

'The suckling pig was better,' William said, and smiled.

'It was.' That was a breakthrough, and John decided to risk everything. 'I liked your father.'

'You and who else? Sorry. You were in England when he died. His funeral was a joke,' he said bitterly. 'There was a big thing, you know, about where to bury him. My mother wouldn't put him in the Manchioneal churchyard or at Seaside. So it was decided to get a priest and put him in the old family burial ground over yonder. I say "family", but only God knows who's in it, because all the baccra Newtons are at Manchioneal, with tombstone and writing, and over yonder it's all brick boxes and no names, probably slaves and women. Uncle Stanley had to give out a lot of rum to get that grave dug, as it's mostly rockstone. He got old Cuffee and his son to dig it – you know Cuffee? Well, when the body was down, and the priest praying with my mother, and she all veiled and covered in black, and your father and mother looking serious, old Cuffee, well in his liquor now, you know, old Cuffee shout out, "Time to cover him up! Which one of de young gals dat pleasure Mass 'Arold will throw de first rock?" Believe it or not, with my mother watching, de pretties' young coolie gal came forward and drop a little dirt in de grave.'

'Did you know who she was?'

'No, master, never seen her before, or since.'

'I heard the funeral was well attended.'

'By local people. Society didn't come from Kingston.'

'A lot of people loved him.'

'Everybody loved him,' William said, opening the door of his rattletrap. 'Okay, Mass John, I gone.'

'Okay.'

That afternoon it rained, so tea was taken in the drawing room with the windows closed. It was a heavy shower, blotting out the sea, falling in sheets on the palms and making pools on the lawn, streaming from the roof and bouncing on the hard green tiling of the steps. The rain made conversation difficult, and the ritual tea was silent. Grace, behind her silver service, looked like a priest at communion. Stanley, unaware of such solemnity, munched his biscuits without fear of being overheard, and passed the cake to Mavis.

Mavis sat in the armchair by the window where Grace herself usually sat to read or sew. Seeing her in that chair, Grace hated her. She hated the largeness of her; she hated the looseness of her figure; she hated the animation of her gestures, the length of her hair, her lips, her lipstick and her very life. Then she glanced sideways at John, who was also watching Mavis, and saw the adoration in his eyes, the tenderness, the desire to protect this strange person. So when John looked at her, Grace smiled her own approval.

The rain was followed by a windless gloom, not the sort of day to show a potential bride her future home, but John, having planned an excursion to Darlingford, would not postpone it.

'Glad to get out of there.'

'Stone Haven?'

'Where else? Your father and mother were looking at me like an insect.'

'They like you.'

'I'm not looking for anybody's approval.'

'Not even mine?'

Mavis said nothing, for it was self-approval that she really wanted, and would never get.

'She's quite unsuitable.'

'It may come to nothing after all,' Grace replied, not believing it; she had seen the sheep-dog admiration on John's face.

There was silence for a while, and Miriam, lying on the leather sofa in the sun parlour, waited breathlessly.

'Where's Miriam?'

'In her room, I think, reading a book.'

In all honour, she should now declare herself, but the temptation was too great. Grace, in the library, had returned to the matter in hand.

'Why do you say she's unsuitable?'

'Who is Arkwright?'

'Does it matter?'

'Of course it matters. As far as I can see he is not much better than a shopkeeper.'

'He's Kingston middle-class.'

'She's not of good colour.'

Even from where she was, Miriam could hear her mother's sharp intake of breath.

'She's the same colour as you are, Stanley.'

'That's neither here nor there.'

Grace was angry, 'It is. That's what you're talking about! Why did you mention it? I can't believe it, Stanley. Have you forgotten who you are? When I married you, you were a black man, and illegitimate. You haven't changed your skin by going to Ascot every year! I married you to prove a black man could be a gentleman. Have you forgotten everything?'

'I hope,' said Miriam, in the doorway, 'that there was another reason.'

'Miriam, this was a conversation between your mother and myself.'

'I know that, Daddy, but I couldn't pretend I hadn't heard.' Miriam turned to Grace. 'Surely you didn't marry him just on principle?'

'No, Miriam. I married him for love.'

Grace turned her back to Stanley. It seemed she was about to cry, and would take no further part in the conversation. Stanley, implacable, addressed himself to Miriam.

'Do you think Mavis is suitable?'

'That's for John to decide.'

'I can express an opinion ...'

'I heard it,' Miriam snapped.

'... the matter of colour is not important,' Stanley went on, 'but John has to consider his career. He is going to be important. At the Jamaica Club they talk about him as a future prime minister. He needs to marry somebody who can be the first lady of this country. She has to give up everything for him, encourage him, support him, and still be herself, confident and powerful. She has to do for John what your mother has done for me.'

Stanley moved to comfort Grace, to touch her, but she avoided him, pushing her chair away, grating on the floor, and left the room, leaving a calm, uncontrite Stanley to face his daughter.

'You mean John should marry white.'

'Not necessarily,' Stanley prevaricated, 'someone who can be first lady ...'

'How do you know who can do that? How does anybody know? The other side of ambition is snobbery, and you're a snob, a British Empire snob, a racial snob ...'

'Miriam, just watch what you're saying.'

'All that is over. The people who are going to be important in Jamaica, you don't know where they will come from! From prison, or a paddy field, or from the slums of Kingston, and good colour, bad colour, white or black will have nothing to do with it.'

'Maybe so. I won't argue with you, Miriam, because I hope you're right, but mark my words, that girl has no substance.'

At first, it seemed Stanley was going to escape to his office, but he went instead toward the bedroom and the sound of weeping. He had wounded Grace once too often, and knew that he must comfort her.

She was sitting at her dressing table, in front of the half-length mirror, so there were two weeping women in the room. Hearing him, she became absorbed in the contents of the drawer where she kept her letters, searching for something.

'I'm sorry.'

'I was looking for . . . I was thinking . . . of the struggles we had, years ago with the Friends, with my family, with ourselves, all that pain . . .'

'And joy, Grace.'

'And joy. All that was not for social advancement, or to prove anything.'

'I hope not, unless you think of life as sacrifice.'

'Would that be wrong?'

'I don't know.'

'We fought our battles for love. Isn't that so?'

He came up behind her, and put his hands on her shoulders. Their eyes met in the mirror.

'Yes, and I still love you, Grace.'

'I know, but it saddens me, Stanley, to see you so much a man of the world, the world as it is, not as it should be.'

Stanley in the mirror bowed his head, accepting the rebuke.

Chapter Twenty-one

It's not every day that a Member of the House marries the daughter of a Prominent Citizen. The Governor was there, without his plumed hat, but in a white linen suit, standing out among the multitude of dark worsteds which traditionally bestowed on black men a colonized respectability. The Governor's dress had more in common with the odd artist and political rebel, Miriam's friends, who turned up in safari suits open at the neck, but then, it was rumoured, His Excellency too was a socialist. The only Rasta was on the street outside the Half-Way-Tree Church announcing, like the Ancient Mariner, to the amusement of the wedding guests, the imminent coming of the Lion of Judah and the reign of Peace and Love.

Some came in chauffeur-driven cars, others in their own, which they parked in dusty side streets where small barefoot boys contended to watch over them, and strolled back toward the church to join the crush of politicians, civil servants, judges, businessmen, planters of all hues, and wives and daughters of all shapes, colours and sizes, fluttering their butterfly fans and shining in dresses of brilliant colours like a rainbow shattered and fallen on the churchyard. These visitors mingled with members of both families, uncles, grand-uncles, great-grandsons, cousins many times removed, but definitely still family; they prolonged the greetings, and the compliments, and the expansive smiles, and the dabbing of the faces, putting off as long as possible the movement from the fiery churchyard to the furnace of the nave.

Grace, escorted by Miriam, had taken her place early. She was in dark blue silk, with a matching hat, a smidgin of powder on her cheeks to hide the pallor. The Governor came over to talk to her; he had requested an honour for her in the Queen's Birthday List, in recognition of her work at Happy Grove School, and he wished to say how pleased he was she would accept the MBE. Paul was there, having flown home from college in Philadelphia in honour of the occasion. Cousin William, his stump in a black leather pouch, was an usher. Stanley, mysteriously, had not arrived.

Miriam and Paul circulated, encouraging people to go in, for the proceedings were running late. The groom, in the custody of the best man, took his place in the front pew, and with the arrival of the Chief Minister there could be no further reason for delay. Busta, his white hair high above the press of the aisle, came down to John and patted him sympathetically on the shoulder.

'Don't try to run now, boy. I can see de man wid de shotgun,' and he waved cheerfully at someone on the bride's side.

The organist struck the first notes of 'Here Comes the Bride' and heads turned toward the door. Paul, sitting behind Miriam, leaned forward to touch her on the shoulder.

'Daddy's not here,' Paul whispered.

John, half-hearing, turned, seemed not to to get the full significance of the empty place beside his mother, and turned back to his contemplation of the stained glass. The bridesmaid led the way. The bride, an iceberg in mosquito netting, was swaying down the aisle on the arm of her father, who looked already diminished, and a small boy and girl trailed behind, fanning themselves with the end of her train, which they sensibly continued to do throughout the service. There was still no sign of Stanley, and no sign of him during the Bishop's ponderous 'Dearly beloved, we are gathered here...' or during the exchange of vows, which Mavis managed clearly and John merely muttered, or the singing of 'Oh Perfect Love' or even when the sweating organist hurled himself into the opening bars of the Mendelssohn, a signal that it was all over and the suffocating congregation could seek the joys of fresh air and, as soon as possible, a drink.

Veterans of the RAF formed a guard of honour on the steps, flashbulbs burst, and a policeman kept the churchyard clear of urchins from the street. As John came down the steps with Mavis on his arm, he saw the Chrysler pulling up, and Stanley, without waiting for Frank to open the door, getting out, but then lost sight of him almost immediately as they were surrounded by well-wishers, kissing and congratulating.

'Let's get out of here, John,' said Mavis, her first words as a bride. 'I'm sweating through this bloody dress.'

John, the politician, was trying to be polite to someone who remembered him well. Mavis tugged at his arm. Paul saw his father, a small, paunchy brown man in a crumpled suit, pushing his way through the crowd toward the bridal party, and intercepted him.

'You're a little late, sir.'

'I was held up. I came by way of St Ann. Stopped in to see Mass Charley.'

Grace and Miriam came up to them then, and Stanley continued to Grace. 'Darling,' he said proudly, 'I've done the deal.'

'You were late for John's wedding.'

'I'm sorry, darling, I'll apologize to John, but I tried my best. Look, see, here it is!' and he pulled out of his pocket an old envelope with something written on it in pencil, and some signatures, including his own. 'That's Mass Charley's signature... signed and sealed.'

Grace thought the end of the world had come. There she was, in the yard of the Half-Way-Tree Church at four o'clock in the afternoon, surrounded by five hundred wedding guests all chattering like parakeets as they dispersed toward their cars and the reception, there she was talking to this strange man, her husband, about a deal, and he was showing her a piece of paper that committed him, at his age, to the ownership of another five thousand acres of land that he did not need, and to a mortgage debt, scribbled in pencil, that consisted almost entirely of noughts. Her back hurt, and she felt faint. She opened her husband's jacket, and gently replaced the envelope in the inside pocket.

'Miriam, can you get me to the car?'

'Where was he?' Miriam asked, as they moved slowly away.

'Don't ask, for if you ask a silly question, you'll get a silly answer. He's been ruining us for the sake of his own ambition.' She turned. 'Paul, bring your father to the reception, and make him promise not to talk to anybody about what he has been doing today, because it's John's day, do you hear?'

Stanley was genuinely bemused. 'I don't understand your mother's attitude,' he said to Paul. 'I tried my best to get here on time.'

'What were you doing, sir?'

'Business, business, but not for my sake, for John, for you, for the whole family. I don't understand her attitude.'

His father was like a child rebuked. Paul was sorry for him.

Chapter Twenty-two

Before day, Gustus was standing in the yard below the bedroom window, calling.

'Mass John, Gustus here.'

John, already awake, swung his legs out of bed and crossed to the window, adjusting the louvres so he could look down at Gustus, a brown man, in brown khaki, the outside son of an important citizen and foreman at the new coir factory, a project of John's that worked, usually.

'Mornin' Gustus.'

'Morning, sar. The generator break down, sar.'

John considered this information. The generator wasn't due to be started for another hour.

'When it break down?'

'Yestoday.'

'Why you didn't tell me yesterday?'

'I was not here, sar.'

That was logical, and irrefutable.

'All right, Gustus. I'm comin'.'

'Yes, Mass John.' Then came the real reason for the dawn call, 'Dem not cuttin' cane today, sar. Say dem gwine strike.'

'What for?'

'Me don't know, sar. Some ignorance.'

Gustus moved away, and John closed the louvres to keep out the first rays of the sun. Mavis came in with a tray of tea and Saltine crackers.

'Who was that?'

'Gustus.'

'Trouble, I suppose,' she said bitterly.

'Nothing special.'

'But something that will keep you away all day and bring you home exhausted. I want to go to Kingston.'

'When the House is in session we'll go to Kingston.'

'It's not good enough, John. You're either on the estate, or in the constituency office, or in the House or at some damn function. You have no time for yourself, or for me.'

'I'm sorry.'

Mavis sat on the edge of the bed, stirring her tea.

'So what am I supposed to do?'

John was putting on his shoes. Dressed for exit he could afford to say, 'There's lots to do in the country if you look for it. Mamma is always busy.'

'I'll tell you another thing, master! I'm not your mother. I'm not cut out for it.'

'Before we married . . .'

'Can you remember that long?'

'. . . You used to be interested in children . . .'

'Children, not black babies with yaws.'

'... You could start a clinic.'

'And tie myself down, a prisoner of all their nasty little parasites. I would never get to Kingston.'

John, in the doorway, 'They say drinking makes you irritable in the morning.'

'Pot and kettle.'

Gustus was waiting at the coir factory when John arrived, and together they walked toward the generator shed. Gustus had disassembled the offending part and laid it on a wooden bench.

'It can be welded?'

'No, sar, dat can't weld. Mus' be new.'

'You 'ave de part number?'

'No, sar.'

'Get it for me, an' put it in de back o' de car. How much you have?'

'Coir, sar? Three ton.'

'I have an order for four from de mattress people.'

'Yes, sar.'

As John rejoined the main road, a man in a blue shirt waved him down.

'You goin' a works yard, sah?'

John nodded.

The man got in beside him. This was Ever Ready, so called for his sexual prowess not his punctuality; he was sideman on the D4.

'Ever Ready, you late.'

'No, sir.'

'What you mean, "no"?'

'I miss me ride, sah. I was lookin' for someting I couldn' fin.'

'Then you're late.'

'No, sah.'

The car rolled slowly into the Hordley works yard, one of the new properties that Stanley thought of as a wedding present. Wheeled tractors, each pulling a line of cane carts, were moving out. Walter, the D4 driver, was parking his Honda bike under the mango tree. The bookkeeper, precise Mr Dawson, was scribbling in the office. He rose and came toward John. Man-Man's chickens, scratching around the old water wheel, ignored him. The Bedford was loading copra for Kingston, George sitting at the wheel reading science fiction.

'Morning, Mr Newton.'

'Morning, Mr Dawson.'

John kept the new bookkeeper waiting until he had instructed the D4 to begin ploughing the field known as Naseberry Piece, listened to Walter cussing out Ever Ready for being late, and written out the purchase orders for George to take to Kingston, including one for the generator part, and had dealt with Miss Tilly, a grandmother who wanted a paper for the doctor.

'It seems we have a serious problem on our hands this morning, Mr Newton.'

'Is that so?' John said, sounding like his father.

'The cane cutters have concocted some sort of grievance.'

'Have you seen Mr William?'

'No, sir.'

On the instant, the Morris Minor bumped into the yard, coming from the other direction.

'I was looking for you,' William explained. 'This is one hell of a business. I know who is the cause of it, this boy Ram John. He's blind with ganja, and stirring up trouble ever since he came here. I told you to run him off the place. From the beginning I told you that boy is going to make trouble . . .'

John listened patiently to his cousin's version of events. The dispute had something to do with the new practice of burning the fields before cutting. It had been done in Trinidad for years, and was quicker and more efficient, but Ram John, who knew everything, had told the cutters that working in ash would give them all tuberculosis, and it was, like birth control, a plan to kill nigger. William had told Ram John to get off the property, which, considering how he had lost his hand some years before, was an act of extreme bravery. The result, unfortunately, was that work had ceased immediately.

'So what do you want me to do, massa?'

'Nothing,' John said. 'I'll handle it.' And went home to his breakfast.

*

Mavis greeted him with the news that the lavatory would not flush because they were out of water. She had sent the yard boy into the pasture to walk the pipe, but the fool had found nothing. Despite the crisis, Esmie had produced pawpaw, cornflakes, and a dish of fish fritters with hot pepper and plantains. While they were at coffee, the old Chrysler, still shiny, arrived, and Stanley came in, with necktie and braces, on his way to a meeting of the Coconut Industry Board.

Stanley, the pragmatist, seemed to have forgotten his opposition to Mavis, and kissed his daughter-in-law warmly, while John munched stolidly at his toast.

'How's Mamma?' Mavis asked, all sweetness and light.

'Quite bright. She's feeling much better today. Yes, quite bright,' Stanley replied, spoiling it by over-emphasis.

'I was thinking of going to see her this morning.'

'Yes. She'd like that. She'd like company.'

'Have some coffee?'

'No, no, I'm not stopping. John, a word.'

John walked with him to the car. Stanley obviously had a weighty matter on his mind for he assumed an air both pompous and conspiratorial.

'I want to make a contribution to the Friends' school, Happy Grove. I think it would please your mother.'

'What sort of contribution?'

'She has always been distressed at the lack of library facilities.'

'You mean books?'

'No. I mean a library building, with new classrooms, and designed in such a way that it can be used as a theatre and for public functions.'

'That's very generous.'

'Do you like the idea?'

'Yes, but why are you asking me?'

'I thought I should consult you, as of course it would involve considerable expenditure.'

'You mean this is a company gift, not a private one?'

'That's neither here nor there. Whichever is the more economical way of doing it. But I want your approval.'

'You didn't ask my approval before you put us back in debt to buy the St. Thomas properties.'

'That's another matter,' said Stanley, 'and in the long run, you'll be grateful to me for that. Land will always be in short supply. God is not making any more of it.'

'That's true, sir, but God doesn't fix the price of sugar.'

'And what is your government doing about that?'

'The best we can,' John said, hoping it was true, for he had no confidence in the Minister of Agriculture, and no faith in the generosity of Tate and Lyle.

'Anyway,' Stanley concluded, 'I shall drop in on that architect of yours, ask him to look at the site and draw me some plans.'

'Why not?'

'Righto,' said Stanley, climbing into his car. John watched the Chrysler down the drive. He wondered what had prompted all this. Did Stanley want a memorial for himself, or to settle some obligation to Grace? To be fair, the man had always been generous, sometimes in a back-handed way. Financing John's first date, he had calculated the price of a movie ticket, a tram fare, and a Coca-Cola to the last halfpenny, and went into shock when asked to multiply by two. At other times he was generous in a private, personal way, setting up a deserving person in business, educating an obscure relative or, not so obscurely, employing William, who would never be more than a passenger. Still, he had private reasons for that. The library would be a public gesture, it would be the 'Stanley Newton Library', inescapable. Could it be he was jealous of Mamma's MBE and had decided the Queen owed him something?

It was late morning before John drove into Stokes Hall, and parked across the road from Harris' house. The union leader lived in a two-room cottage set in a food garden on the steep slope opposite the Chinaman's shop. John pushed open the wicket gate and started up the path, calling out for Harris.

A middle-aged black man with a high, shiny forehead appeared in the doorway, pulling on his shirt. He was wearing blue serge trousers and carpet slippers.

'Mr Newton, I was just coming to see you.'

'I'm saving you the trouble, Mr Harris.'

'Well, it's an honour and a pleasure, sir. Come in, come in.'

John went into a small, square room with a small, square table.

The walls were lined with newspaper, and there was a photograph of Harris himself, with Bustamante, his prize possession and tangible proof that he was the union man in the district. Harris made John sit down, and found a bottle and two tumblers. He washed the glasses, already clean, as a gesture of hospitality, dried them, and poured them each a rum.

'You don't get rum when you come to my office.'

'That's why I don't come.'

'No, that's not why. You call out my cane cutters for a reason so foolish you dare not tell me.'

'Me! Dare not! Mr Newton, you're a joker. Seriously sir, de men dem can't work in dese condition.'

'They've been doing it for years in Australia, and in Trinidad.'

'Me don't know about dose places. Dis is Jamaica people we talkin' 'bout now.'

'They been doing it since the beginning of crop . . .'

'Giving you a fair trial. But dey are comin' home dirty, coughin' up ashes.'

'I know for a fact it's easier to cut burnt cane. I've done it myself.'

'We talkin' bout sickness.'

'You see anybody sick?'

'They want sickness money.'

'You know I arrange for Doc Hart to treat everybody free and the estate take care of it. And you know they are making more money already in premium because the cutting is easier.'

'Suit you.'

'Suit everybody.'

Harris shifted his ground. 'Mr Newton, just because people make a complaint, you can't throw dem off de property. De time for dat is past.'

'De man is a rascal.'

'I know de man is a rascal, sir, and you know de man is a rascal, but he is a union member.'

'He use bad language to Mr William.'

'No, sir.'

'Ask.'

'If I find out he use bad language, I will discipline him myself.'

John thought about that one. 'All right.'

'Yes, I would teach him manners! But Mr Newton, what about dese other fellows? What you can do for dem? They mus' bath every day, and wash clothes, and dey don't even have enough money to buy soap.'

'Soap?' said John. 'Suppose the property issue soap, to all the cutters.'

'And loaders. De women mus' get as well, and no yellow laundry soap, you know. Lux toilet.'

'I'll have another rum with you.'

Harris poured. That was settled, between friends. After all, Harris was Busta's union man, Newton was his MHR. Together, with courtesy and respect, they would find something the people would accept.

Harris drank, leaned forward, and spoke confidentially. 'Mr Newton, I hear the PNP union are setting for you in Port Antonio.'

'Which one?'

'The dockworkers.'

'So tell me.'

'Stay out of it, John, do you hear. I beg you.'

Mavis was frightened. If they were plotting against John, they would get him, and they would probably get her. 'The only thing you can do is stay out of it,' she said.

Stanley, who had driven down from Stone Haven to join the conclave, was of the opposite opinion.

'He can't do that,' he said patiently, as if she were a child, which infuriated Mavis further.

'Why not? He can go to Kingston. He has other business.'

'He can't. Tomorrow, the wharf will be full of everybody's fruit. The ship will be in. If the PNP close down Port Antonio, how can he ignore it?'

'He doesn't own the wharf, he doesn't run the union. It's not his quarrel.' Mavis was close to tears.

'He is the MHR,' said Stanley slowly, enunciating the initials, giving them their full significance.

John said nothing, looking from one to the other. Mavis got to her feet, angry at his silence.

'So what are you going to do? I suppose you're going to listen to your father. You won't listen to me. John, it is a PNP union. They mean to destroy your career by putting you in a situation where you can't win, and they'll kill you if they get the chance! If you go and defend the growers, they will say you're a capitalist, and you're anti-union. If you take the union's side, you will offend all the little small farmers who are supposed to love you. Stay out of it.'

'He can't, my dear,' said Stanley, shaking his head.

Mavis stormed into the house. The door to the drawing room was half-open, impeding her progress, and she shoved it roughly aside so it swung, and swung back again, banging to emphasize her departure. Father and son, unimpressed, waited for the air to clear. From inside came the sound of Mavis' voice, taking it out on Esmie, who had apparently made no provision for supper.

John knew that Mavis was right. His father was also right. In Jamaica, each political party had its own unions. They were inseparable. In a country where there was never enough work, a vote for the winning party was a vote for a job. There was an election pending, and while John's support in the countryside was as strong as ever his position in Port Antonio had always been shaky. It was possible that Harris was merely slandering a rival union, but the story had the ring of truth.

'I believe it,' John said, 'but what can I do?'

'I don't know, boy. You're the politician.'

'You want me to referee and get punched by both sides?'

'At least you'll be in the ring. The one thing they'll never forgive you for is not being there.'

'If they mean to strike, why have they kept it a secret?'

'Because they're going to wait until all the fruit is cut, and can't go back on the tree, then hit the Company for some foolishness to which it can't possibly agree.'

'They'll be throwing away their own wages, and persuading the Company to leave out Port Antonio.'

'You tell them that, they won't listen. This is a political business. Wages don't mean anything if the PNP can get rid of you.'

'Harris is right. I can't take the Company's side. I can't argue for the union against the growers. I can't argue for the growers against the union, especially as our own fruit will be trying to get onto the wharf.'

'You can argue for a solution. I don't think you'll get one, but you have to show your face.'

At Darlingford, John and Mavis were at supper. Esmie and the yard boy had gone home. The watchman, who smoked ganja and slept in a room behind the garage, had not arrived yet. They were alone but for the constant attention of the moths, and the roar and hiss of the sea at the foot of the cliff. Esmie had left them a red pea soup, thick and hot, the eating of which made them sweat. They avoided looking at each other, absorbed in their own thoughts, aware of the conflict to come.

John had brought his last drink to the table, and she rebuked him for it. Only a drunk brought rum to the table, she said. Halfway through the soup, John announced he was going to Port Antonio.

'What do you think you're going to do there?' she demanded.

'I don't know yet.'

'You'll just go round to Harvey's and drink with him and fall asleep on the sofa.'

'At least I'd be there first thing in the morning.'

'Well, I'm not sleeping in this house alone.'

'I can't take you with me.'

'Why not?'

'Never mind.'

It had been on the tip of his tongue to say that you don't take a quarrelsome woman to a union meeting, but that would have enraged her, and opened up the whole argument about whether or not she was good for his career. Known as the mildest and most diplomatic of men, it was something of a joke in the party that he was married to a woman some called honest and outspoken, others called a loudmouth.

'I can stay at Bonnie View.'

'The place will be closed up by the time we get to Port Antonio, and it's probably full.'

'John, I'm not staying here.'

John pushed his plate aside, rose, and refilled his glass.

'What's wrong with this house?'

'It's creepy,' she said, 'and I hate it. You don't notice it. You only come here to eat and sleep. I'm here all the time. It's empty, and it echoes, and it's isolated.'

'Watchie will be here.'

'Watchie is useless. He's stoned all the time. I could be murdered, raped and murdered, and he wouldn't know.'

The tone of her voice had hardened, and the Alsatian, asleep on the living room floor, raised his head and dropped it again.

'You're perfectly safe.'

'I am not! I am your wife, the rich man's wife, the politician's wife, and I am here alone. I am the target for any lunatic from the village. Look what happened to William. His hand was chopped off. You know what it's like to be awake in that room all night? Listening to the sea, listening to anything that moves, leaf or lizard or coconut rat, waiting, sick to my stomach and terrified, because I know I am going to get killed! I told you I had to have a place in Kingston.'

'We will,' John agreed, trying to appease her, 'as soon as we can arrange it. As soon as I can afford it.'

'You'll never afford it, because you give everything away to every beggar and liar that comes to the door. You think they love you for it. They despise you. They think you're weak and gullible.'

'You can stay at Stone Haven, if you like.'

'I'm not staying with your family. I'm tired of your family. Your father hates me, and your mother hates me. She puts up with me in Christian charity! Nobody's going to put up with me.'

John said nothing, sitting on the windowsill, watching her clear the table, banging the plates and the silver, dumping them in the kitchen for the cockroaches in the night and the maid in the morning. He did not want to discuss his family. She had declared her views on that subject often enough. They all thought they were God's gift: Miriam, who was arty and an intellectual snob; Grace, who had come out to save the souls of Jamaicans who didn't want saving; Stanley, who was just an illegitimate half-breed trying to become a gentleman, a nouveau riche not half as rich as he thought he was; and John himself, giving his time and money to all those blasted niggers, all greedy and ungrateful. Politics in Jamaica was a joke, and he was a fool! The niggers were incapable of self-government, incapable of democracy! They came from Africa under whip and gun, and whip and gun was the only rule they could ever understand! The only way they could be stopped from murdering decent people in their beds!

As she moved, talking all the time, he stopped listening, and merely looked at her. She had put on weight since their marriage, and needed now to wear full skirts to mask the size of her hips. Her face had coarsened somewhat, he thought, from the effects of drink, but who was he to talk. She applied her make-up sloppily. Nowadays, he found it harder to be aroused by her, bringing to bed the resentment caused by her constant nagging. He had withdrawn from her and found her flesh no temptation but a duty. He performed it, knowing she did not enjoy it either, merely demanded it as her right while despising him for his lack of ardour, and his inability to arouse her. Both of them had hoped a child would come to change their lives and their attitude to each other, but a child had not come, and his attempts to father one grew fewer. Nowadays he hated to lie beside her. One night, suddenly awake, he had found himself, in his pyjamas, standing in the middle of the living room, not knowing how he got there.

'I'm going now,' he said, pushing himself up from the windowsill, and walking across to the bookcase to pick up his car keys. She followed him.

'You're not going! You're not leaving me in this damn place! You're taking me to Kingston. You take me to Kingston tonight. I'll stay there until this business is over. They beat up old man Stewart in Annotto Bay last week, and they're going to kill you, John. The PNP has orders to kill, that's the only way they'll get into power. You're taking me to Kingston tonight, do you hear?'

John went out, down the steps, across the lawn to his car. She was still on the verandah, talking at him, shouting at him. He thought he heard something to the effect that he was a coward, and a queer, and that was what was wrong with him. He started the car, and moved off down the drive.

She was screaming. He looked behind and saw her on the verandah in the light from the drawing room, screaming her head off, like a witch in a bonfire.

The line of lorries stretched back from the entrance to the wharf, past the power station, the Standard Bakery and Lee Phong's and all the way down Harbour Street to the Cenotaph. The other way it stretched along the harbour front between the swamp and the sea. Interspersed among them were mule carts similarly loaded with green bananas swathed in damp trash, and donkeys with a bunch of bananas on either side of their hampers, led down from the Rio Grande valley in the cool of the morning.

The men were congregated by the gates, the truckdrivers, the donkey drivers and the sidemen, those who worked for large farms and those who had brought their own few carefully nurtured stems, their cash crop for the month. The men strolled or squatted, surprisingly patient, resigned, waiting. It was still early, already hot, and most had not eaten, but they were patient, expecting the matter, whatever it was, to be settled soon, and the long day to begin, unloading, checking, and stowing the fruit into the cool dark hold of the banana boat which could be seen, mast, funnel, and boat deck, over the top of the wharf building, its bow and stern clear at either end.

There was a policeman there, reinforcing the gateman, and inside, under a royal palm a few yards away, a knot of dockers whose job it was to see that the gates remained closed. Their fellows had taken over the compound and were massed around the zinc-roofed bungalow which housed the offices of the Company. The door was open, and another policeman guarded it, but the windows were shut, so although the dockers could see the figures of men moving and gesticulating inside, the words of their conference could not be heard.

The leader of the dockworkers' union, a man named Gladstone, sleek as a black seal, his moustache carefully trimmed, his teeth very white, a ladies' man with an educated voice, was supported by two labourers, hard-handed men, there to see they were not betrayed. The Company's agent was white, in white shirt and tie, looking harassed and trying to be reasonable. The police sergeant, like a bandmaster, sweating into his tight collar, was already resigned to trouble. Harvey, the pilot who had brought the ship in at dawn, relaxed in a corner with a bottle of beer. John, in a light grey suit, brushed and shaved after his night on Harvey's sofa, was inquiring into the nature of the dispute.

'Damn foolishness!'

'It may be foolishness to you, Mr Alcock, but it's life and death to my workers!'

Harvey smiled into his beer.

'They want double rates to load the ship. If we are going to have rubbish like that, Gladstone, we just have to close down Port Antonio and use Oracabessa and Bowden.'

'De ship is 'ere now, an' de fruit is 'ere now. We want twice times,' said one of the hard-handed men.

'Why, Gladstone? On what grounds?' John asked.

'There was no ship last week, Mr Newton. We had no work last week.'

The police sergeant laughed and the company agent cried out in exasperation.

'Damn foolishness!'

Gladstone was unruffled. 'You got paid last week, sir, and...' turning to the police sergeant, 'and you got paid last week.'

'You are not employed by the week. You are employed piece work to load the ship.'

Harvey smiled again. 'If you have two ships in a week, Gladstone, you work half-rate?'

'It pleases you to joke, Mr Brown. If there are no bananas, and no ship, we are hungry. My men have women and children. They must eat every day, whether there is a ship or not. Eh, Mr Newton? Your government is not going to feed us if we have no work, but it is your job to feed us, and it is the Company's job to give us work.'

'Somebody fill up your head with a lot of communist rubbish.'

'You have work, Gladstone. The ship is here, the fruit is here. Load it. If you carry on like this, it will be your responsibility if the port is shut down.'

'Gladstone,' John said, 'this is not the time to start this business.'

'It is the only time you will listen.'

'I appeal to you,' John said, 'the fruit is cut, and in the hot sun it will spoil. You will damage a lot of people. Load today and talk tomorrow.'

'Talk today, and load tomorrow!'

'But you and I can't settle this,' John insisted. 'We can't make a deal for Port Antonio. It has to be on a national basis.'

'Whatever settlement is reached here can apply everywhere else.'

'No, it can't be done like that. You have my word, I will take the matter up with Busta, and with Manley, to convene a meeting to discuss pay and conditions for dockworkers islandwide.'

'When the ship is loaded, you don't have to agree to anything, Mr Newton.'

'There will be other ships.'

The police sergeant interrupted, 'Mr Newton, a word.'

He drew John aside, and into an inner room.

'They come to cause trouble today, Mr Newton. Reason will not prevail. Gladstone looking for a fight, sir. From early morning I get through to the police in Kingston, St Ann's Bay and Morant Bay. We just have to keep talking until they arrive, because we must protect life and property.' The sergeant's face shone with the glow of duty done, affection for his elected member, his drinking friend, and the prospect of exercising his men in crowd control.

John smiled his thanks, concealing his dismay, for police reinforcements was the last thing he wanted; they would be a challenge to the dockers, and could ignite the violence inherent in the situation, the anger that lies just below the surface of patience, the sudden, mindless blood lust of the oppressed.

'Thank you, Burkey. Let's hope we can settle it before they get here.'

He went back to reason with Gladstone, to explain to him that whatever the justice of the case, and that justice lay in the stomachs of hungry children, nothing would be solved in this way, but Gladstone was adamant. His purpose was to humiliate John, to show that his writ did not run in Port Antonio, and to demonstrate to dockers and farmers alike that their MHR was a stooge of the Company, and an enemy of the people.

'Work today and talk tomorrow, that is your motto, Newton, so the rich stay rich and the poor stay poor!'

There was a cry from outside, a shout, followed by the long babble of someone haranguing the crowd. John went to the door to listen.

A stone crashed into the zinc roof above John's head, and the police sergeant grabbed him by the arm and pulled him back into the office, barring the door. The Company agent was closing the wooden shutters. The dockers outside, seeing the notables take cover, increased their shouting, and one stone became a volley, rattling on the roof, crashing on the verandah. They were throwing bottles, sticks, husks, anything that could be picked up, and they were shouting, 'Double! Double!'

Inside, the policeman appealed to Gladstone, accusing him of starting the trouble, ordering him to go out and restore order.

'You set dem to do dat. You go outside!'

But Gladstone merely smiled, and the hard-handed men stood between him and the law. The agent had taken cover behind his desk, and only Harvey stayed still, smiling like Buddha behind his beer. John stood alone in the middle of the room listening to the staccato thunder of the stoning.

Something heavy hit the shutters of the window, and John, suddenly angry, shouted, 'No, no! Nobody throw stone at me!'

He wrenched at the bolts, pulling open the shutters, and vaulted through the open window, and ran toward the crowd of dockers, shouting 'No!'

A rock hit his head, bringing him to a halt. He swayed, momentarily dizzy, and sank to his knees, but rose again to a silence as the men looked to see what they had done. The blood was running down John's face, but he seemed unaware of it, walking toward the first man he could reach, taking both his hands and saying, 'No . . . no war . . . no war.'

The man, a big, thick-lipped fellow with a red shirt and a woollen cap, looked back at John, and down at his hands, held firmly in John's clasp, and at the blood, unnoticed, running down his face.

'A'right, Mr Newton. A'right . . . done.'

John, still holding the man's hand, led him to the entrance, signalled for the gates to open, and waved the first truck in. He climbed onto the tail gate as the truck went past, and rocked slowly across the compound. Then he gestured to the sideman to give him the first bunch and, putting it on his head, carried it into the wharf. Putting it down, he saw that Gladstone had followed him.

'That's enough, Mr Newton, unless you want to join the union. I shall inform my people,' he added gravely, 'that you have accepted my recommendation to refer this matter to Kingston.'

Chapter Twenty-three

Miriam and her cameraman, Lennie, in a blue Toyota van, with Georgie Boy, sound engineer, crouched among the equipment, negotiated the snarled traffic on the Half-Way-Tree Road, cut across on Oxford Road by the Jamaica Development Bank, turned south past Up Park Camp, and west again into Franklyn Town. They were looking for Hungry Man's house on Fernandez Avenue, just behind the Nelson Oval. It was in an area of modest bungalows, built between the wars and inhabited then by professional people, merchants and civil servants, the sort that now were moving up the plain into the shelter of the mountains, building viewing terraces and swimming pools, installing burglar alarms and learning to like Alsatian dogs. But the houses in Fernandez Avenue still served, roofed with shingle or red painted zinc, patched and half-hidden in vegetation. Oranges and pawpaw grew into the windows; the yards were full of chickens and rusted machinery, and the houses full of life.

Hungry Man was at 9B, and he was expecting them, they hoped. Miriam pushed open the iron gate, causing a bell to ring, but this provoked no reaction. She avoided the rain puddle on the little path, and climbed the two steps to the verandah. The narrow double doors were open. She knocked on one of them, and looked into the dark interior. A pile of musical instruments, guitars and percussion, lying in a tangle of wire, told her she had come to the right place. There was a man in khaki dismantling a plug. Beyond him, a table, some straight chairs, a salt and pepper set and a bottle of Pickapeppa sauce made up the furniture. On the wall there was a photograph of Michael Manley with Haile Selassie and a walking stick, quaintly entitled 'Joshua receiving the Rod of Correction'.

'Mawnin' sir. Is the Man here?'

The electrician ignored her, absorbed in his task. Miriam looked back toward the van to see Lennie and Georgie Boy unloading the gear.

'Who dat?' said a voice from somewhere in the house.

'It's Miriam Newton, from JBC,' said Miriam clearly, identifying herself to the oracle. The oracle was unmoved.

'We must be early,' she said to Lennie and Georgie Boy, loudly enough to be heard. She knew she was late, but wanted to be polite. 'We'll wait on the verandah.'

After a while, a man came out of the bedroom buttoning the waist button of his trousers. He was naked from the waist up, and barefoot, but fully dressed by virtue of the dreadlocks which hung in long coiled curls to his shoulders. He was below medium height, and slender, but superbly built, each muscle outlined against his tawny skin. Some forgotten overseer or passing sailor had put cream in the coffee of his complexion, and his features were more Ethiopian than West African, more aquiline and predatory.

'Miriam?'

'Yes.'

'All right.'

'This is Lennie, and Georgie Boy.'

'Peace and love.'

He paused to look at Miriam, taking his time, judging her.

'Five star,' he said.

He moved past her to the verandah to look up at Long Mountain and take stock of the day.

'Chairs round de oder side. It rain in de night.'

Georgie Boy went to fetch them and, with Lennie's assistance, set up a semi-circle. Hungry Man remained standing, looking down at them. Miriam thought it was time she said something.

'I thought before we did anything about an interview, we could just chat.'

'Tea coming,' said Hungry Man, and sat down. 'Your brother is Minister of Communications?'

'Yes.'

'That's how you got started in television?'

'My brother wouldn't give me a job. He knows I'm PNP.'

'Is that a fact? I watch your programme, Miss Miriam. Is not bad.'

'Thank you. But not good?'

'Is too cute, you know. Too what they call folksy.'

'It has to entertain.'

'Who? Entertain who?'

He was an arrogant bastard, Miriam thought, but it might all be pose, pure pose.

'I was lucky to get it on.'

'That's true,' he said generously. 'How you manage dat?'

'As you know, our output is mostly English and American repeats, junk that has paid for itself already or we couldn't afford it. We argued that if Jamaican television was to be anything, it should have a few minutes presenting Jamaicans to themselves, so that their ideas about themselves, their images of themselves are not made by Desi Arnaz, Roy Rogers, or Susannah York. They said okay, but it had to be cheap. The cheapest form of television is a talk show. I said I would find interesting people to talk about themselves, next door neighbours, people you've never heard of, eccentrics, anybody except politicians.'

'You get too many Aunt Jemimas and Uncle Toms,' Hungry Man said.

'Which one are you?' Miriam asked.

She was nettled. He had no right or reason to attack her, and she wasn't going to take it. Hungry Man considered her, expressionless, and then went on as if she had not spoken.

'You want some angry people, a gun man from Trench Town, a convicted murderer from Spanish Town gaol.'

'That's a good idea. Can you help me find one?'

A handsome young woman in traditional Nigerian dress brought in a tray of tea and a small table to set it on. The ceremony of passing round the mugs gave Miriam time to think. Despite his rudeness, there was a quality of vulnerability about him, she thought, as if there were two persons there, an angry one, and a frightened one, both beautiful.

'I will want to ask you about your background . . .'

'No.'

'Your family and all that, you know . . .'

'No.'

This wasn't going very well. 'I will be bound to ask you about the name, "Hungry Man", how you came by it.'

'How you come by yours?'

'From my father and mother.'

This was the cue he was waiting for, and Hungry Man moved from feigned indifference to the eloquence of the preacher as he moved from educated English into dialect at will or whim.

'And with the name you took the whole baggage of your family, their history, their father and grandfather history. I and I reject it all. I and I is the father of myself. For generations, white people practise genocide against us. We was in Babylon. Our names erase, our language erase, our culture erase! We was made to scramble for the leftovers, to eat like dog off the floor of their civilization. My name is what I am.'

'Will you talk about all that?'

'If I want.'

'I am in sympathy with what you're saying . . .'

'Don't lie to me, girl. You're from the plantocracy, just visiting, patronizing black people . . .'

'And don't you insult me! I'm asking a serious question. How can we build a nation, how can we survive in the twentieth century on something so unsophisticated as Ras Tafari?'

'Unsophisticated! Unsophistication is power! Ras Tafari is power. Power to convert, power to transform. You tell me how something so unsophisticated as Christianity took over the Roman Empire! Rome doubted, Christians believed! Belief is power. Ras Tafari has power to convert, to transform, to purify by the fire of Judah. We shall purify! We shall have Rasta science, Rasta government, Rasta medicine. Erase. Ras. Ras puts back what was erased.'

'Will you talk about your music?'

'No.'

'You can't say no; as a great performer, and a great musician, in my opinion, you just can't ignore it. I won't ask you to perform.'

'I know dat. If I was going to perform you'd have to talk about fee, right?'

The telephone rang, and was answered by the handsome Nigerian girl, who came back into the doorway.

'Is dat Yankee man, Marty Somebody.'

'What him want?'

'He want see you today.'

'No.'

'What you doing today?'

'Nothing.'

'He says he's flying back to New York tonight.'

'If he want see me bad enough, he'll stay till tomorrow.'

'You will say something about your music,' Miriam pursued.

'My music is nothing without my religion, and my philosophy. The one is born of the other. The music is ours alone. You don't hear any Beethoven in it, or any Frank Sinatra, or any sitar music. My music come from de belly, de belly of a Hungry Man. Music bindeth up all wounds. Music is the solace of affliction! Music fire! Music is the cry of the distressed and the celebration of joy. It is a prophecy of peace and love to all the brethren and sistren.'

He eased his crotch in his tight trousers. 'You want me say something like dat?'

Stanley, on the Stone Haven verandah, was complimentary about the interview, scathing about Hungry Man.

'The boy's name is Hector McNab,' he said in his best no-nonsense voice. 'He was never hungry in his life. His father was a pharmacist in Black River, and when he retired, he bought a little property near Montpelier. The boy went to Jamaica College, and played cricket! Everybody is bound to know in the end.'

'You don't understand, Daddy. He's trying to make a statement.'

'He's trying to make money.'

It was the kind of thing she should expect her father to say, Miriam thought. He considered all socialists and Ras Tafarians to be rascals and charlatans.

Michael Manley, he said, should be publicly flogged, and all Ras Tafarians forced to have a haircut as dreadlocks were a place for breeding fleas and hiding ganja. Miriam loved her father, and some small corner of her heart agreed with him, which is what Hungry Man meant when he said that even by accepting her name she took on the baggage of her family. She loved Hungry Man too, for his courage. There was nothing left in him of McNab the pharmacist, retired coconut grower of Montpelier.

The interview with Hungry Man led to others. Miriam called his bluff, and was able to add to her gallery of preachers, cobblers, female bank managers, professional beggars and school children a genuine, self-confessed and unapprehended political murderer. With Hungry

Man as her passport, she moved as easily downtown as uptown. The old colonial centre of Kingston was being deserted by the better shops and wealthier shoppers, who now patronized malls and plazas further up the plain. Financial institutions were moving to New Kingston, on the site of the old race track, and the downtown hotels had gone seedy or been pulled down. King Street, Orange Street, Parade, which in Stanley's heyday had been the business centre, had become a market, a mile-wide open bazaar, where stalls filled all the pavements and people all the streets. There was no need for Rasta to go back to Africa. Africa had come to him.

Miriam arrived at Fernandez Avenue about noon to find Hungry Man in bed. There was a cup of tea beside him, the guitar propped against the wall, and the litter of the previous night's session all over the house. She was embarrassed to be neat and clean.

'Come nuh, man, what you doing in bed? We going to country.'

'I and I not going.'

Miriam thought of a ritual protest, of turning it into a joke, but the way it was said was so casual it could only be definite.

'You're not going?'

'No.'

'My family are expecting us.'

'Call them and tell them we not coming.'

'There's no telephone at Stone Haven.'

'Dat's deep bush.'

He looked directly at her, staring her down. Miriam sat on the bed beside him.

'Come nuh, man. You can't disappoint de people.'

'Dey won't be disappointed. Dey'll be overjoyed.'

'What about me? I arranged all this, and you said you would come.'

'Gal, you want me to jump hoops. You want me to balance a ball on mi nose. You want me to be polite to dem, and dem to be polite to me, you want to spend de whole day telling lies. If dem want to see me, dem can come here, but dem don't want. You want it. You want to measure me against dem. You want to put me in dat frame and see if I still pretty.'

'Maybe it was a bad idea, but I arranged it.'

'Disarrange it.'

'You're afraid.'

'Afraid o' what?'

'You boast that you're the father of yourself. But this person you have made may be a shadow. You think you'll disappear in my mother's drawing room? If my father calls you Hector, will you suddenly turn into a little boy from Black River?'

Hungry Man laughed, showing his beautiful white teeth. Ripples of laughter shook him, and he pulled himself higher on the bed, enjoying it, enjoying her. He put a pillow behind his back and sat up so their eyes were on the same level.

'No, darlin', I won't turn into anything. That's why I can't be bothered to go. If we spend one day being polite, we wasting time. If your mother and I and I start talk religion, or if your Daddy and I and I start talk politics, we are all wasting time. Take off your clothes.'

It was to be unconditional surrender, when she had not planned it. Those were his terms. Sometimes it takes more courage to surrender than to fight. He was looking at her dispassionately, waiting. If he would only throw her a crumb. He did.

'Take them off, sweetheart,' he whispered, asking.

'Now?'

'Now.'

'In broad daylight?'

'Broad daylight is best.'

She glanced toward the open door.

'Leave de door. Nobody in de house.'

Slowly, Miriam took off her blouse. She wore no bra, and her firm high bosom had no need of one. She sat, without embarrassment, and he, with no movement but his eyes looked at the line of her arms and shoulders and the curves of her breasts. She stood up to take the jeans off, stepping out of them, standing in front of him in her panties only.

'Take dat off too.'

She did, and quickly climbed on to the bed with him.

It was later, when Miriam had made coffee, found some saltfish and ackee in the refrigerator, heated it up, and served it with fried plantain, hard-dough bread and a scotch bonnet pepper, that she asked the question that had been niggling at the back of her mind.

'Where's Naomi?'

'I sent her out.'

'Did she know why?'

'She won't mind.'

'How do you know?'

'It's not her place to mind.'

'Aren't you sleeping with her?'

'What you think?'

Miriam decided the conversation was getting nowhere. 'It's none of my business,' she said coldly.

'Naomi is all right. She's cool. You'd get along with her.' Hungry Man paused. 'You want to move in?'

'Not in the circumstances. I don't usually live with my men.'

'Tsch, you want a one-one. Freedom is the thing, man. I believe in freedom for women. I and I don't want put a sign on you saying *Trespassers will be prosecuted* as if you was your Daddy's banana walk. I and I does what I want. Naomi does what she want. You can do what you want.'

'Thank you,' she said, but he went on as if she did not agree with him.

'In Babylon you can own people as well as things. I and I say you can't own people. So when I say come and live here, I mean you can come because you want me, and you want to, but don't put condition on me, don't put condition on Naomi.'

'Funny how your freedom would work though. You'd end up with two women and each of us with half a man.'

'You can leave if that's not sufficient.'

Just then, Naomi came in. Miriam heard her footstep on the verandah, and looked up to see her in the doorway. Seeing her again, Miriam was struck by her beauty. She was Jamaican, but the Nigerian dress suited her for she was very black, with a big healthy body, soft, slanting eyes and a wide smile.

'Hi, Miriam.'

'Hi.'

Naomi approached and looked down at their plates. 'You found de saltfish and ackee. Is good eh? Is de likkle pieces of bacon in it. Any leave?'

'Yes.'

'I better grab some before Greedy Man eat de whole damn thing.'

She went into the kitchen, found a plate and a fork, helped herself, and came back to join them.

Grace was in town for a visit to the chiropractor, and Miriam went to pick her up at his office, and take her to lunch. The people we love do not change, and then they change utterly. Grace, who was just sixty, looked suddenly old. There was a lot more white in her hair, and she was paler. She was standing very straight at the top of the steps, and very still. Then Miriam noticed, beneath her mother's dress, a bulge made by the top of a back brace.

Miriam took her arm to help her down the steps.

'Thank you,' Grace said. 'I can manage.'

But she did not withdraw her arm, and let some of her weight rest on her daughter. The flesh in Miriam's hand felt soft and wasted, and she noticed how carefully her mother turned to get into the car, putting her legs in one by one, avoiding pain.

'Doctor give you a hard time?'

'He's very gentle, very considerate, but sometimes . . . Never mind, I can bear it.'

'It doesn't matter whether you can bear it or not. Is it doing you any good?'

'We have more important things to talk about.'

'No, we don't. What's the matter?'

'Doctor says I must have slipped a disc. He's recommended the brace, and it does help.'

Miriam looked at her, not believing a word. 'How long will it take to mend?'

'A month or two, he says, a few more visits. You can start the car, Miriam. It gets hot, just sitting here.'

Grace said she was in no mood for a big lunch so they went to the new air-conditioned pharmacy at Half-Way-Tree for a chicken sandwich and a cup of coffee. There, surrounded by cosmetics and medications, they discussed Miriam's pregnancy.

'Have you told the father?'

'Yes.'

'What does he say?'

'He's happy, and he wants me to have it.'

'So you've talked it over?'

'More or less.'

'Did you suggest you might not have it?'

'Hector doesn't believe in that. He feels very strongly about it. He believes that life is sacred, and if it has come into being, it must be protected.'

'I know that's the Pope's position. I didn't know that Haile Selassie endorsed it.'

'Birth control is a plan to kill nigger, Hector says. White people tell black people not to have babies in order to perpetuate dominion.'

Grace smiled, 'If so, it will never work. Black people are too good at having babies.'

She was in pain, and the conversation painful, this attempt to treat this awful thing as if it were natural, as if it were normal. Yet it was both those things, and she must be calm and wise for as long as the burning in her back allowed.

'Are you sure it would be healthy?'

'What do you mean? Are you worried about VD?'

'Are you smoking ganja? And what about him?'

Miriam bit her lip, refusing to reply. It was impossible to talk to someone who thought in those terms.

Grace went on, 'I asked that question because I don't know the answer. Do you?'

'I'm not going to answer you.'

'Is the boy planning to take any responsibility for it?'

'You mean marriage?'

'Yes.'

'He doesn't believe in that.'

'I see. He has very convenient beliefs.'

'I've said that.'

'To him?'

'Yes. But I don't believe in marriage either. He will not be the only person in my life. I may not be the only person in his. He wants the freedom to pursue his career, and . . .'

'If he's successful, you may never see him again. But if he fails, he'll be back to demand his rights. I know Jamaican men, I've seen it often enough. Responsibility is not in their vocabulary. Either way, you have the baby.'

'That's not a punishment, Mamma. It's a gift.'

'I just want to know what provision he is making for the child.'

'I don't know, but I'm not interested in the money, and I'm not interested in your kind of respectability, the kind of marriage that sounds like a property settlement. Besides, Hector doesn't have any property.'

'He can offer you the profits of his labour.'

'I don't want them, I can work for myself. I want the child, and I want to look after him, and I want to keep on working! In your day, you found a man to look after you, and provide for you in a world of men. But that was yesterday. I want a baby, and I don't see why I should give a man twenty years of my life in order to have one. Things are different now, the world is not made up of families, it's made of individuals. Things and people move too fast. You have to believe in yourself, and in yourself alone!'

Grace considered her, her child's face, glowing with earnestness, with courage, and with beauty. She disagreed so deeply with what Miriam was saying. It was wrong, and it was not Christian. It was against the rules of God and man. She feared for her, but even at that moment she remembered when she herself had thrown her father's wisdom in his face and followed her own heart, her own religion, and her own principles for good or ill. She reached out and took Miriam's hand.

'Oh, darling girl,' she said, 'may God protect you.'

Hungry Man's single, 'Honey from the Lion', was into the charts, so he and the Dread Commotion were booked on a tour of England, coinciding with the release of his first English album. Miriam drove him to the airport with Naomi who was going along as head cook and bottlewasher to the band. It had been agreed that there would be no jealousy or upset. Naomi had nothing else to do, while Miriam was both pregnant and working, so a tour of England would have been impossible. Discreetly, Naomi sat in the back seat. The group, with their instruments and luggage, came in a van.

Of course they were all recognized at the terminal, checking in for the flight to London, but there was no demonstration as reggae stars are a dime a dozen in Kingston, and produce no more reaction than a laugh, a touching of hands, and a 'Right, man, right!' Their manager, a busy little gentleman of Lebanese extraction, bustled about with the documents while the singers sat on their suitcases. He came over to warn them, before the baggage went out of their hands, against carrying substances into England. The tour might be jeopardized if they were caught, and everything, he assured them, was available there.

Naomi, in a beautiful full length robe of gold and green with a matching headdress, flowed away to the bookstall for magazines, leaving Miriam to say goodbye to Hector.

'Okay.'
'Okay, Hector. Good luck.'
'Look after yourself.'
'Don't worry.'
'Peace and love.'

It would not do to kiss or embrace in public, but he lifted a gentle hand to her cheek and she closed her eyes. Then he turned and ambled off toward passport control, joining Naomi on the way. Miriam stayed where she was, the keys to the car in her hand, watching them. Immigration allowed them through with a salutation, and as they moved toward the departure lounge, Hungry Man waved once more to Miriam, put his arm around Naomi, and disappeared.

He was off to conquer the world, and he would, she believed. Under the cool, the casual masculinity, he had been terrified, a slim young black man under cover of dreadlocks, scared stiff, and he would remain scared until he sang. They would love him, because that's what he sang about, peace and love, and he was good. Wasn't it strange, she thought, driving along the Palisadoes Road, that the gospel was now preached not by people like her mother, but by pop singers, that the spokesmen for church and state were now so careful, so critical or hypocritical, so content with disaster, so proud of the apocalypse, and so corrupt, that the young no longer listened. They listened to the singers, because, if only in the act of singing, they believed in love and in the perfectibility of man.

She decided she would not think about Naomi. Yes, she would. She loved Naomi, her smile and her slow warmth. She would keep him steady, rock steady, and hold him together. The words came unbidden:

> Brown skin gal,
> Stay home and mind baby.
> Brown skin gal,
> Stay home and mind baby.
> I'm going away
> In a sailing boat
> And if I don't come back
> Stay home and mind baby.

When Hungry Man came back from England, Miriam brought him to Stone Haven. The tour had been a success and the album was selling. He might have stayed on as long as he liked, but he wanted to be in Jamaica when Miriam's baby was born, and, like Stanley, he didn't want to pay English income tax. They stopped at Hordley on the way out, and she showed him round. Hungry Man, in his King's Road gear, looked weird in the works yard, but he surprised her by knowing more about it than she did. The retired coconut grower of Montpelier had not been completely forgotten.

They took tea on the verandah. Grace had acquired a rocking chair, which Stanley, alluding to her Iowa background, said was reverting to type. He himself had to be summoned from his office when the tray was produced, which laggardliness could be passed off as diligence, but which Miriam knew was the only protest his courtesy would allow to the presence of a hairy Rasta on his front verandah. Hector was deferential, and called Stanley 'sir'. Stanley rose to the occasion by talking about old Jamaica folk songs, and illustrating them in his vibrato baritone, as if he thought Hungry Man was a musicologist. All the while, Stanley was looking at the creature as if measuring him for a suit.

He admired Hector's finely cut features, his expressive brown eyes and delicate hands. He was a good-looking boy, if you could ignore the dreadlocks, which Stanley couldn't. They talked politics briefly, for they would not agree. Stanley was now a staunch supporter of Bustamante, whom he had once characterized as a rabble-rouser. That epithet was now reserved for the new anti-Christ, Michael Manley. Manley, to Hector, was insignificant, a mere John the Baptist to the reign of Ras Tafari. Stanley pressed him on the fiasco of Haile Selassie's visit to Jamaica, and Hector calmly explained that primitive, literal Rastas worshipped the Lion of Judah, and sought a physical return to Africa from exile in Babylon, but Ras Tafari spiritualized was more akin to such ideas as 'black is beautiful' or to the Black Muslim movement. It was a realization of identity, a rebirth of pride, a growth of consciousness, a logically consistent faith, and a source of philosophy.

Stanley, listening, decided the boy was mad.

When Grace, who had been silent through all this, asked Miriam to help her to her room, Hector excused himself, tactfully, and went down the front steps, as far as the retaining wall of the drive, allowing Grace an unobserved departure.

He put a foot on the wall, and leaning forward, took in the view. Below him, the pasture sloped to the driveway of the old Williamsfield house, and beyond to the cricket field, overgrown, with a rusted roller abandoned in the corner. The coconuts in the grove on the other side of the main road were moving in the sea breeze which tugged at his own locks. There was a glimpse of the calm green waters of Innes Bay, and beyond and to his right the indented coastline stretched as far as he could see, promontories reaching into the Caribbean, fountains of spray falling in rhythm on top of the weathered cliffs. To his left the dark-green hills rose into cloud, and overhead the john crows circled, with no flapping of their wings, riding the currents of the air.

A high babbling cry attracted his attention. There on the next hill, below the wall of the Williamsfield house, he saw the figure of a woman in a white garment like a nightgown, her arms gesticulating like a broken windmill, yelling at the top of her voice. It was, though he did not know it, Miriam's Aunt Cynthia who had gone quite mad and now fancied herself as a prophet. Every afternoon as the sun set she stood on her imagined mountain top hurling hellfire at the sea.

Stanley, listening, and looking at Hungry Man, his foot on the wall, remembered Harold and the one-handed William. He thought of the baby in his daughter's belly, sired by that lunatic boy, and he remembered his own courtship of Grace, the noble beauty of her, her faith, and her quiet good sense. She had been his way out of the madness of Jamaica, but she was tired now, and in pain. Miriam was lost. John was unhappy with that woman, he knew; and Paul, well there was hope for him, in England studying to be a vet. He might turn out to be useful on the farm.

The light was fading, and the madness dragged at him like quicksand. Then he remembered he had not worked out the projected reaping of coconuts for March. He could get that done before supper. He could go back to his desk before the Rasta man returned.

Chapter Twenty-four

At two o'clock in the morning, John was found by the watchman of the Coral Sands Hotel lying in the garden below the balcony of his room. He was barefooted, in his pyjamas. The watchman tried to help him to his feet, and then realized that he was badly hurt. He left the Minister lying there, ran to the lobby and reported to the night clerk who telephoned for the police and an ambulance. When the ambulance men arrived, John was alive, but unable to speak. His ribs were broken. It was later realized that the splintered bones had punctured his lung, liver and spleen. He died shortly after being admitted to hospital.

The watchman, questioned, claimed to have seen a man on the balcony pissing into the garden. But that was earlier. An hour later, on his rounds, he had found the Minister lying on the lawn. He had not seen him fall, and had heard nothing. From the position of the body the police deduced that the Hon. John Newton had fallen from the balcony, landed on the concrete kerbing between the flowerbed and the lawn, thus breaking his ribs and causing the fatal injuries.

There had been, or so it was believed, no one else in his room at the time. His wife had not attended the party retreat and remained in Kingston. After dinner in the main dining room of the hotel where he had been invited to sit at the right hand of the ageing Bustamante, he had retired to his room. There, he had been joined for a nightcap by the Minister of Finance and the Minister of Agriculture and Lands. Both these gentlemen maintained that John was cheerful, and had not been drinking heavily. In fact, according to the Minister of Agriculture, he was being particularly abstemious, as if aware of some new burden to be placed on his young shoulders, and confined himself to beer. Feet up at the end of the day, this late-night gathering had been convivial but restrained. There had been some discussion of political problems and of party matters, but not including the question of party leadership. The Minister of Agriculture had been the last to leave, at about midnight, he thought. The door was locked from the inside.

The theory then constructed was that John, having seen out the last of his guests, shut the door, undressed, donned his pyjamas and went to bed. An hour or so later, feeling the effects of the beer, he had risen to relieve himself and, being half-asleep and in a strange place, mistook the balcony for the bathroom. Moving groggily, he had put out a hand to steady himself, found only the air, lost his balance, and toppled over the balcony rail, landing on the concrete kerb. Stunned and confused by the fall, he had not been able to cry out, or his cries had been unnoticed in the neighbouring rooms. Weakened by loss of blood, and in great pain, he had dragged himself a few yards and collapsed. When the watchman found him, it was too late. Barring such flights of fancy as a drunken memory of flying, or murder by a fellow minister with a cricket bat, it seemed an acceptable theory, and it was later strengthened by his wife's disclosure that John had for some years been prone to sleepwalking.

Much depended on the watchman's sighting of a man pissing from a balcony. Cross-questioned, he thought it was the same balcony, but could not swear to it. He thought the man had been in his pyjamas, but could not swear to that either and, as the incident had been earlier, and he had not actually seen a fall, he could not be sure that he had seen Mr Newton, or even a man on Mr Newton's balcony. What about the restrained conviviality of the visiting Ministers? And were there women involved? He had heard laughing and talking and raised voices, but could not positively identify the room, or the time, or the number of occupants, as he had been on the other side of the hotel. Pressed, his answers became more vague, and more defensive, until at least one detective became convinced the watchman had been asleep until starting the round on which he discovered the dying man.

The testimony of the Minister of Finance and that of the Minister of Agriculture were more consistent and, being eminent persons, more to be respected. The late-night meeting had been convivial, they agreed, but restrained, totally unremarkable, an innocent prelude to a profoundly unexpected and deeply shocking accident to a dear colleague. They could not say whether anyone else had been admitted to the room after their departure.

It did not take much imagination to picture the Ministers' party as something rather more exuberant, and perhaps rather more drunken. Despite their testimony, there could have been a bit of good-natured horseplay, some pushing and shoving, who knows? They were all relatively young men, of volatile temperament, and strong. There could have been a quarrel, a fight over a woman. Newton, instead of changing afterwards, might have been entertaining in his pyjamas. Even the locking of the door from the inside proved nothing, for from the balcony to the ground was but a short drop for an athletic man like the Minister of Agriculture.

It might have been suicide, but this was discounted, not only because he was a healthy young man with the world before him, successful and respected, but because only someone who intended to fail would try suicide by jumping from a balcony no more than ten feet high. It would be macabre in the extreme to aim one's ribs at a low concrete kerb eight inches wide in order to be quite sure that death was slow, and agonizing

So if he did not jump, and was not pushed, what was he doing in the garden?

There were as many theories of John's death as there were minds to ponder it. Some were simple – he had struggled with a burglar; some domestic – his wife and her lover had hired a man to kill him; some political – he had been murdered by the two Cabinet Ministers, jealous of his future; some geo-political – he had been eliminated by the CIA because they could not bribe him; some financial – a quarrel with his cousin over money; Michael Manley had ordered it; Castro had paid for it; he was not dead at all, he had been seen since, and positively identified, both in Montego Bay and on the streets of Kingston.

Miriam had heard that Mavis was unfaithful. She believed that John had been too busy, too busy in negotiations over the national airline, too busy with a flood control project for Kingston, too busy with 'Christmas work' for the unemployed, too busy finding the right architect for a housing scheme, too busy with his cook's health and his yard boy's papers, too busy to notice.

But John had known, as Miriam found out one night shortly before his death. Instead of going home after some function, he had come to Hungry Man's place to find her, and they had sat on the back verandah waiting for the mountain breeze, John with his jacket draped over the back of the chair, his tie at half-mast, and a drink, often replenished, in his hand. They had talked all night, not about Mavis' infidelity, not at first, but about Jamaica, which was by then his only love.

'The country is going to the dogs,' John said. 'The sugar price is down, the world price of aluminium is down, the bauxite workers are on strike. Farm labour is impossible to get for no one will work the land for wages too low to live on. They drift to town, and the slums of Kingston fill all the plain between the mountains and the sea, and stretch westward into the swamps of St Catherine. In the shanty towns, strange religions are engendered and gangs armed by the marijuana trade contend for territory. Drugs replace food, and prostitution, love. In the tourist towns of Mo Bay and Ocho Rios, it is becoming more profitable to beg than work, more profitable still to steal.

'The army is always ready to take over,' John said, 'so we must keep them weak. The CIA is even readier. They report to the American president that Jamaica's problems are insoluble, so he should support anyone who can keep order.

'You, Miriam, are a socialist. Every right-thinking person should be a socialist,' John said. 'They are on the side of the angels. But socialism is one of those theories invented by clever men to explain all human life, capitalism is another, so is Christianity. They are like model railways, they work well on the nursery floor. Socialism has something to say, but belief is heavy baggage. If you believe in one model, you must falsify everything else to make that model work. A politician who believes passionately in some damn solution, final or otherwise, is a dangerous man. In politics, you can be right, right about everything, and still wrong. You can be right that our independence is a sham, that we are still colonized, you can be right that we are exploited by the UK, the USA, the supranational companies and so on, but you can be wrong to take them all on at once, for the big bully boys from overseas will beat you, and the people will pay for your defeat.

'In the old days,' John said, 'Jamaica was a slave society administered by a hybrid middle class and ruled from London. What is it now? A slave society administered by a hybrid middle class and ruled from Washington. What we are seeing is the pauperization of the Third World, the Empire of the Banks. You can make a name for yourself by being against it, but you can't stop it!

'We must start from our insignificance,' John said, 'and within that strive, not for Paradise, we're not going to get there, but just to keep going. So far, my darling, we're a great success. We haven't had a civil war yet, we haven't had a racial or religious war. There has been no revolution. We don't have some jack-booted fool strutting around Port Antonio cutting off people's heads and sticking them on bamboo poles as the British did in the days of slavery. People still vote, still throw the rascals out and put another set of rascals in. The Americans send the CIA but they've kept the marines at home, so far. Castro sends agricultural instructors, but they can't speak Jamaican. Our people bear hardship without wishing it on their neighbours, and everywhere you go in this country, if you stick your head out of the window, you can hear somebody laugh.'

Night and the bottle ended.

'Time to go home,' John said.

Miriam walked with him to his car.

'I've decided to leave Mavis,' John said. 'I can't stand it any longer. It's no good for her, or me. I'm not there most of the time, and when I am, I'm no sort of a husband, but the hatred I get from her makes it impossible for me to approach her.'

'You haven't told her yet,' Miriam replied, 'that's why you're trying it out on me.'

'That's right.'

'Nobody will blame you, John.'

'Except her . . . and myself, for failure.'
John got into the car.
'Okay, sis.'
'Okay.'

Miriam believed John died of love. He had loved Mavis, and however strong he was in public life, in private he was weak and vacillating. He had no power to hurt her, and could not endure her misery; he died because it was the only way of leaving her. He had loved his wife too much to be able to reject her; he could not raise his voice at her, or hit her, or order her about. He had given her all the authority he gave his mother, whom he idolized, with whom he could not quarrel, and who, saint-like, could do no wrong. So he felt the fault was his, the wrong was his, the guilt was his. The torrent of her hatred and abuse, her wit directed at him, all were just. Indeed, it was his own fault to give such power to a woman, but once given he could not take back, or suffer it. He died walking away from the bed. So Miriam believed, but she was a romantic.

On the night after John's death, Stanley phoned Paul in England with the news, and suggested that he come home for his brother's funeral. Paul was, by then, a junior partner in a veterinary practice and there was nothing in the way of his departure but a horse with arthritis and a bitch to be spayed. He was reluctant to travel so far for so melancholy a reason, but reminded himself that funerals were for the living not the dead. John would know nothing about it, but the living would approve the gesture.

Two days later, he was once more on the road from Kingston to Stone Haven, perched this time in the front seat of a Jaguar beside Frank, whose grey hairs were beginning to show from under his chauffeur's cap. There was something odd about the drive, not just the heat, not the half-forgotten island smells, not the thick, humid air. Something visible had changed. They were up in the hills beyond Nine Mile before Paul realized what it was. All the roadsides were clean, or being cleaned, not only of litter, old packages and bottles, but newly cut. An army of men with machetes was cutting the grass and trimming the bushes for all of the fifty miles. As they came down into Yallahs, there was a banner across the road which read, 'Good night, Star Boy', and at Johnson's Pen another, 'John-John, Rest in Jesus'.

'We're not even in his constituency yet,' Paul said to Frank, and Frank replied, rebuking him, 'He was Minister to the whole island.'

Paul kept silent, and reflected that for much of his brother's career he had been off the island, and had no real knowledge of the esteem, or lack of it, in which John was held. On a previous visit, he had watched John electioneering and at a Chamber of Commerce lunch. His brother had grown heavier for too many such luncheons, and paler for the hours spent at his desk. Everybody said John was wonderful, but what he saw was a pompous drunk, a small time politician with his stomach pushed out in front of him. The role makes the man. John, so diffident and shy, had learned to love the sound of his own voice, to rock back and forth on his heels, hands in the pockets of his jacket, making sure his voice carried to the back of the room, making sure he got a laugh in the first minute, praising something, honouring someone, promising that the future would come, which is true enough, though a logical impossibility.

Paul wondered, knowing his Jamaica, whether it was John or death itself that was to be honoured, and enjoyed. Jamaica is a great place to die, for no passing goes unremarked, or uncelebrated. In contrast, he recalled English hearses on the A30, pushing the speed limit, followed by one miserly carload of mourners, or perhaps only by holidaymakers looking for a chance to overtake; he thought of crematoria in London, puffing gently, of discreet knots of relatives waiting for a taxi, widows ordering announcement cards, and lawyers rubbing their moist hands. In Jamaica, the people love death; it is their goal and expectation, their triumph, a reality in every household, and a spirit in the brooding land. Death is the victory of divinity over all mortal presumption. In a conflict between God and man, who would be on the side of man? To die young and full of promise is not to be regretted but a cause for celebration.

Frank brought him back to earth. 'Your brother was the Minister of Communications, Mister Paul, so the Public Works must put on a show and clean up de roadside.'

'Yes, Frank. Quite so.'

The body followed behind them on the same route, seeing nothing.

The hearse was escorted by police on motorcycles, black men in uniforms trimmed with white and red, while Jamaican flags fluttered from the cars behind, black, green and gold. The coffin was visible through the glass panels of the hearse, and in the villages old men bared their heads as it went by, and along the open road the cortege passed other people, men, women, and children, dressed for church, walking in the same direction.

The coffin arrived at Stone Haven in the late morning. It was lifted out, and placed on carpenter's trestles in the cool of the garage.

Asnith came in to Stanley, who was sitting in the living room, reading his Bible.

'Gustus is here, busha.'

'Yes?'

'Dey wants to know, de people dem, if dey can look 'pon Mass John, sir.'

'Yes. Tell Gustus I put him in charge,' said Stanley. 'Tell him one at a time, hear?'

In the hot noontime they drifted into the yard, in twos and threes, moving slowly, standing about and, under Gustus' eye, going in, and looking down. Some said nothing, some clapped their hands and cried, some prayed.

After a while, Stanley came out on the back verandah with Paul, and stood watching. Those who saw him stared, or touched their forehead, or muttered some condolence.

'Is the grave dug?' Paul asked.

'Yes,' Stanley said, 'at Seaside. I'm putting him next to Montclair Hoffman. Montclair was my friend, and the first black headmaster of Happy Grove. John is the first Minister of an independent Jamaica to die in office. The ground is stony,' he added, typically, 'but well drained.'

Miriam, in the last weeks of her pregnancy, waddled into her mother's bedroom to help Grace get ready for the church. She found her sitting at the dressing table, a black dress covering the back brace and her grey hair unfastened about her shoulders, the brush lying in her open hand.

'Let me do that, Mamma.'

Grace let her take the brush, and watched in the mirror as Miriam applied it with smooth gentle strokes.

'I don't know how I'll make the church,' Grace said.

'You can stay here. Watch from the window.'

'I brought him into the world, and I shall see him go out. But if I try to climb the steps and stumble, I may fall, or cry out. I don't want to be a burden, but tell Stanley to send for two strong men to carry my chair.'

'Yes.'

'Have you seen Mavis?'

'I heard her in the kitchen. She's arranging about the food and drink.'

'We want to make sure there's sufficient. They'll all be coming back here to Stone Haven. There's nowhere else for them to go. I'll do the pins, Miriam.'

Miriam watched her mother's swift, skilful motion, coiling her hair at the back of her head with the left hand and pinning it with her right, but she noticed that her mother winced slightly as she raised her arms.

'I think I'll get this cut, next time I go to Kingston, get a more modern style. What do you think?'

The grave was near the side entrance to the church, which the children had used when they went to Sunday School. It was away from the choir, and the pulpit, and handy for arriving late, or leaving early. This time the family had to run the gauntlet of the main aisle and sit in the front pew, where Grace had already been installed, facing the coffin, the lectern, the platform, and the stained glass window of Christ knocking at the door. The coffin was open, and stood between two vases of white calla lilies which had arrived from the Rio Grande valley.

Paul approached the coffin tentatively. Thoughtfully, Miriam had told him this was not compulsory, but Paul believed it was better to do things than not to do them, better to regret an experience than to avoid it. He would not see his brother, but his brother's body; he was not sure whether the dead face, product of the undertaker's art, would affect his memory of the living one.

John looked so much smaller. The face, framed in the satin lining, was pale and powdered, his hair beautifully combed, the skin smooth, waxy and unlined, the mouth firmly closed. He looked ten years younger. It was John, made into a doll, but John nonetheless.

Paul went back to his seat at the far end of the front pew, and watched the rest of the family file past the coffin. Grace did not go, but William did, and Miriam, disapproving, and Stanley, protected by solemnity, and last of all, Mavis. Mavis wore full mourning dress, black hat and veil. She waited until the others were all seated to pay her last homage, to exercise her rights as the widow, the only one standing in the still church. She looked down at John's face, briefly, and slammed the coffin lid as one slams the door in the face of an intruder.

The noise echoed through the church like a gunshot. Paul caught his breath. Mavis might not have known, he thought, how heavy the lid was for she had made no attempt to lower it gently; it might have been an expression of her impetuous temperament, or the violence of her grief. It might have been something else. As she sat down, Paul looked at Stanley, whose face was set in stone.

Paul could not concentrate on the prayers, or hymns, or on the preacher's eulogy, but half turned instead to look at the congregation. Behind him were the local people, cousins, aunts and uncles, friends, overseers, bookkeepers, clerks, shopkeepers, planters and professional men, row after row of black and brown, with the odd white face of an expatriate or a missionary, the men stifling in suits, the women with too much make-up. He had been too long off the island, for most of them he did not know. Leaning slightly forward he could see, across the aisle from Mavis, the Prime Minister, in a grey suit, enormous, leonine, his craggy face topped by a huge mane of white hair. The great man obscured his Cabinet, but behind him were judges, consuls, permanent secretaries, row after row of people representing things and institutions. Did they all know John, Paul thought, or were they there only to impress each other, to remind each other they were all part of a community, one small and struggling nation that had lost a son, so come to honour him in his mother's church?

'Abide with me' was being sung, and it was time to carry the coffin to the grave. The Minister of Finance and the Minister of Agriculture were the first pallbearers, then Carlton of the RAF and Mr Mullins, the overseer at Darlingford, and finally cousin William and Paul.

Mavis walked behind, then Stanley, led by Miriam making sure the old man saw the steps. Grace waited in the emptying church.

As they came out into the sunshine, Paul saw a sea of automobiles filling all the space between the church and the school, and was dimly aware of policemen keeping back those who could not get into the church. The coffin was heavy, and he was glad when they had covered the short distance describing the semicircle that brought them to the eastern slope and the freshly-dug grave. With the discreet help of the undertaker's assistants, their burden was placed in position on the tapes, and the widow's wreath on top of it.

Paul stepped back and looked around. It was a brilliant, sunny day. The afternoon breeze was coming in off the sea, the afternoon clouds drifting toward the mountains. The preacher took his place at the head of the grave, and the wind blew away a leaf of his worn Bible. The congregation that had been in the church stood silently in the churchyard, many of them clustered round the grave, but they were not all for, Paul realized, the whole hillside beyond and below the graveyard was solid with mourners, men in black suits, women in white.

The crowd extended from the graveside all the way to the Mission Home, down to the elementary school, and as far as the road and the cliffs overhanging the sea. They were all looking up toward the group around the interment in the shadow of the church. The preacher began to pray, but his voice was lost in another sound, like the sound of the sea itself. Someone, way down the hill, had started to sing, and it had been picked up by the vast semicircle of the crowd, the deep voices of the men and the high female descant, blending and rising in volume. They were singing,

'... He's the lily of the valley,
He's our bright and morning star ...'
and their voices soared and sank with the melody, drowning the graveside prayers, lifting the spirits of them all, releasing all their tears and all their joy in him. The unknowns who were not in the church laid claim to John, and sang him to his sleep.

Alone, in the empty church, Grace wept.

*

Stanley had circulated in the churchyard, both before and after, issuing invitations to Stone Haven after the interment, varying the phrase to suit the hearer. To some 'to take some refreshment', to others 'for a cup of tea' or 'a bite to eat' and to a few 'Come and wash down the grave dust.'

Tea was laid out in the sun parlour, and there was a cold buffet in the dining room of ham, chicken, roast beef and salads. Frank ran the bar on the side verandah, assisted by Tumpy, who sat on an upturned box solemnly chipping pieces off a hundred-pound block of ice insulated in sawdust, and sipping occasionally from his own lukewarm glass of rum.

Grace had retired to her room, but Stanley, attended by Miriam, held court in the drawing room, for everyone had to see and offer condolences to Mass Stanley, so tragically bereaved.

'Please accept . . .'

'Busha, this is my wife, Rose . . .'

'Some consolation . . .'

'We feel for you, sir, we feel for you . . .'

'He made a contribution . . .'

'. . . can be proud . . .'

'. . . sadly missed . . .'

'. . . we have few such, few such . . .'

Stanley nodded gravely to all of them, and seemed to remember most. He had always loved ceremony, and rose to this occasion with dignity, thanking them all, accepting consolation. The Prime Minister, going early, came to say goodbye, looming over Stanley, and even further over Miriam. He squeezed the old man's shoulder.

'Stanley, my boy, God bless. It's not natural, eh? The boy should have buried us. Never mind. We must carry on. When donkey dead, Quashie mus' walk.'

With darkness falling, the tea-drinkers departed, but the bar was still busy. The party spread out onto the front verandah and the lawn, and broke up into smaller groups. Voices grew louder, and the conversation changed, for the language of grief is limited. The mourners turned with relief to births, marriages, contracts, sport, the making and losing of money, and political intrigue.

The Minister of Agriculture, several sheets in the wind, accosted Paul on the way to the bar.

'You young Paul? The brother? I want you to know, I want to tell you to your face, because I know what some people are saying, I had nothing to do with it, as God is my witness.'

The Minister was a big man, with a Clark Gable moustache and very white teeth. His lip quivered, and there were tears in his eyes.

'I believe that, sir,' Paul said. 'I believe it.'

By this time, Frank had given up serving, and contented himself with opening bottles while the mourners helped themselves. Tumpy was running short of ice. Miriam had persuaded Stanley to sit down out of the way, and was getting him some refreshment when Paul spotted her and put an arm around her.

'Miriam, tell me something. I saw you looking in the coffin in a most disapproving way. What was wrong?'

'What I saw was a disgrace.'

'What?'

'The undertaker put lipstick on the man.'

'How do you know?'

'I could see it.'

'Miriam, that's his job. He has to make the body look presentable.'

Miriam was not assuaged. 'I think it's a disgrace. By the way, Daddy wants to see you.'

Paul made his way through the drinkers to where his father sat in the sun parlour. The old man was saying goodbye to the Chairman of the Banana Board and his wife. Paul waited. Stanley saw him, called him over, and introduced him to the departing guests. 'This is my youngest, who came out from England for the funeral.'

Paul shook hands, greeting and saying goodbye, all in one.

'Sit down, boy,' Stanley said. 'I want to talk to you.'

'You should be in bed,' Paul replied. 'We can talk tomorrow.'

'I don't have too many tomorrows. It's time you came home for good.'

'One of these days.'

'Soon. You can have the Darlingford House.'

'What about Mavis? Doesn't it belong to the widow?'

'It belongs to the property, and she doesn't want to live there anyway.'

'John not cold yet, and you putting me in his bedroom.'

'You can have it repainted, and so on.'

'I won't give up being a vet.'

'There's no need. You can run Darlingford and practise your vet business at the same time.'

'I'll think about it, Daddy. I'm doing quite well over there.'

'That's what worries me. You might like it, and want to stay. Besides, if you were a failure, I wouldn't want you.'

'What about William? He's my senior, and should know more about it than I do.'

'William is not up to it,' Stanley said, flatly, in a tone that allowed for no discussion.

Paul saw William then, watching them. Avoiding him, he went out onto the verandah. He put one foot up on the concrete bench rail, drink in hand, looking at the people on the lawn, and across the little valley at the dark silhouette of the church.

'This country is a cross between a madhouse and a graveyard,' he thought, 'and I want no part of it. No part of it. John crow roasting plantain for you . . . waiting to make you his rotten feast. But unfortunately, all this is part of me. England is nothing, a frivolity, a place to chase women and to gain experience, just somewhere else. But this has always been my place, from the beginning, from when I was a little boy playing in the yard, mouthing silent orders to imaginary labourers, imitating my father. I wanted to be here all along, but while John lived there was no place for me. Daddy won't last much longer. He'll die too, and leave me his kingdom, or his prison . . .'

Before Paul could develop this line of thought, embellish the soliloquy, the Minister of Agriculture came out of the drawing room, crossed the verandah, and started down the steps. On the third step, he slipped, turned sideways, one leg buckling under him, tried to recover, staggered again down two more steps and fell, mercifully, on the grass. His glass was still firmly clutched in his right hand. He was quickly surrounded, and helped to his feet, as if nothing had happened.

'I think it's time,' Stanley said to Paul, 'to close the bar.'

Chapter Twenty-five

It was agreed that Paul should serve out his contract with the veterinary firm. This suited Stanley because the estates could stagger along for another year and, rather more than a field manager, he wanted a chauffeur-companion for his annual trip to England, which this year was something special. Stanley's interest in education and in the Anglican synod had finally been brought to the attention of the Palace.

Even so, the irrepressible old man was oddly silent on the drive from Southampton to London.

'You haven't told me.'

'About what?'

'Miriam's baby.'

'Oh yes. It's a boy. Seems healthy enough.'

'Is she working?'

'No. She wanted to look after it herself, and she couldn't breast-feed it on television. You know what Miriam is like. We persuaded her to come back to Stone Haven for a while. She's in her old room, the pots and pans room, and Mrs Parkyn brought back the crib, your crib, John's crib.'

'Where's the father?'

'McNab? He's in Japan.'

'They like reggae in Japan?'

'Hopefully,' said Stanley. 'With any luck he'll stay there.' And then he added, 'It's a nice little boy.'

They lapsed into silence as the car, a new one, proceeded slowly through the wet green countryside toward the wet grey city.

Stanley was gazing out of the window, fidgeting, seeing nothing.

'There's something I have to tell you, I'm afraid. It's about your mother.'

'You said she was the same.'

'Not exactly. Well, we're not sure. I've never been satisfied with this chiropractor business. Mamma seemed to think if it hurt it was doing her good. She wasn't making any improvement. Sometimes, it seemed to me, it was making it worse. You know how stubborn she is. I finally persuaded her to have another examination. I got Dr Stockhausen to look at her. He is of the opinion ... it might be cancer. Anyway, I've arranged for her to go to New York, to Columbia ... they are supposed to be the best.'

'When?'

'In about four weeks' time. I'm going over to be with her.'

'After the Investiture?' There was the merest hint of criticism in Paul's question.

'The earliest it could be arranged,' Stanley replied firmly.

The bad news accounted for Stanley's abstraction when they were alone, but it made no difference to his public persona. He was in vintage form when they went to Lord's for the second Test against the West Indies. The place was jammed with vociferous blacks, scenting revenge for centuries of slavery, and apprehensive whites fearing the same thing. A steel band played at the nursery end, and with Worrell at the wicket, Father Time himself was dancing a calypso. They could not find a seat, and Stanley, disdaining the clamour of his countrymen, decided to negotiate for the Members' Pavilion.

'You can't get in,' said Paul. 'You just can't do it.'

'No harm in trying,' Stanley said mildly.

They went round to the porticoed pavilion entrance, and started up the steps only to find their way blocked by a large man in a suit with an official badge.

'Sorry, sir. Can't come in here without a pass.'

'I'm Stanley Newton, from Jamaica.'

The doorman was not quite sure what difference that made, but he was not employed to be rude, only to keep people out. He hesitated, contemplating this confident little man in a brown suit and a crumpled raincoat, his binoculars over his shoulder. The young man with him, in grey bags and university blazer, looked quite respectable. They were clearly not hooligans or limbo dancers, but just as clearly not members of the MCC.

'Is Mr Griffiths here?' asked Stanley. 'I've come to see him. You can tell him I'm here.'

Griffiths was the Secretary of the MCC and the mention of his name offered the doorman an escape route. He wouldn't have to send the little man away. Mr Griffiths could do it.

'What did you say the name was, sir?'

'Newton. Stanley Newton from Jamaica.'

Paul was pretending to be invisible. He dreaded the impending humiliation and hated his father for courting it. Even more, he hated the possibility that Stanley might succeed, and prove him wrong. He had seen the old man do it before, borrow a seat on the Centre Court from the President of the All-England Club, and one memorable day at the Royal Agricultural Show, he had watched him duck under the velvet ropes and go into the stand by way of the red carpet laid out for the Queen, that being the easiest and quickest way in. Waiting for Griffiths, Stanley had engaged the doorman in conversation, found out how long he had been at Lord's, where he lived, and how many children he had, and was explaining to him why one had to cut down the whole tree to reap a bunch of bananas when Griffiths arrived.

The doorman introduced his new friend, 'This is Mr Newton from Jamaica, sir.'

Griffiths wasn't sure whether he recognized the little man either, and the young one was absorbed in a study of the score card.

'How nice to see you,' Stanley said, shaking hands. 'We met at Sabina Park, and you told me to look you up. This is my son Paul. He's a veterinary surgeon.'

'You chose the right day,' Griffiths said, not without irony. 'Come in, come in. I expect you'd like to have a look around.'

Twenty minutes later, they were seated among the members, right behind the bowler's arm, and close to the wicket gate through which the warriors take the field. Stanley's eyes were not what they used to be when he played the game himself, so as the day wore on he relied more and more on a running commentary from Paul. After lunch, like most of the members, he slept, stirring slightly when Worrell reached his century, and rising to clap him into the pavilion when the great man was finally out.

At the tea interval, he told the doorman he'd be back, and set off for a stroll around the back of the pavilion to stretch his legs. Paul was dispatched for paper cups of tea, and on his return found Stanley in animated conversation with someone else. This was Hurst, lawyer and fellow-member of the Kingston Cricket Club, who was staying with relatives and following the cricket. Hurst was almost bald, which made his nose seem longer, and he carried a little belly below the waistband. He was wearing his Cambridge blazer and his Kingston CC tie. They sipped tea and marvelled at the delicacy of Worrell's stroke play, agreeing that no one had played the late cut better since Ranjitsinghi. Stanley invited Hurst to lunch.

'... at the Grosvenor, one o'clock, next Tuesday.'

'I think I could make it,' Hurst said doubtfully, 'I'll check with my wife.'

'Bring her along. It's a small celebration. I'm going to the Palace in the morning for the Investiture.'

'Your OBE! God damn it, Newton, I forgot all about it!'

'Yes, that's it. I'm having a little lunch, in a private room, I've asked the High Commissioner, and the manager of Barclays Bank.'

'You don't want us, man.'

'Yes, I do,' Stanley said, 'I want an old friend.'

'We shall definitely be there, Newton, definitely. One o'clock, Tuesday.'

On their way back into the pavilion, the doorman greeted Stanley by name, and the members seated around nodded amicably and hoped he was enjoying the match. He was, said Stanley, and Paul, paralysed, waited for the invitation to Stone Haven, and the bit about cutting bananas, but they never came.

With the score at 317 for 4 and half an hour to stumps, Stanley, who had been fidgeting again, excused himself, stepping carefully over the members' feet, and hurried up the steps toward the interior. Paul saw him in brief conversation with a man at the door, and then he disappeared inside. A couple of overs later, looking round, he saw his father at the top of the aisle, gesticulating, a sort of semaphore which Paul interpreted to mean that he wasn't coming back, and he wanted to drive somewhere. His raincoat, which usually hung open, was buttoned over his paunch. Paul, in his turn, climbed over the members' feet.

'I thought we'd leave early and avoid the crush. Do you remember where you left the car?'

'I hope so.'

Paul made him wait by the main gate, and drove back ten minutes later to find him forlorn among the newspaper vendors, peering anxiously for the car like a lost schoolboy. He was silent all the way to the hotel, and then asked Paul to come up to his room. There the reason for the buttoned raincoat became apparent. His trousers were wet from crotch to knee. This simple fact did not distress Paul as much as his father's embarrassment. 'I'm having a little trouble going to the bathroom.'

'So I see.'

'What do you think I should do?'

'How long have you had this trouble?'

'Some time now. It's worse over here.'

'It's the cold weather,' said Paul, taking charge. 'We'll have to get this suit cleaned, for a start, and we don't want you wetting up the Queen's carpet.'

Gwendolyn, Paul's latest, knew a doctor, pill-pusher to the stars, who, she promised, as she popped briskly into bed, was the best diagnostician in England. She phoned him there and then, for his speciality was being available, and he arranged to see the gentleman from Jamaica in the morning, in Harley Street. Stanley, he advised, must have a prostatectomy, as soon as convenient, and for the Investiture, if only to ensure his peace of mind, a bag strapped to his leg. They were as common as handkerchiefs in the House of Lords, he assured Stanley.

Paul took his father shopping, to an emporium conveniently close to the street of doctors, where trusses and catheters, bandages and crutches were displayed in the window like nightgowns and lingerie. There, a white-haired gentleman with the manners of an undertaker selected a bag for Stanley, and instructed him in its use.

And so it came to pass, that wearing what he called his 'contraption' hidden under his striped trousers, and a morning coat hired from Moss Bros, the son of the randy Reverend Newton of Manchioneal went to the palace to see the Queen.

*

This then was the summit of his achievement, the medal in its little box lying on the satin bedspread in his room. He was reminded of the medal he had won for recitation at the Titchfeld School in Port Antonio, forty-five years before. He had given it to his mother, and she had been very proud.

Things become important by the way they are celebrated. He had a limousine to take Paul and himself to the Palace, and he had taken a private banqueting room for lunch, a room painted in French grey and cream, with velvet curtains, tasselled and pleated, and tall windows overlooking the park. The tablecloth was damask, and gladioli stood in vases against the walls. He was at the head of the table, watching his guests sip champagne while they joked, the accents of the Jamaican contingent self-consciously broad in that atmosphere.

'Well, Mass Stanley, what you an de Queen have to talk about for so long?'

'That's between me and Her Majesty.'

'No, sir, you can' keep dat secret. Paul tol' me she talk to you longer than anybody else.'

'Daddy was doing all the talking. The poor Queen could only listen.'

'Did you tell her how many tons of cane to a ton of sugar?'

'Lawyer, lawyer, as I was coming out, I heard this Englishman behind me, very posh. "Can't understand it, dear boy," he says. "She always talks longer to the tinted people".'

'Button-holed the poor woman.'

'The Queen asked me if I had come over especially, and I said no, I came every summer, but I couldn't stay too long or I'd have to pay English income tax, and she laughed and said that was one problem she didn't have.'

The prawn cocktails were consumed, and silent English waiters bore away the empty goblets.

This then was success, and it would cost a bit. He had disdained the roast beef as being merely a Sunday dinner, and ordered a whole saddle of lamb, something you couldn't get in Hector's River. He wanted the others to enjoy themselves, and to remember it. Paul, who seemed to be becoming an expert in these matters, had chosen the wine and brought along a girlfriend whose name he couldn't remember, but she was a stunning little thing, and she treated him, Stanley, with such easy affection and respect. A nice girl, with good manners. Paul seemed to have a way with women, which wasn't always a good thing. Look at poor Errol Flynn, everybody suing him for his money. Nice girl as she was, whatever her name was, he was glad Paul wasn't planning to marry her. She didn't look the type to settle in Manchioneal. Not like Grace . . .

The High Commissioner, a tall black man who had been a famous athlete, and been at school with John, was doing his duty by the bank manager, discussing their mutual interest, contract bridge. Hurst was talking to Paul. It had been a good idea to invite him, even though his wife was a scarecrow with dyed hair and much too thin. Paul had placed her on his right though she was the only person he didn't want to talk to, which suited because, for once, he did not want to talk. Looking at Hurst, Stanley remembered him when young, and remembered going to see him to ask for help in establishing his inheritance, in legitimizing himself, as if, after Jesus, any child born of woman could ever be called illegitimate. He had seen little of Hurst over the years, except at the cricket, but to have him there was, what was the word, poetic, and he knew that Hurst also remembered.

He watched the waiter carving the saddle with great interest. He himself loved to carve, and this chap knew what he was doing. You had to know the anatomy of the animal, move swiftly without haste, and own a sharp knife.

The Queen had liked the joke about the income tax. Really rich people liked jokes about money, and she was really rich.

'Hurst,' he said, 'have you heard the one about John D. Rockefeller giving the doorman a dime. The doorman complained, "Mr Rockefeller," he said, "your son always gives me a dollar," to which John D. replied, "He's got a rich father".'

Everybody laughed, and Gwendolyn clapped her hands. The waiters were handing round the lamb, and serving the redcurrant jelly, parsley potatoes and peas. Stanley, having shown he was enjoying himself, and contributed his joke, returned to his musings. He should have told the Queen that one as well. What lovely skin she had; it must run in the family. Considering how many people she saw every day, how had she managed to convince him that she was genuinely interested in him? They all wanted to know what he had said to her, and he had told them something, but not all of it. Some things weren't for telling.

'Four years ago, ma'am, you gave my wife the MBE.'
'Is she here? Did she come with you?'
'No, ma'am. She's not so well.'
'I'm sorry to hear that. Please give her my best wishes.'

Grace should have been at the Palace, where Paul had been, on one of those little gilt chairs with the red seats. Even though she hated travelling abroad, and hadn't come for her own medal, she'd have come for his, and be sitting in the empty place at the end of the table. At Stone Haven, she would be in bed now, because of the time difference. The morning breeze wouldn't have started yet, and the quickstick trees outside the window would be still, and the church tower clear against the background of the sea. He hoped she was not in pain. Paul was asking him what he was thinking about, and persuading him to a glass of burgundy, which he accepted. If he couldn't have one today, when could he? The irony was that if he had been a drinker he would not be there. Harold was in his grave. He imagined Harold's flesh, like his own, rotting and melting away, leaving dried wisps along the bone to moulder into dust.

Paul was saying he should be smiling, so he smiled, but continued with his thoughts. He had run a good race, played a good innings, whatever silly way you wanted to say it, but it was ending. The contraption strapped to his leg under the table told him it was coming to an end.

He'd given his children a good start, the best he could. Poor John. God must have been short of faithful servants to call him so soon. Miriam could have done better, but who knows. The girl has courage, and that's worth more than luck. With the Rasta man gone, she might do better, and his grandson was a fine little fellow. Paul, laughing with the blonde girl, seemed to have discovered the secret of life; he enjoyed himself so easily. He hoped the boy would be tough enough. John hadn't been tough and, like Harold, he had been a drinker; and like Harold, he hadn't married well, but he had cared about the people. Oh Absalom, my son, my son. Life wasn't easy, and he supposed he should be thankful to have done as well himself, and reached this peak, the summit of his achievement.

What was it, and why had he been honoured? Not for giving a library to the school, or making money himself, and surely not for paying so much interest to Barclay's Bank, Dominion, Colonial and

Overseas. Perhaps he was being honoured for marrying Grace, for siring children, but that was nothing special, and they were just people, talented and flawed, happy and unhappy people, nothing special.

He decided honour was being paid not to him, but to his neighbours, to all those who lived on that green and breezy end of Jamaica, where the trade winds daily left their burden of rain to climb the heights of the Blue Mountains, to all those who lived in that small corner of the world, unheard of and uncared for, except by each other. The community of which he was the head was being honoured, as the man who lived in the big yard, who gave the jobs and directed the enterprise of carpenter, cane cutter and washerwoman. They were being honoured for simply making a community, unique and similar, made out of loyalties and responsibilities, honoured by the head of a greater community, made also out of loyalties and responsibilities, owing its final allegiance to Almighty God.

Suddenly, he remembered Frank, saw him clearly, as he always saw him, the back of his head against the windscreen, and the Jamaican roads swinging from side to side. He made a mental note to give his gold watch to Frank.

'Your mother is a remarkable woman.'

Paul said nothing. This he already knew. He was there to find out what was wrong, what had been done, and what remained to be done. The eminent surgeon smiled; he was a mild-looking, professorial man of about fifty, with thinning sandy hair and rimless glasses.

'A remarkable woman.'

A large brown envelope full of X-ray photographs lay on the desk in front of him. He selected one of these, fitted it into a viewer, talking as he did so, and switched it on. Grace's backbone, against a black background, became sharply visible.

'When I showed this to my students, I asked them whether this person was alive or dead. The verdict of the class was that she was dead.'

Paul sat very still. There was a faint feeling of nausea in his stomach, and his palms were clammy. The eminent surgeon's pale blue eyes were watching him, so he nodded, meaninglessly. The man went on.

'See. See how the vertebrae have collapsed and fused? The cancer has destroyed the bone and left the spinal cord unprotected. Here. And here.'

Paul nodded again.

'She was being manipulated by a chiropractor? This is unbelievable. The pain must have been intolerable. I would not expect anyone to endure the pain she has endured. It was necessary to operate in order to relieve the pressure on the spinal cord . . .' He paused, contemplating Paul as he would his class of medical students, '. . . Are you particularly squeamish, young man?'

'No, sir.'

'I realize I'm talking about your mother, and it's hard to take, but I think you want to understand, don't you?'

'Yes.'

'Ah.' The eminent surgeon resumed his professional manner. 'When I made the first incision, here, the pressure was so intense that the blood hit the ceiling of the operating theatre . . .'

With that image before his eyes, Paul was still able to realize that the man was truly impressed. He was not enjoying telling the gory detail; he was excited by having in his care someone who was making medical history, and whose ability to bear pain was apparently unlimited.

'. . . she has lost a lot of blood, and our problem now is healing. Her blood will no longer clot.' A thought struck him, and he changed the subject. 'I gather you are the only member of the family here?'

'My father is in the main hospital.'

'Is he? As a patient?'

'Yes,' Paul said, and reading the surgeon's mind went on. 'He thought as this whole business was already costing so much money, he'd have his own operation at the same time instead of staying in a hotel.'

The surgeon smiled, relieved; he could see he was dealing with a businessman.

'A prostatectomy,' Paul explained.

'Well, that's no problem – should come out like a peanut from a shell. Now, as for your mother. I'm using a new drug, I won't say it's an experiment for it's been highly tested, but I will say it's her only chance. It may assist coagulation, giving a chance of healing, and therefore a chance to live. If she lives, and I repeat it is a big if, I have to warn you that the backbone is too far gone, it cannot be repaired, and if she survives, she will be paralysed.'

Paul took a deep breath. 'Why don't you let her die?'

The surgeon sat down and pressed his fingertips together, nodding in appreciation of the question, and the boldness of the questioner.

'That is possible. We could just make her comfortable and let her go. If she were other than she is, that is what I might do, but your mother is very special. In the conversations I have had with her, I have encountered a woman of rare intelligence and spirit, and humour. While that spirit lives, I must do everything I can to keep her alive.'

'Will she be out of pain?'

'I can't promise that she will be out of pain. No. But I want your support, and I will presume you are speaking for your father.'

'You must do what you think best.'

The eminent surgeon smiled, rose, and came round the desk to shake Paul by the hand and show him out.

'Can I see her now?'

'I think she's back in her room, but she'll be sleeping. Tomorrow will be better.'

Paul took the elevator down to the ground floor and walked across the lobby toward the revolving doors to the street. Then he changed his mind, retraced his steps, re-entered the elevator and pressed the button for the seventh floor. His street shoes sounded loudly in the corridor; he passed a patient in slippers, and a cleaning woman pushing a trolley with rubber wheels. He found his mother's room, and pushed the door open. The nurse at her bedside, taking her pulse, looked up in alarm.

'You can't come in now, sir, please.'

Paul raised a hand to indicate that he would be no trouble, and whispered, 'That's okay.'

Grace's eyes were closed, her white hair on the pillow, her body under a white sheet. The splash of dark red in the transfusion bottle was the only colour to be seen, and from it the red tube connected to her arm. She was breathing. Paul nodded to the nurse, and went out.

At the end of the corridor, as on every floor, there was a little lounge with a coffee machine, magazines and five or six chairs, a place for visitors and family conferences. Paul made himself a cup of coffee, and sat down to think.

It would be better if she died, but that man would not let her go. He had admitted she would spend the rest of her life in paralysis and pain, with no hope of recovery, but he still would not let her go. There were people queueing up for places in the hospital, so he wasn't doing it for money, not in that sense, but Paul was certain that if his mother had been an old woman in the slums of Kingston with a handful of coppers knotted in her kerchief, there would have been no talk of spirit. Before humanity became a consideration there had to be money, or at least insurance. His mother was making medical history and, if she survived, the surgeon could go on showing that X-ray to the interns and asking them whether the woman were alive or dead. It could become his party piece. Statistically, if she survived a fortnight, his operation had been a success. If she survived six months, she might go into the records as cured. The coagulant agent would be adopted nation-wide.

It was easy to criticize the eminent surgeon, but, after all, the man was doing his best, and what would he, Paul, do in his place? He wished for his mother's death, as he himself might one day wish to die, but would he kill himself, or her? Would he, as the euphemism went, let her go? If he could not, neither could the doctor. They were both caught in a great irony, that all the money made to buy security, all the comforts of the hospital, all the technology of the operating theatre and the skill of the surgeon, all the research and the marvellous new drugs, all the tender-loving care of the nurses, all these things intended to foster and to cure, were in this instance instruments for the prolongation of pain.

There was a tunnel connecting the annexe where his mother was to the main building of the Columbia University Hospital where his father was. Paul avoided it, preferring the windblown litter and the noise and fumes of the street to the safe, fluorescent, air-circulated gloom of the tunnel. He needed, in between dying parents, to have a glimpse of life, such as it was, of Cadillacs flexing their knees over the bumps, and neon signs doing spelling bees, pointing out bars and bargains and the long view of the wide river and the George Washington Bridge.

His father was asleep. His operation had been a success and he was comfortable. It would be better to come back tomorrow. Paul looked briefly in at him peaceful on the pillow. He decided that not even his father's Machiavellian mind could have devised the scheme for simultaneous operations, thereby saving himself, anaesthetized, cocooned, the anxiety, the waiting, the consultation with the doctor he, Paul, had just been through, and hearing, as he had just heard, that Grace's life depended still on the efficiency of a drug with a name he had already forgotten.

Yet Stanley may have been imperfectly cocooned, or there had been a miscalculation by the anaesthetist, for when Paul came to see him on the following day his father, though tossing and turning, was still asleep. In the night, he had managed to pull the drip out of his arm, wrench the catheter out of his penis, and damage the sutures which had closed the incision over his bladder, all this while struggling unconscious with his private devils. He now had to be watched constantly, and sedated for his own protection. What might have been a swift recuperation was indefinitely extended as, at his age, the half-open incision would be slow to heal.

Paul offered to sit with his father for a while and the nurse accepted eagerly, instructing him to make sure the old man did no more damage to himself or the hospital's equipment, and showed him the button to press if he needed help. Paul pulled the straight chair up to the head of the bed, and sat down to watch over his father. The tubes running in and out of him made Stanley look like part of a Rube Goldberg invention, an artificial man. Nearly seventy, his short, black hair was as thick as ever, only occasionally laced with grey. There was more grey in his beard, and he needed a shave. He had a prominent mole just outside the smile wrinkle on his right cheek. His nose was broad and rounded. Closed eyes emphasized the strength of his mouth and chin, determined even in repose.

Sometimes he muttered words Paul could not catch, and moved restlessly. As a precaution, he held his father's hand, the palm so much lighter than the weathered, wrinkled skin on top. The nails were professionally manicured, as always. The grip on Paul's hand strengthened as Stanley entered another nightmare. Words, disjointed, names and sighs and sudden exclamations of terror were punctuated by breathing silences. Paul was witness to a dreaming he could not see. He thought he knew his father's life, but people and landscapes, bits of conversation came tumbling out which he could neither place nor understand. He felt his father falling, recoiling from some terror, striking weakly at an adversary who did not budge. More mundanely, he laughed at jokes, quoted a sum of money, said good morning to someone passing by, and called a mule by name. With complete conviction he expressed concern, shook his head sadly, clicked his tongue at tragedy and cried, 'Shame, shame'.

Suddenly he was heading down a mountain side, bracing himself.

'You're dashing along. Slow down, slow down,' he said, terrified.

'It's all right, Daddy, it's all right,' Paul said, soothing him.

His father looked at him, bleary and unseeing.

'Who's that?'

'It's me, Paul. I'm sitting beside you.'

'If you're sitting beside me, who's driving the car?'

His mother recovered first. She still needed blood, but she was able to take some nourishment by mouth. The use of a bedpan was a major achievement. It took some time, and required two nurses, and during it Paul was banished to the coffee machine. A young intern came regularly to change the dressings on her back. Paul accused his mother of flirting with him, at which she blushed, for she would not even let the young doctor in unless her hair was brushed, and she had, with the nurse's help, applied the merest hint of rouging on her cheek. She lay on a sheet of Saran wrap, because her skin was so worn by lying down she would have stuck to the sheet. A television set was brought in, mounted high on the wall, so she could watch it from her pillow. Religious programmes she watched without expression, though her right hand would keep the beat for the hymn singing. She shook her head sadly at the news, and she smiled at 'Amos and Andy'. She loved 'Amos and Andy', and Paul, watching her, reflected ruefully that for this his mother's life had been saved, so that she could be paralysed and watch 'Amos and Andy'.

Esther Simms came to visit. She wore a dark grey suit, sensible shoes, and a scarf. Her hair was blue rinsed, her teeth whistled slightly, and her skin was untouched by the sun, but she could walk and that was a victory over the helpless woman in the bed whose friendship she had betrayed, whose husband she had taken, though not for long. It was not mentioned; it no longer mattered. The treasons of the body are meaningless, in time. They were still friends; they shared the work they had done together in the mission field, the school, people they knew. How is Wilbur Smith, and do you know what happened to Martha Miller? Paul Khadurian? He has a hardware store in Plainfield. Are you keeping well? God in his mercy. This is my youngest. I remember you.

Esther was surprised to hear that Stanley too was ill, and in the same hospital. Mercy me. She had a train to catch, and could not visit him. You would give him her regards.

'She's still a pain,' Grace said to Paul after she had left, 'once an old maid, always an old maid.'

The time came when Stanley was well enough to visit. He shaved, put on his cream pyjamas, his paisley dressing gown and the slippers he had bought in Regent Street. He sat in a wheelchair with his bottle attached. Paul pushed him along the corridor to the elevator, which took them to the basement, and through the block-long tunnel to the annexe, passing other wheelchairs and men in white with stethoscopes around their necks. Another elevator conveyed them to the seventh floor, where Paul pushed again along another corridor to his mother's room.

They had chosen a time when Grace would be at her best. The nurse had helped her into a bedjacket, and arranged her hair.

'Well, Stanley, look at you!' she said in a firm voice as the wheelchair came in.

'Darling, how are you feeling?'

'As well as can be expected,' she said.

A kiss was not possible, but Paul manouevred the wheelchair so Stanley was on her right, the drip being on her left, and Stanley took her hand, and held it.

'You've had a bad time too.'

'I don't remember much of it.'

'We are a pair.'

He squeezed her hand.

'Dear Stanley,' she said.
'My darling Grace.'
In that exchange, a marriage, mourned, celebrated, reaffirmed.

A month later, the operation was officially a success. She was healed; she could move her head and her right arm. She was put on a stretcher and taken out of her room. Paul travelled with her in a smooth-riding ambulance as far as Idlewild. The ambulance was allowed on the runway and drove right up to the plane, where the stretcher was placed on a fork-lift and offered up to the door. The cabin crew installed her in a cubicle curtained off from the other passengers for the six-hour flight to Kingston. There, strong men carried her down the gangway, tilting dangerously, and placed the stretcher in the rattling oven of a Jamaican ambulance for the twisting, bumpy ride to Stone Haven. The servants gathered round to watch as she was lifted out and carried into the house, through the library and the dining room, across the hall into her own bedroom. Tenderly, she was taken off the stretcher and put to bed.

She was sweating and pale. She asked for water and her pills. She was in terrible pain.

Chapter Twenty-six

Asnith was getting older, and quarrelled with everybody. As a result, there was a constant stream of housemaids coming and leaving again before the family were quite sure of their names. Asnith herself was a fixture, because, as Stanley said, she knew how to season. When Grace was brought home to die, Stanley thought the noise of Asnith's quarrels and the instruction of new maids would be too much for her, so he sent for Sunshine.

Sunshine had been Grace's first servant, back in the days when they lived in the old Williamsfield house. She was near sixty now, and had raised a family of her own, four sons and two daughters; two had gone to England, one was a schoolteacher, two had disappeared and no longer sent money, the youngest was still at home. Sunshine agreed to come, for old time's sake, for a short time. She understood, though Stanley did not say so, that she would not need to be at Stone Haven for long. She was still there six months later.

Grace's illness kept Asnith almost too busy to quarrel. She had all the servants to feed, Sunshine, Tumpy, now a grey-haired man with a deep voice and powerful arms and shoulders, Katrina, washing and ironing up by the water tanks, Frank, who always seemed asleep as he had to be waked for his meals or whenever Stanley wanted to go anywhere, and Miss Gertie, mad as ever and too frail to wax the floors, who came, nevertheless, every Friday for a square meal and her pay. After gumming her way through the stew peas and yellow yam, she could be heard praying in the back yard, praying to the God of Abraham and the God of Isaac, praying that Grace should be spared. In the heart of the house Grace herself lay like a sacrifice on the high altar of the fourposter in a stupor induced by pain and morphia.

Asnith also had the nurses to feed. Two of them had moved in, Kingston girls. They shared the nursery, opposite Miriam and the baby in the pots and pans room. Stanley himself had moved into the guest room off the front verandah, for Grace had insisted that his own room was too close to her groaning and he would not sleep. The nurses had to be fed separately, of course, in the house, and then Mass Stanley and whichever of the family happened to be there. Though Asnith complained that there were just too many sets of meals, it made her the most important person at Stone Haven, except for Grace. She never begrudged Grace her trays, a delicate soup, a bit of fish, or a rice pudding, trays which Sunshine carried in and handed to the nurse on duty.

All these meals were made on the old wood-burning Caledonia stove in the outside kitchen connected to the house by a covered way, for Asnith scorned the new gas range in the pantry, believing firmly that the bomb-shaped containers of gas hidden in the croton hedge would one day blow up and destroy them all.

Only Sunshine saw Grace regularly, and reported back to the servants, and thus to the village, where, after six months, people began to feel that Missis Newton, bedridden in the big yard, had always been so, and would always be, for only her death would re-establish, however briefly, the memory of her life.

'She shame to dead,' Asnith declared. 'She not going dead wid so much people here.'

Sunshine disagreed. 'She will dead when she ready. She jus' waitin' for her God to call her.'

Stanley would go into her room in the mornings, and in the middle of the day, and at the day's end, but his visits were brief. He could not bring himself to sit down in the rocking chair with the patchwork cushion reserved for visitors. He would go in to see her, knowing that he should, but being there, he always thought of something else he had to do immediately, in the office, at Holland, or in Port Antonio. He could not bear her suffering, and the rebuke implicit in her look when he made his excuse to go. He had loved her so much, but now he experienced an actual physical revulsion at her still body, her face, still nobly moulded in the bone, but the flesh stretched thin and wrinkled. His revulsion extended to himself, included a sad disgust at his own body, his wrinkled neck, old man's breasts and sagging stomach, the grey in his pubic hair, and his shrunken legs. He and Grace were one flesh, and they were dying together. So he remembered something else he had to do, stayed briefly, asked her how she felt, called her darling, kissed her on the forehead, told her he would be back soon, and left. Day after day.

Apart from the nurses, and Sunshine, Miriam was Grace's most constant companion. The baby, whom Stanley had nicknamed Mighty Mouse, learned to crawl around Grace's sick bed, and was lifted on to the fourposter from time to time to look wide-eyed and wondering at the old person on the pillow, who would smile at him, and say loving words, until, tired, she turned away. The baby's voice, crying after a fall, or thirsty in the night, or laughing when Sunshine jiggled him up and down or Tumpy pulled him on a handcart under the quickstick trees, the baby's voice shattered her death-bed silences and was woven into Grace's dying dreams, recalling John and Miriam and Paul. Once, when the little messenger laughed joyously outside her door, Grace said, 'I heard the baby Jesus.'

*

Grace was brightest in the middle of the morning, and at such a time the new pastor came to pay his respects, a young man from Wichita, Kansas. He had been a ball player at college and wore tennis shoes, cotton trousers, and a sport shirt with short sleeves showing his sunburned forearms. Grace interviewed him, finding out about his family, farmers like her own, his faith, and what had led him to the mission field, and how he thought he might be of service in Jamaica. The young man, though strangely dressed, answered her modestly, and with great courtesy.

'Did you give him the job, Mamma?' Miriam asked, after he left.

Grace was worried, 'You think I was too hard on him?'

'No, Mamma, no, you just kept him in his place.'

'Oh dear. Well, never mind.'

The headmaster of Happy Grove came wearing a jacket and tie. Grace was in pain that day, talking was an effort, but she wanted desperately to talk to him. He was the first headmaster of Happy Grove not to be a Quaker. Eminently qualified in every other way, a Jamaican with a degree in chemistry from Howard University, and a Diploma in Education, he was also, it was rumoured, a supporter of the PNP. Under the new government, he told Grace, the school would be expanded, and incorporated into the state system of grant-aided schools. The days of religious schools privately funded from overseas were over. Jamaicans would educate Jamaicans, and the responsibilities of citizenship would take precedence over the inculcation of religious sectarianism.

'Have we done so badly, Mr Taylor?'

'No, Mrs Newton. You have done so well that our turn has come.'

'Will you refuse assistance from the Yearly Meeting?'

'Oh no,' he smiled. 'We will want to maintain a connection with the church.'

'People who give like to have a say in how the gift is used.'

'Understandable, Mrs Newton, but it must be second to our independence.'

'Will you still teach virtue and the love of God?'

'We will teach – loyalty and the love of country.'

'That's not quite the same thing. I'm sorry, Mr Taylor, I am tired now.'

She turned her head away, leaving the headmaster without an audience. He, glancing at Miriam, realized that he should go. Miriam went as far as the verandah with him.

'I hope I said nothing to upset her.'

Hearing the man express what she thought was her own point of view, Miriam was not so sure. She realized she had more sympathy for her mother than she thought she had.

'As long as two and two will still make four, Mr Taylor, it will be all right.'

One mid-morning, dozing, Grace was awakened by a shrill babbling just outside her window. There was someone in the croton hedges which housed only lizards.

It was Aunt Cynthia, in full tirade. She was announcing that Grace's illness had been improperly diagnosed, that it was a mere weakness which the body itself could counter if it were strengthened. The answer was chicken soup. She, Cynthia, had made her a chicken soup but she was being kept out of the house.

Miriam looked out of the window, down into the face of Cynthia, looking up, brown, moon-faced, with dark, sunken eyes; she had remembered her lipstick but forgotten her teeth. She wore a straw hat and carried a thermos, presumably full of chicken soup, in a basket.

'Who's that? Miriam? Hear me, darling. They stop me on the back verandah, tell me I can't come. Every day I come to see Grace, and they turn me away, turn me away like dawg . . .'

'Miriam, go see if you can calm her down,' Grace said.

Help was already at hand. Sunshine was running around the corner of the house, and Frank, awake, was approaching from the direction of his room behind the laundry.

'Come, Miss Cynthia, come . . . Missis Newton sleeping, and you don't want wake her, mam.'

Sunshine took gentle charge of the basket. 'Gimme the soup, I promise she get it. I will heat it myself and gi' it her.'

'Come, Miss Cynthia, come.'

Aunt Cynthia was led away, protesting that the soup of itself was no good. It must be reinforced by prayer, a prayer to drive out the devils come to take revenge on Grace for all her pride. She, Cynthia, knew these devils by name, and could conjure them.

When Paul came home for good, the doctor told him that he was just in time to see his mother alive; she would be dead within the week. In spite of this prognosis, the sight of her youngest revived Grace, and she lived on, until Paul no longer expected her end and immersed himself in his new life, which was his old life. He was not much concerned with refurbishing John's house, for he was still single. But he wanted to learn everything there was to learn about the property, the names, the fields, the crops, and how to unravel the eccentricities of his father's accounting. He planned to start a dairy and to breed pedigree cattle. He carried on a veterinary practice from the boot of his car. His arrival at Stone Haven varied according to the number of goats, dogs, pigs or cattle waiting by the roadside, but he tried to be there for late afternoon tea to join his father, William, and any others come to pay their latest or their last respects.

In the darkening sick room, Grace moved her head.

'Is that you, Miriam? Call the nurse.'

Miriam, standing by the bedside, took Grace's hand. The eyes looking up at her were dim with anguish.

'I think it's time for my injection.'

Miriam adjusted a strand of hair, and let her hand rest on her mother's shoulder.

'Call the nurse,' Grace repeated.

'I don't think it's quite time yet, Mamma.'

'Miriam, don't be cruel.'

Miriam looked at her, trying to empathize, to feel what she was feeling, needing and helpless. Grace avoided her look, turning her head away.

'Mamma, it's not time.'

'Miriam . . .'

'Yes.'

'I have been a good and faithful servant. Why does my God punish me with a long and painful death?'

'I don't know.'

'Is this my reward, Miriam? Is there a God at all? Have I lived a life of service for nothing?'

If, Miriam thought, controlling her tears, if this is more than the whimper of a body in pain, if she now questions, at the hour of her death, the justice, even the existence of her God, then I must try to answer her, as honestly as I can.

'Mamma, we do not live for reward or punishment. We do good for its own sake.' She looked at her mother, the stubborn mouth clenched shut, wilful and unconvinced. 'Heaven or Hell, Mamma, or God himself, may exist or not exist, but your life is its own glory.'

Grace sighed, 'Well, you are educated. You know more than I. Call the nurse.' She closed her eyes, dismissing her daughter.

Looking at the still face, Miriam thought she might not see her alive again, and bending, kissed her on the forehead. The skin was slightly clammy beneath her lips. Miriam went in search of the nurse and found her reading on the back verandah.

'Nurse, she wants you.'

The nurse looked up, disapproving. 'She wants her injection?'

'Yes.'

'It's early. It's not the pain, you know, it's just the injection she wants. You understand me?'

'Does it matter? It's not for us to make a moral judgment on that, only to keep her comfortable.'

'I can only do what doctor says.'

'Give it to her,' Miriam ordered, 'on my responsibility.'

The men were on the verandah, smoking, moving about, drinking rum. Some cousins had arrived, and news was being exchanged by those who had not seen each other for a while, using the occasion to tighten the bonds of family loosened by time or distance. Stanley sat in the middle of it, abstracted, responding when greeted, but, as increasingly of late, withdrawn into his own dreaming. Occasionally, his fingers tapped on the wooden arm of the verandah chair, or his palm turned upwards gesturing to accompany an unspoken thought.

'Paul, a word.'

Paul went to him, and taking an elbow, assisted him to his feet.

'Come,' Stanley said, leading the way down the steps. 'Come with me.'

They crossed the lawn together, father and son, one tall, square-shouldered, easy, the other smaller, paunchy, shuffling, arms at his sides, the palms turned backwards. They went round the corner of the house to that part of the yard which lay between the bedrooms and the quickstick trees. Beyond those trees, there was a piece of bush land on the hillside sloping toward the sea.

'I think this is the right place for a grave.'

'What's wrong with the churchyard? By John?'

Stanley lowered his voice, and leaned closer to his son. 'I want her near the house, where I can see the grave from my window. You don't know these people. They will dig to get a little piece of the body to use for obeah. I want her under my window.'

'All right, Daddy.'

'There's room there for me too.'

Stanley took Paul's arm, to be led back to the family on the verandah.

Stubborn to the last, Grace would not die with all her loved ones round her. She wanted to die alone, as if dying were a shameful thing, an admission of weakness, the failure of a life, something to do without witness but Almighty God.

She was proud, and puritanical. After the long humiliation which she had endured, paralysed, having to rely on strangers to complete her most intimate functions, feed her, clean her, bear away the little waste her wasted body made, after the shame of begging for an impersonal needle to spread poison through the recesses of her body, begging for that release, after the horror of such humiliation, she wished the dignity of dying on her own.

So it was that on a Monday morning, when Miriam had taken the baby to the beach, when Stanley was in Kingston for a meeting, and Paul in the fields, she decided to be about her own business, which was to die.

She told the nurse to fetch Sunshine, and told Sunshine to send Tumpy for the pastor. Tumpy took the road he used to take carrying Stanley's letters to her forty years before, moving slowly on his bent leg, knowing he need not hurry, no life would be saved. He went past her bedroom window, down the drive and by the path to the village, under the barbed wire into the school yard, and behind the main buildings, carefully skirting the soursop trees that were always full of wasps, to the garden of the Mission Home.

'Mrs Newton want you.'

For a moment, the new pastor was not sure who he meant.

'Mrs Newton?'

'At Stone Haven.'

Grace wished to die alone, and this last wish was granted. When the young stranger came, white, in his white clothes and soft white tennis shoes, when he came through the darkened rooms, when Sunshine led him to the bedroom, he found her on the high bed, white, bloodless, cold.

The young man prayed, not knowing her. He prayed for an old dead woman, not having known her young, and beautiful, not having known the mother of a family, a school and a community, but nonetheless, he prayed.

She was laid to rest, as Stanley planned, beyond the quickstick trees, in the small burial ground, where he could see her from his bedroom window, knowing that he would lie beside her soon.

The grave faces east, so if her faith be justified, she will watch the sun rise from the sea on Resurrection Day.